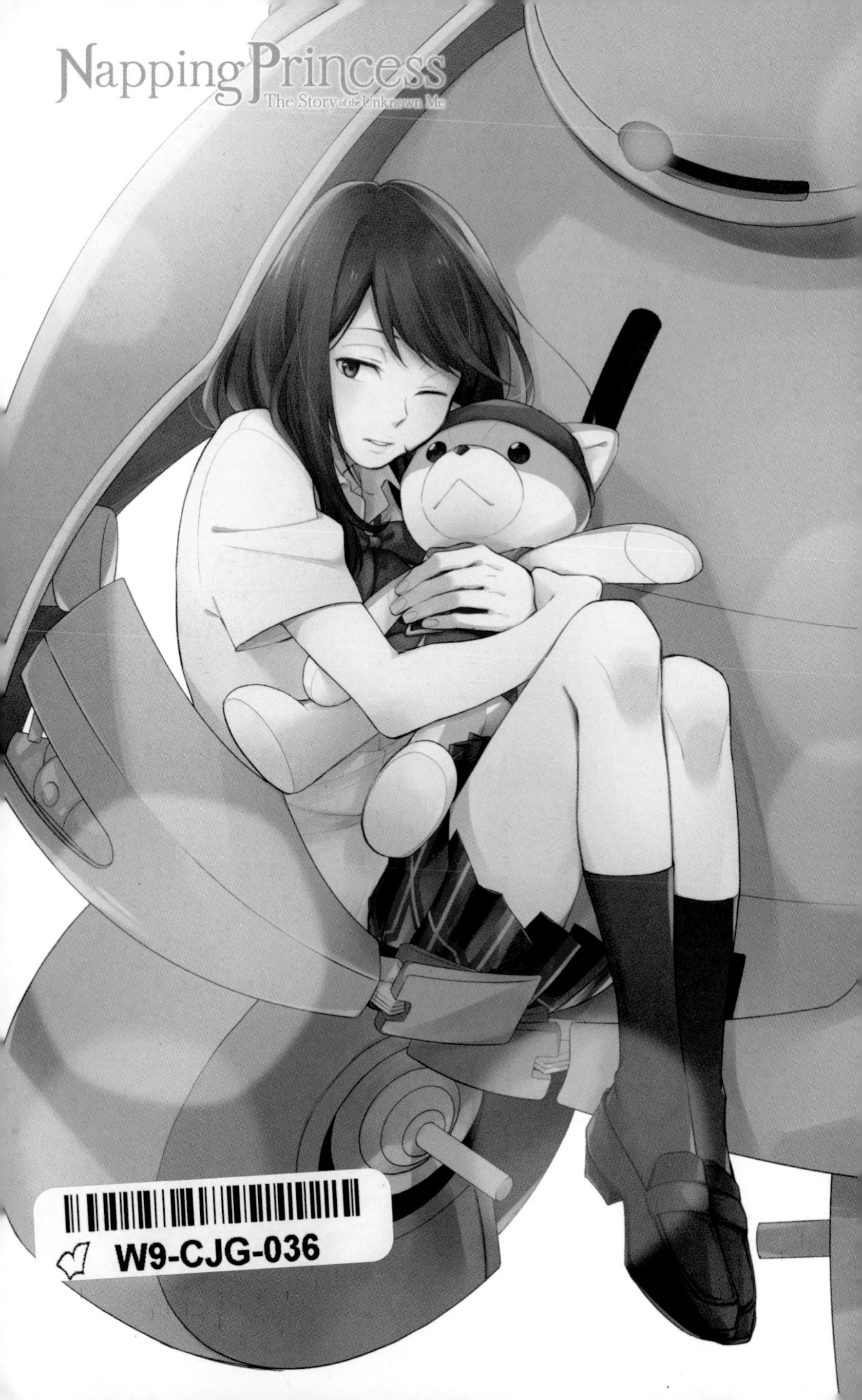
Napping Princess
The Story of the Unknown Me

# Contents

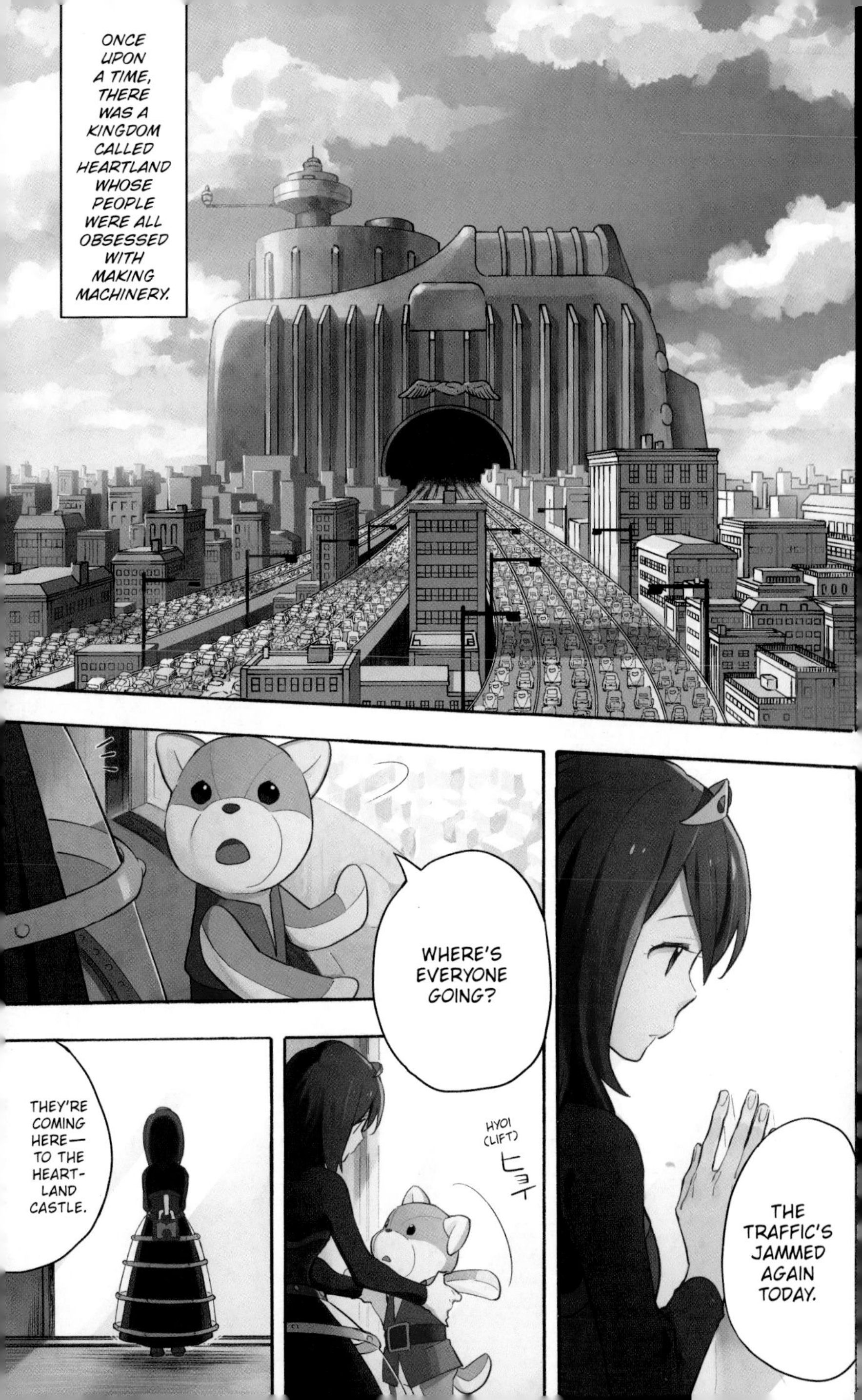
ONCE UPON A TIME, THERE WAS A KINGDOM CALLED HEARTLAND WHOSE PEOPLE WERE ALL OBSESSED WITH MAKING MACHINERY.
THE TRAFFIC'S JAMMED AGAIN TODAY.
WHERE'S EVERYONE GOING?
HYOI (LIFT)
ヒョイ
THEY'RE COMING HERE— TO THE HEART-LAND CASTLE.

# Scene I

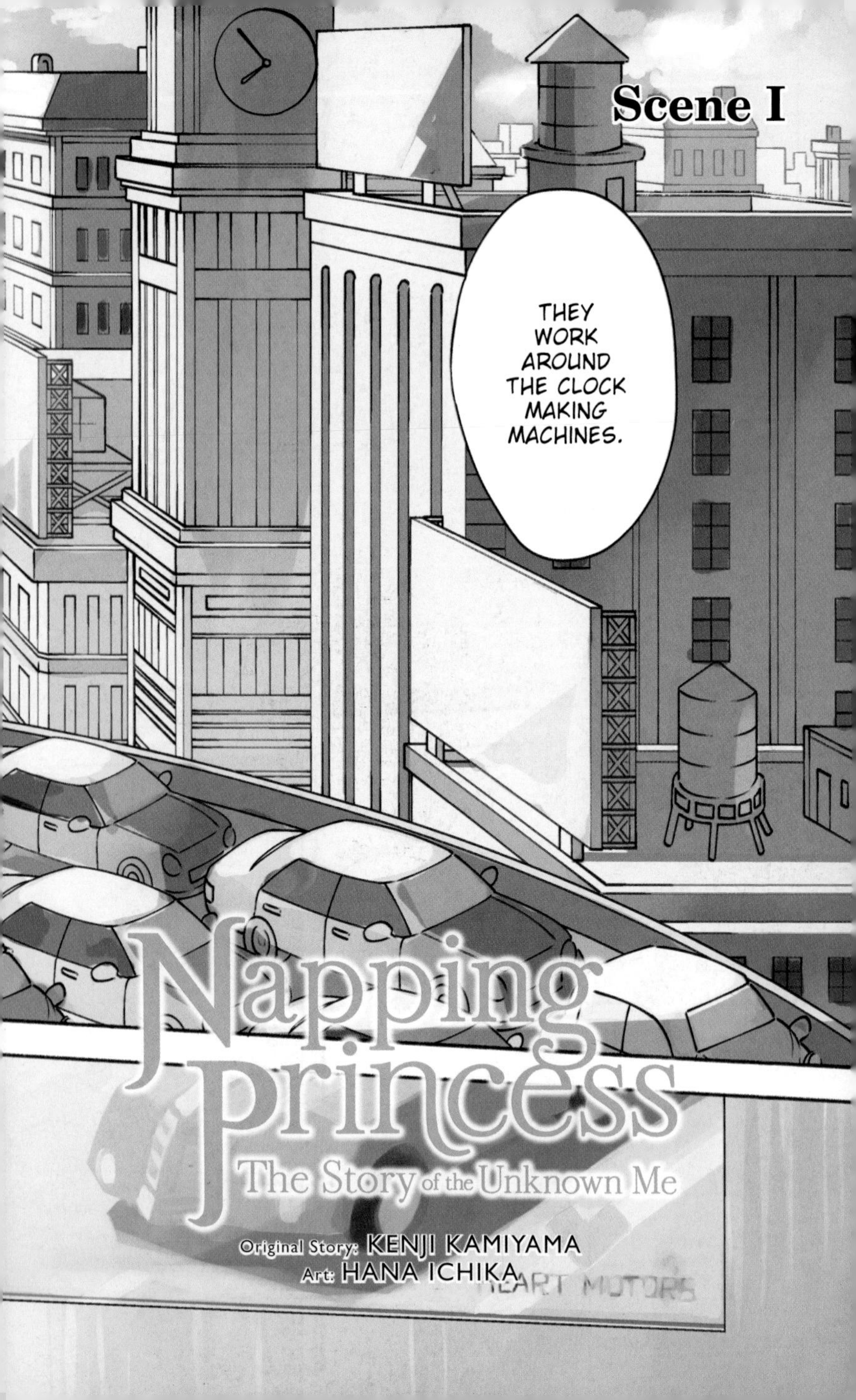
THEY WORK AROUND THE CLOCK MAKING MACHINES.
ART MOTORS

# Napping Princess
## The Story of the Unknown Me

Original Story: KENJI KAMIYAMA
Art: HANA ICHIKA

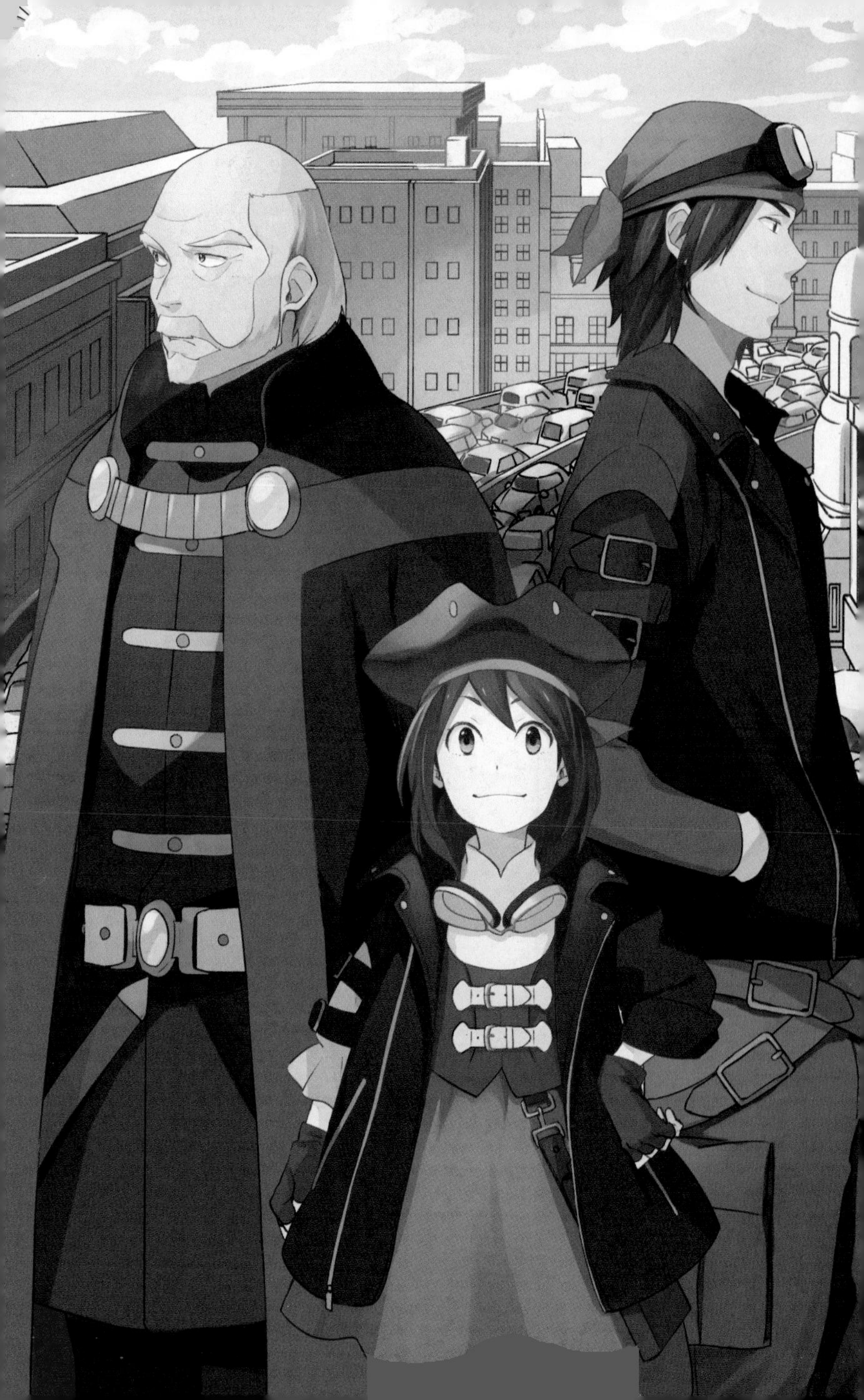

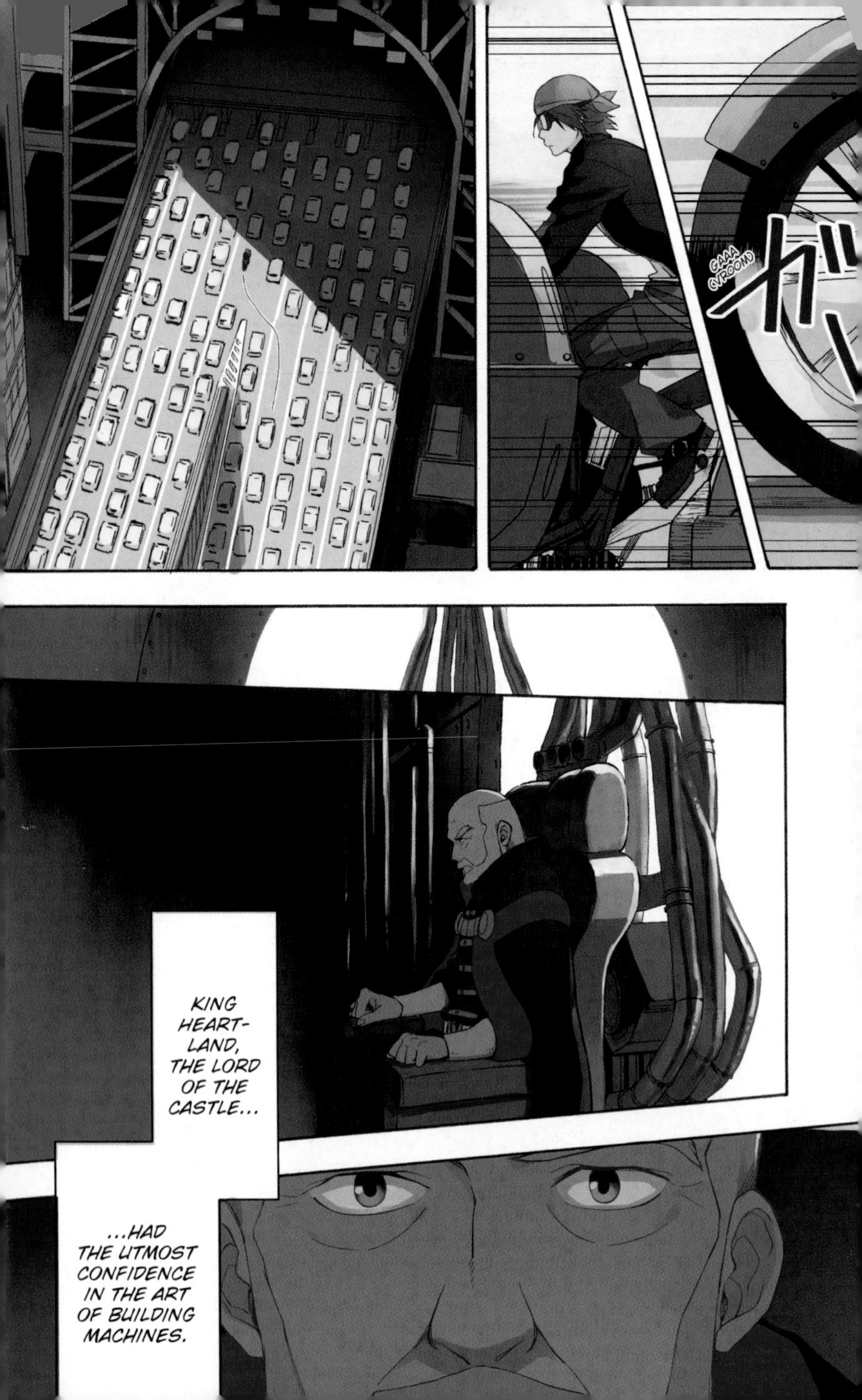
GAAA (VROOM)
KING HEART-LAND, THE LORD OF THE CASTLE...
...HAD THE UTMOST CONFIDENCE IN THE ART OF BUILDING MACHINES.

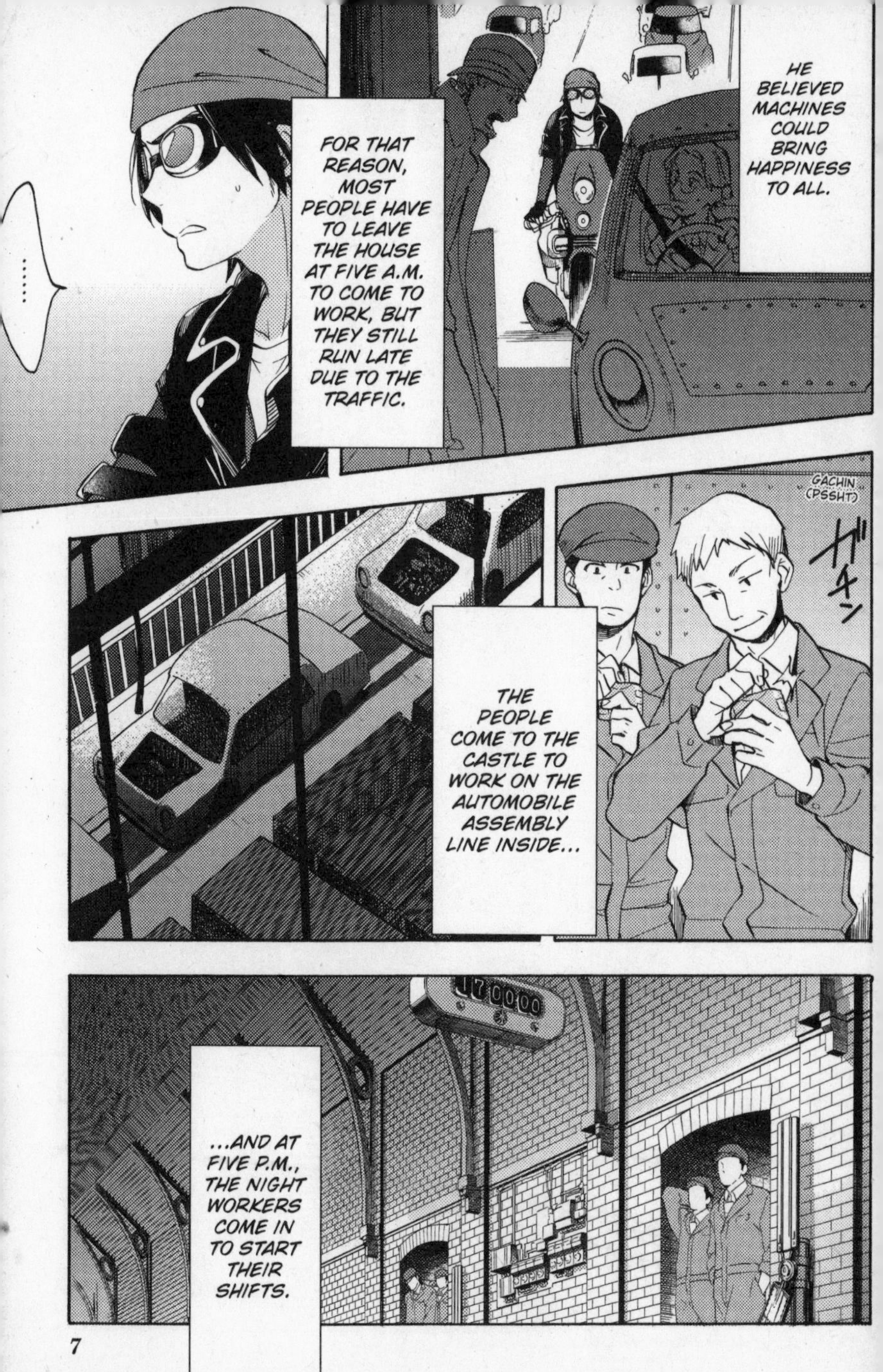
HE BELIEVED MACHINES COULD BRING HAPPINESS TO ALL.
FOR THAT REASON, MOST PEOPLE HAVE TO LEAVE THE HOUSE AT FIVE A.M. TO COME TO WORK, BUT THEY STILL RUN LATE DUE TO THE TRAFFIC.
......
GACHIN (PSSHT)
ガチン
THE PEOPLE COME TO THE CASTLE TO WORK ON THE AUTOMOBILE ASSEMBLY LINE INSIDE...
...AND AT FIVE P.M., THE NIGHT WORKERS COME IN TO START THEIR SHIFTS.

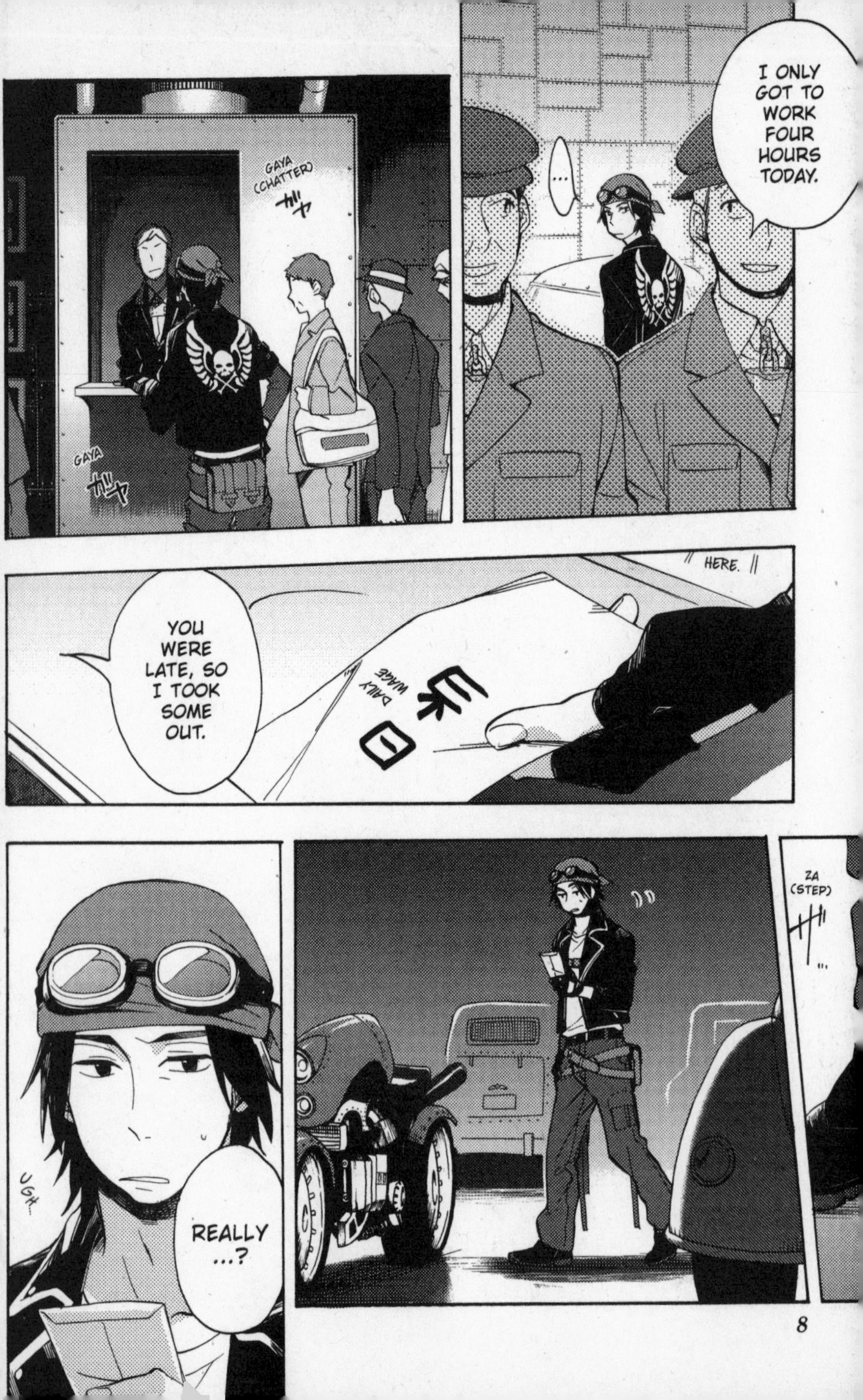
I ONLY GOT TO WORK FOUR HOURS TODAY.
...
GAYA (CHATTER)
ガヤ
GAYA
ガヤ
HERE.
YOU WERE LATE, SO I TOOK SOME OUT.
DAILY WAGE
日給
ZA (STEP)
ザッ
...
UGH...
REALLY ...?

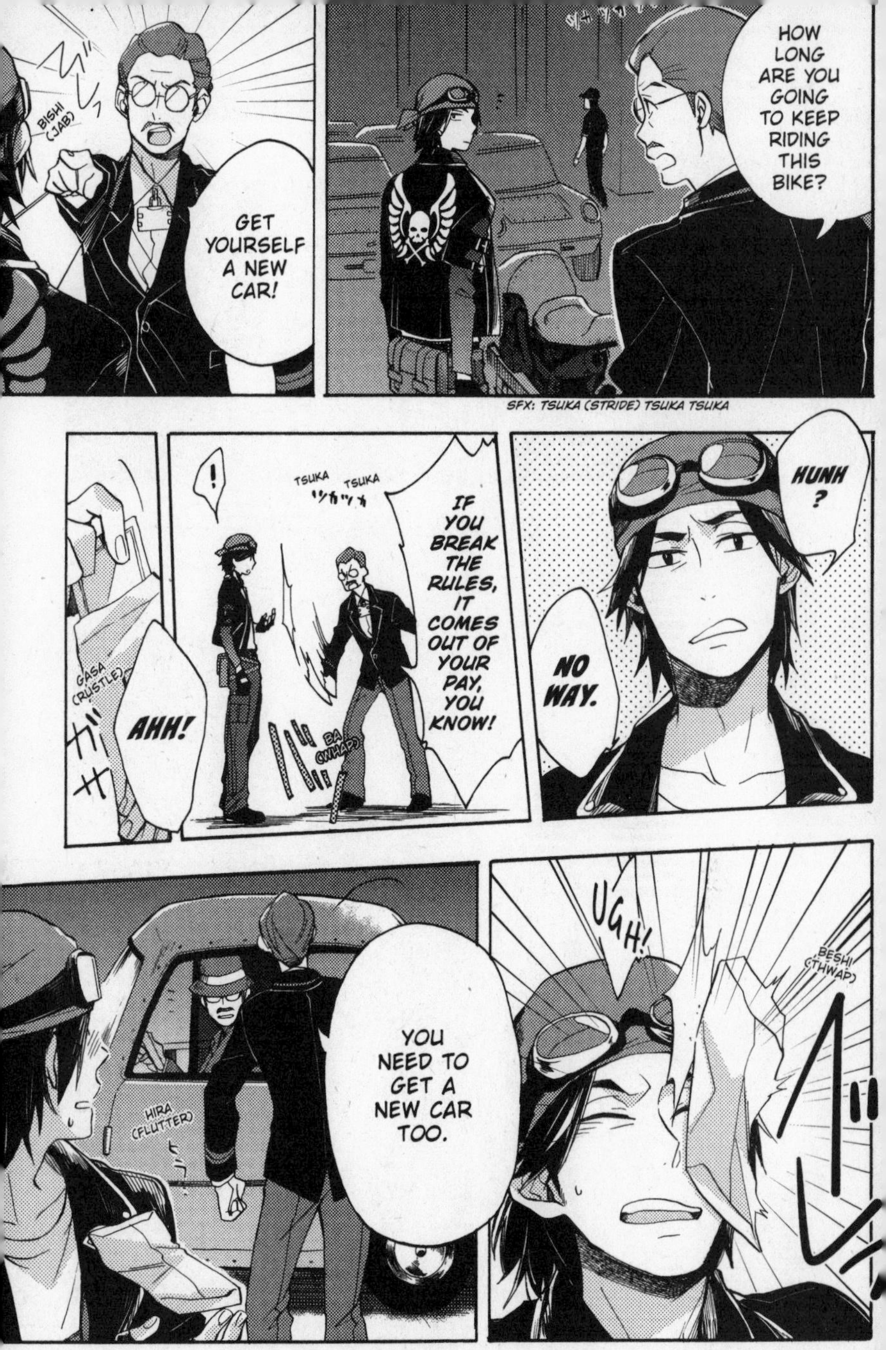
HOW LONG ARE YOU GOING TO KEEP RIDING THIS BIKE?
GET YOURSELF A NEW CAR!
BISHI (JAB)
SFX: TSUKA (STRIDE) TSUKA TSUKA
HUNH?
NO WAY.
!
TSUKA TSUKA
IF YOU BREAK THE RULES, IT COMES OUT OF YOUR PAY, YOU KNOW!
BA (WHAP)
GASA (RUSTLE)
AHH!
UGH!
BESHI (THWAP)
YOU NEED TO GET A NEW CAR TOO.
HIRA (FLUTTER)

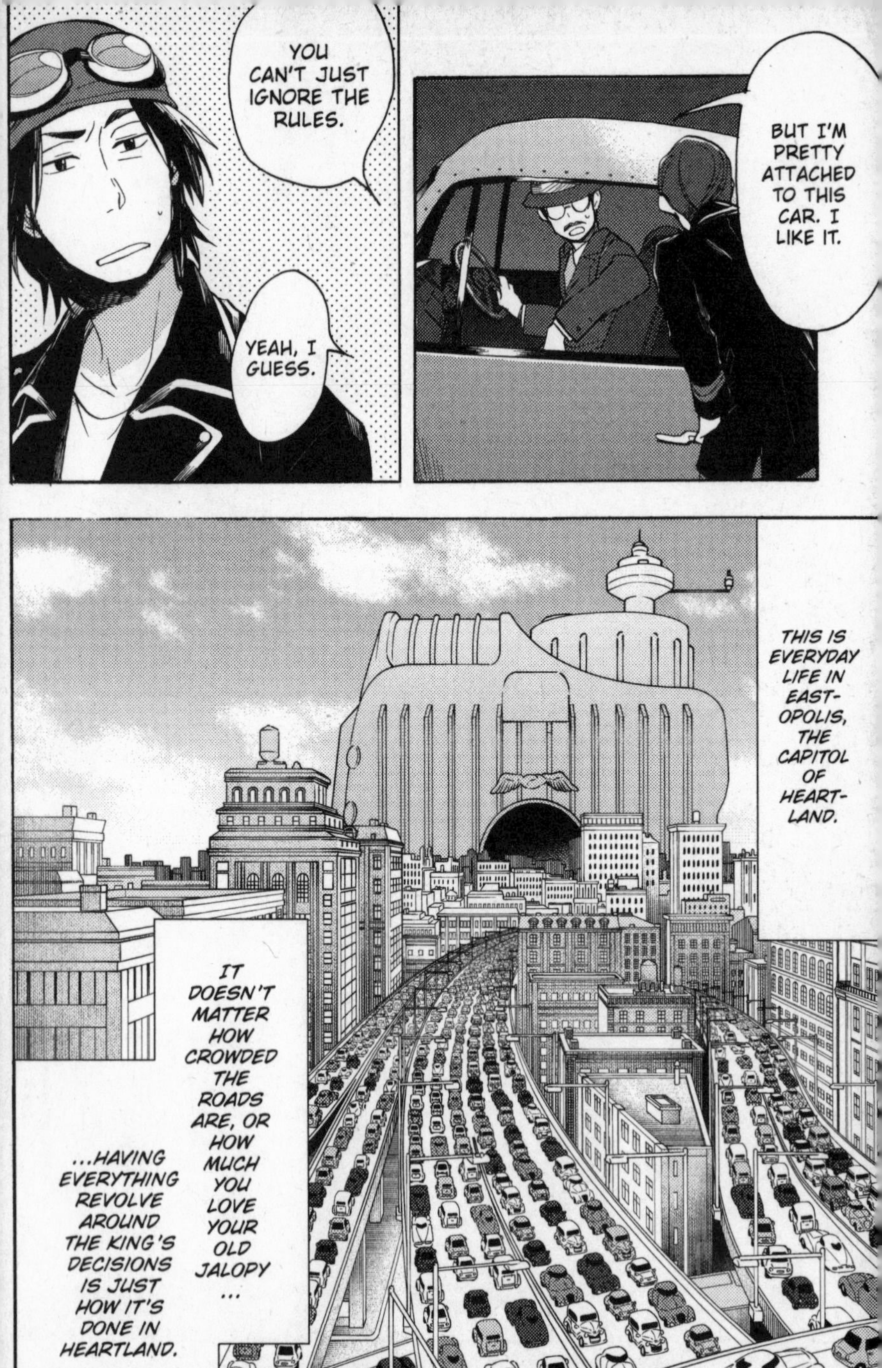
BUT I'M PRETTY ATTACHED TO THIS CAR. I LIKE IT.
YOU CAN'T JUST IGNORE THE RULES.
YEAH, I GUESS.
THIS IS EVERYDAY LIFE IN EAST-OPOLIS, THE CAPITOL OF HEART-LAND.
IT DOESN'T MATTER HOW CROWDED THE ROADS ARE, OR HOW MUCH YOU LOVE YOUR OLD JALOPY ...
...HAVING EVERYTHING REVOLVE AROUND THE KING'S DECISIONS IS JUST HOW IT'S DONE IN HEARTLAND.

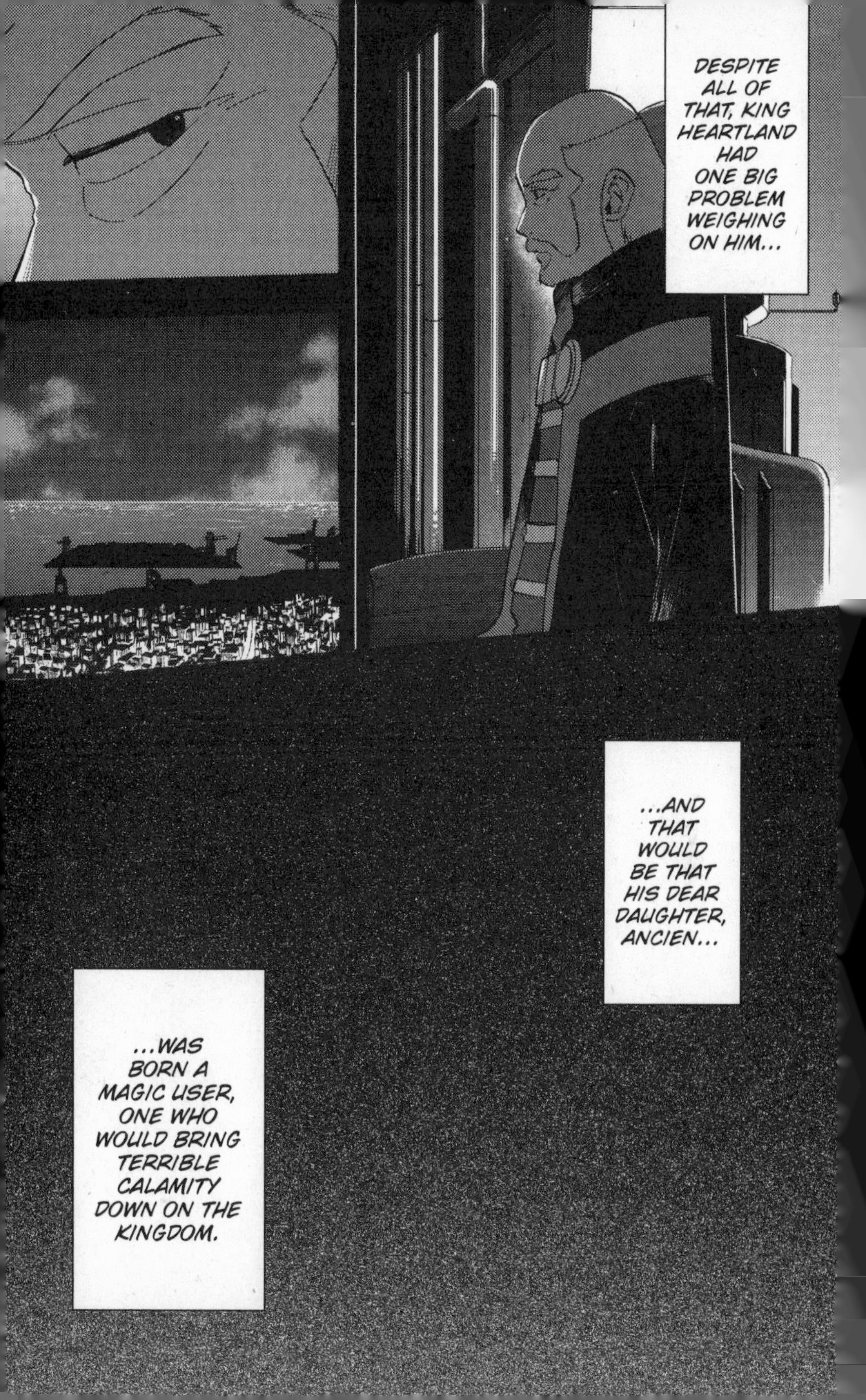
DESPITE ALL OF THAT, KING HEARTLAND HAD ONE BIG PROBLEM WEIGHING ON HIM...
...AND THAT WOULD BE THAT HIS DEAR DAUGHTER, ANCIEN...
...WAS BORN A MAGIC USER, ONE WHO WOULD BRING TERRIBLE CALAMITY DOWN ON THE KINGDOM.

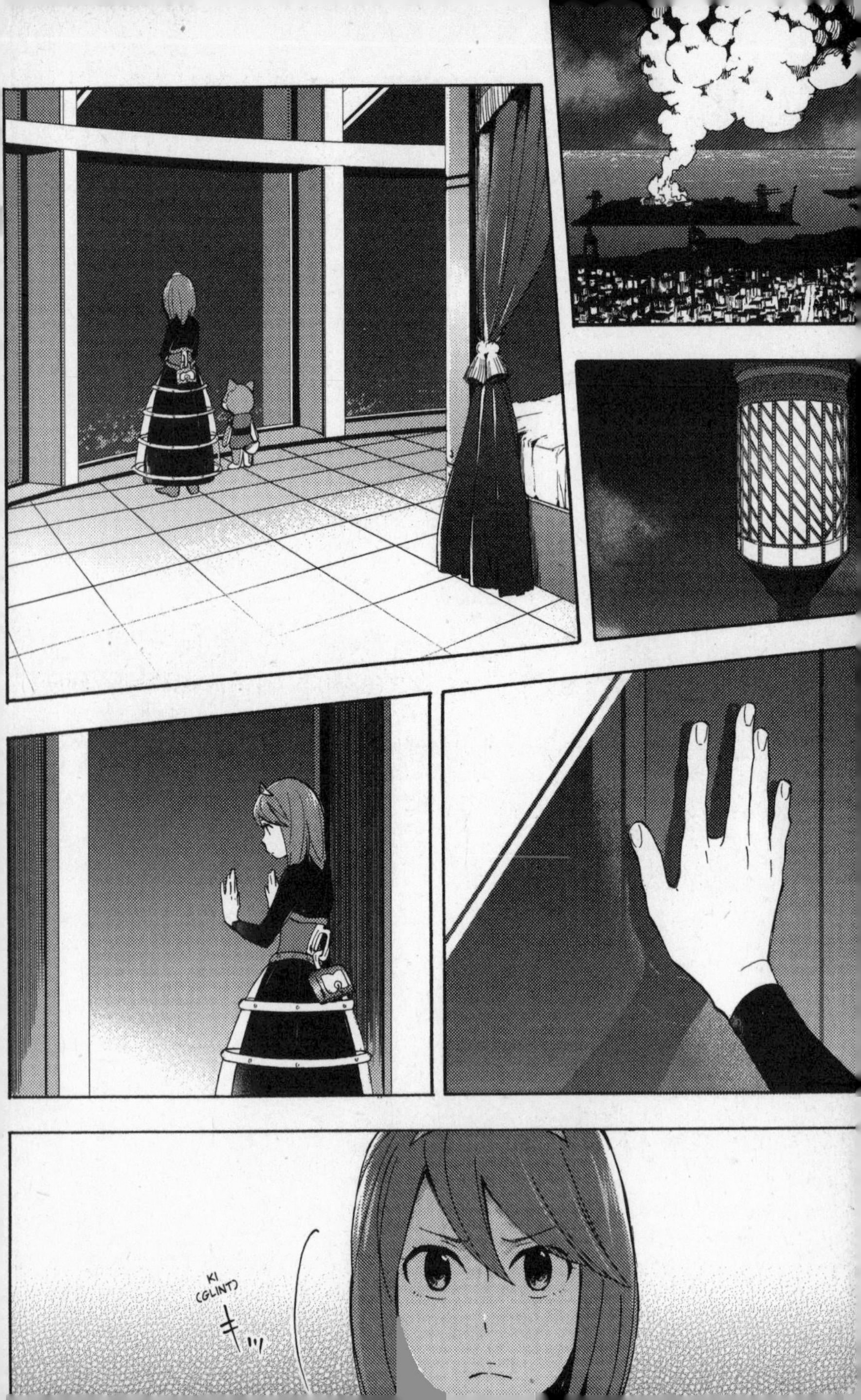
KI
(GLINT)
キッ

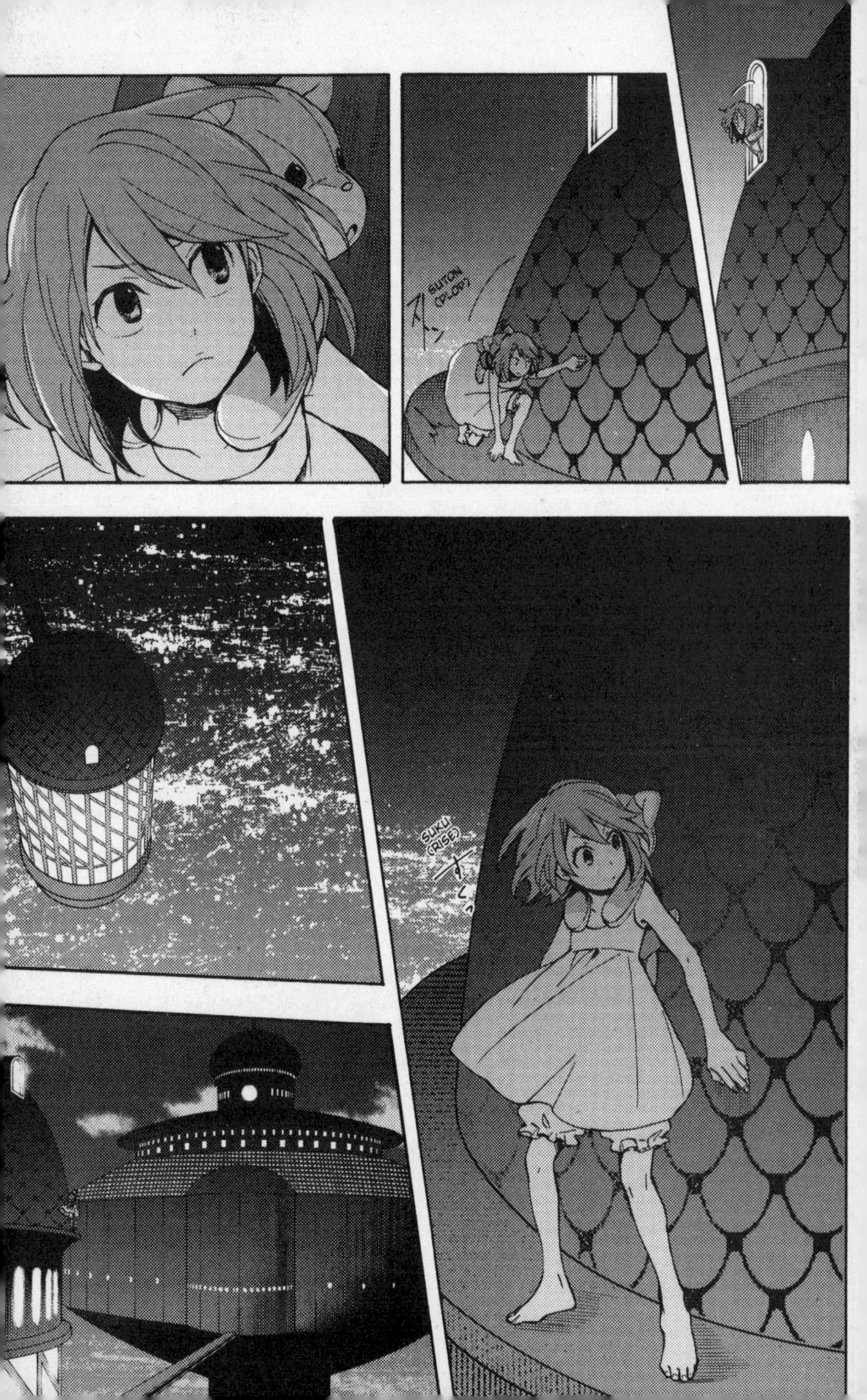
SUTON (PLOP)
SUKU (RISE)

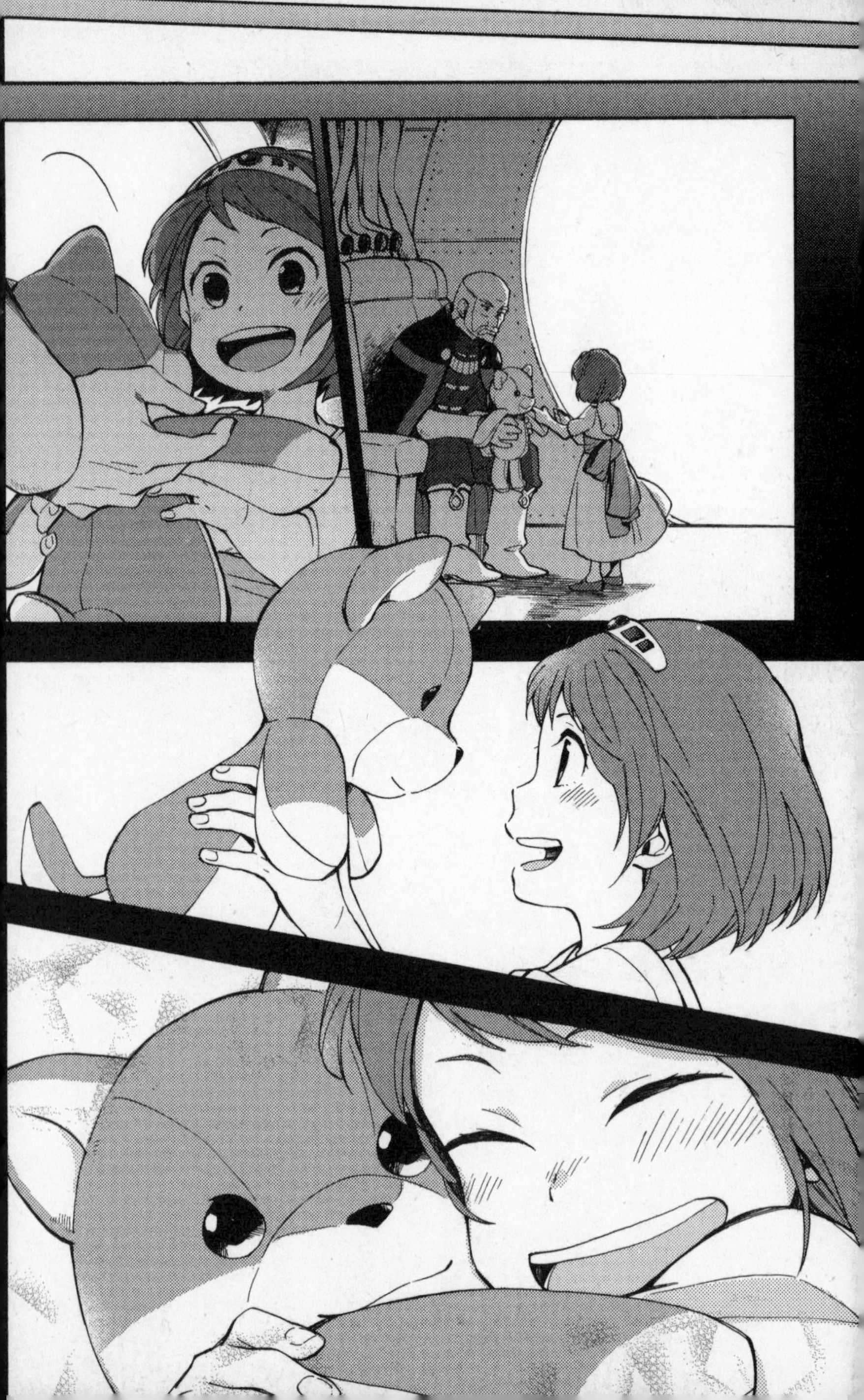

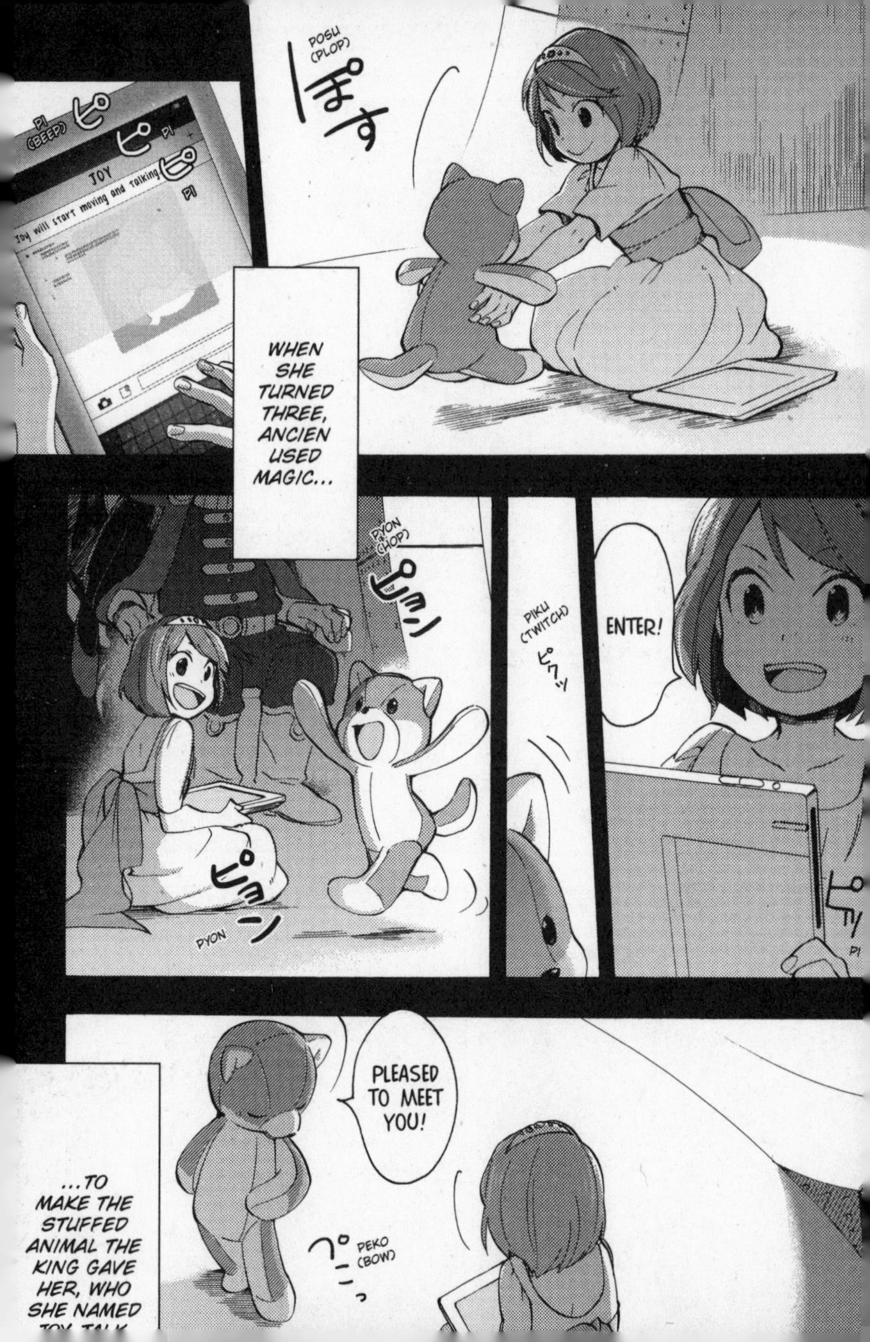

POSU (PLOP)
ぽす
WHEN SHE TURNED THREE, ANCIEN USED MAGIC...
PI (BEEP) ピ
PI ピ
PI ピ
JOY
Joy will start moving and talking
ENTER!
ピッ PI
PIKU (TWITCH) ピクッ
PYON (HOP) ピョン
ピョン PYON
PLEASED TO MEET YOU!
PEKO (BOW) ぺこっ
...TO MAKE THE STUFFED ANIMAL THE KING GAVE HER, WHO SHE NAMED

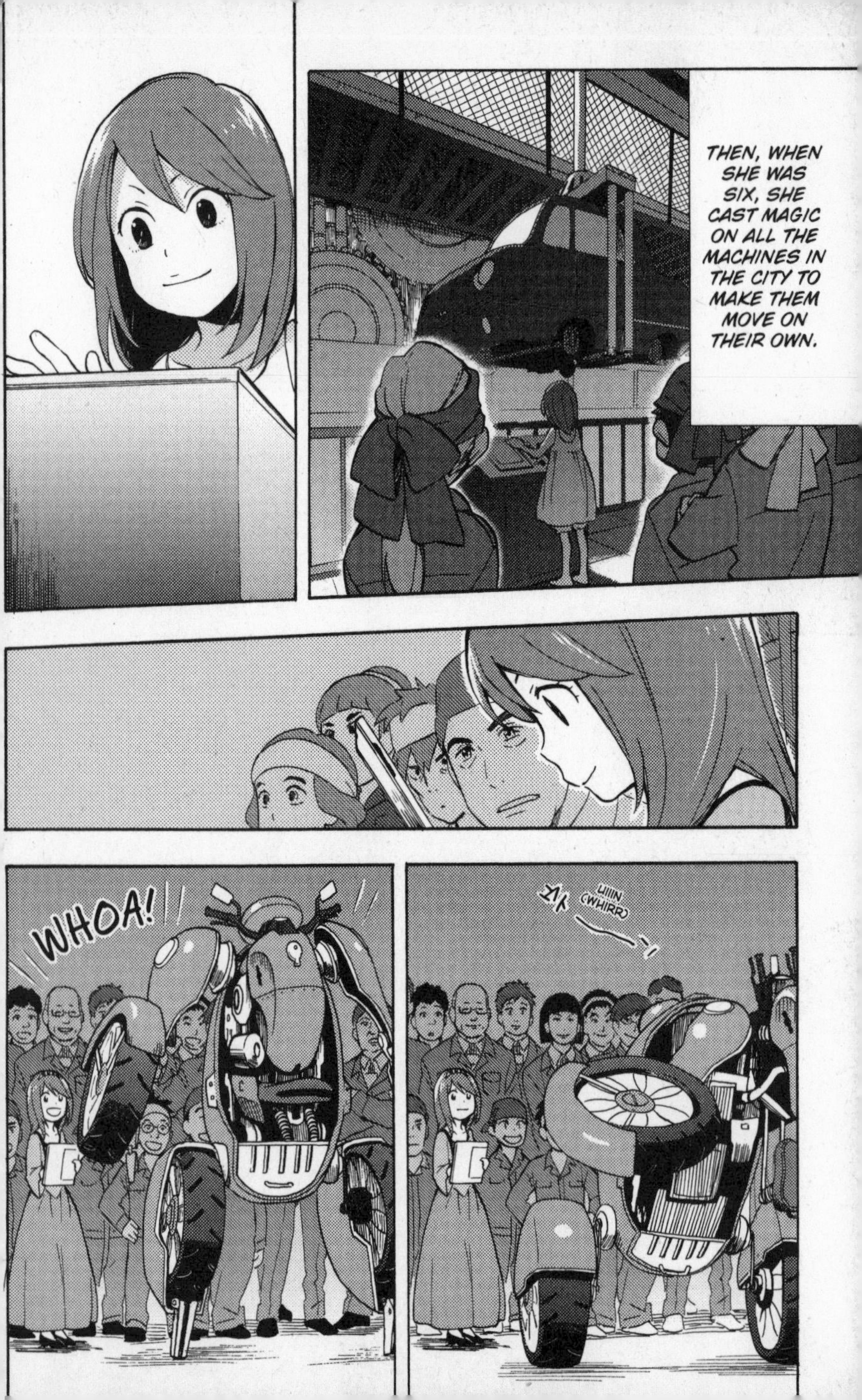
THEN, WHEN SHE WAS SIX, SHE CAST MAGIC ON ALL THE MACHINES IN THE CITY TO MAKE THEM MOVE ON THEIR OWN.
UIIIN (WHIRR)
WHOA!

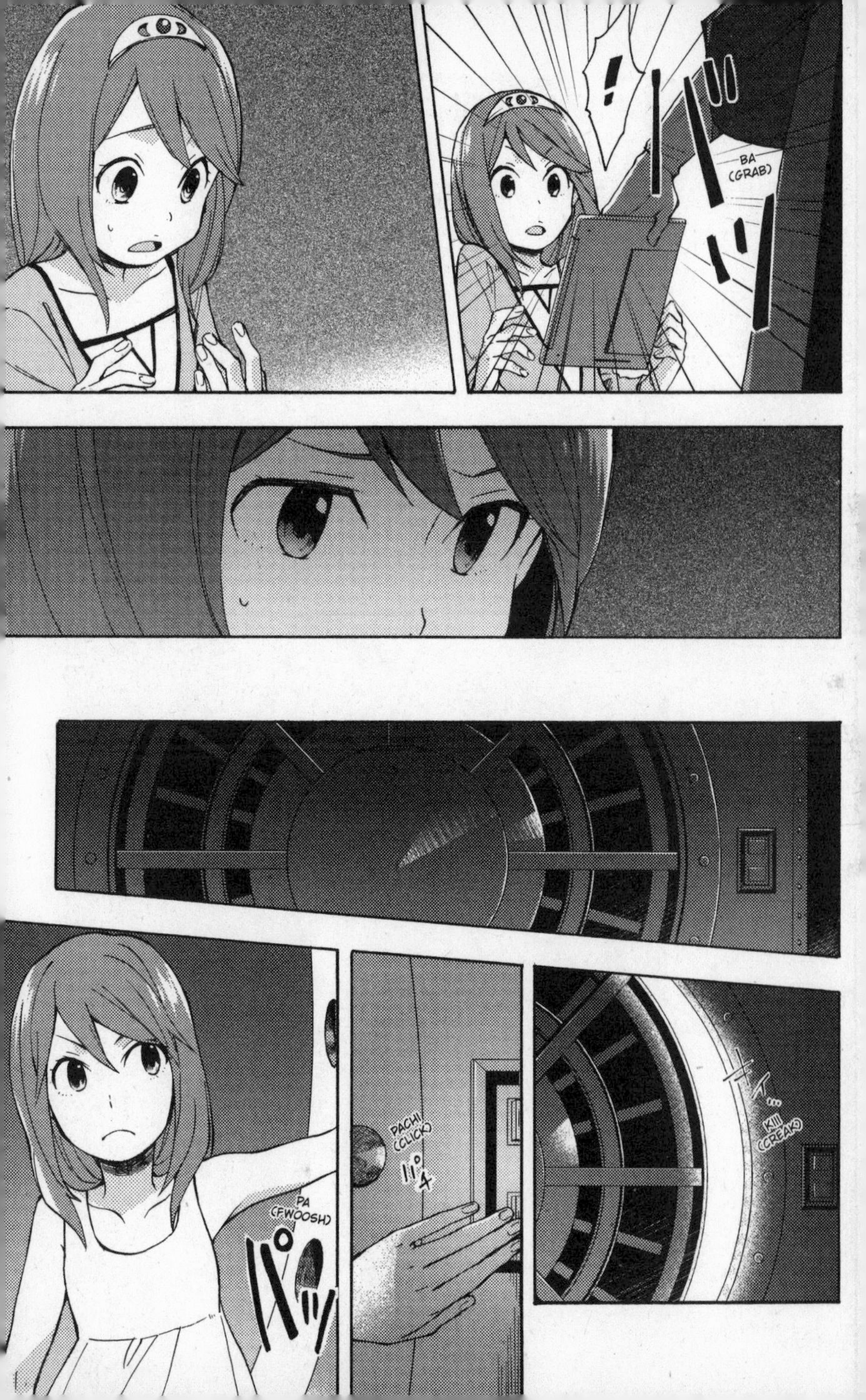
BA
(GRAB)
KIII
(CREAK)
PACHI
(CLICK)
PA
(F-WOOSH)

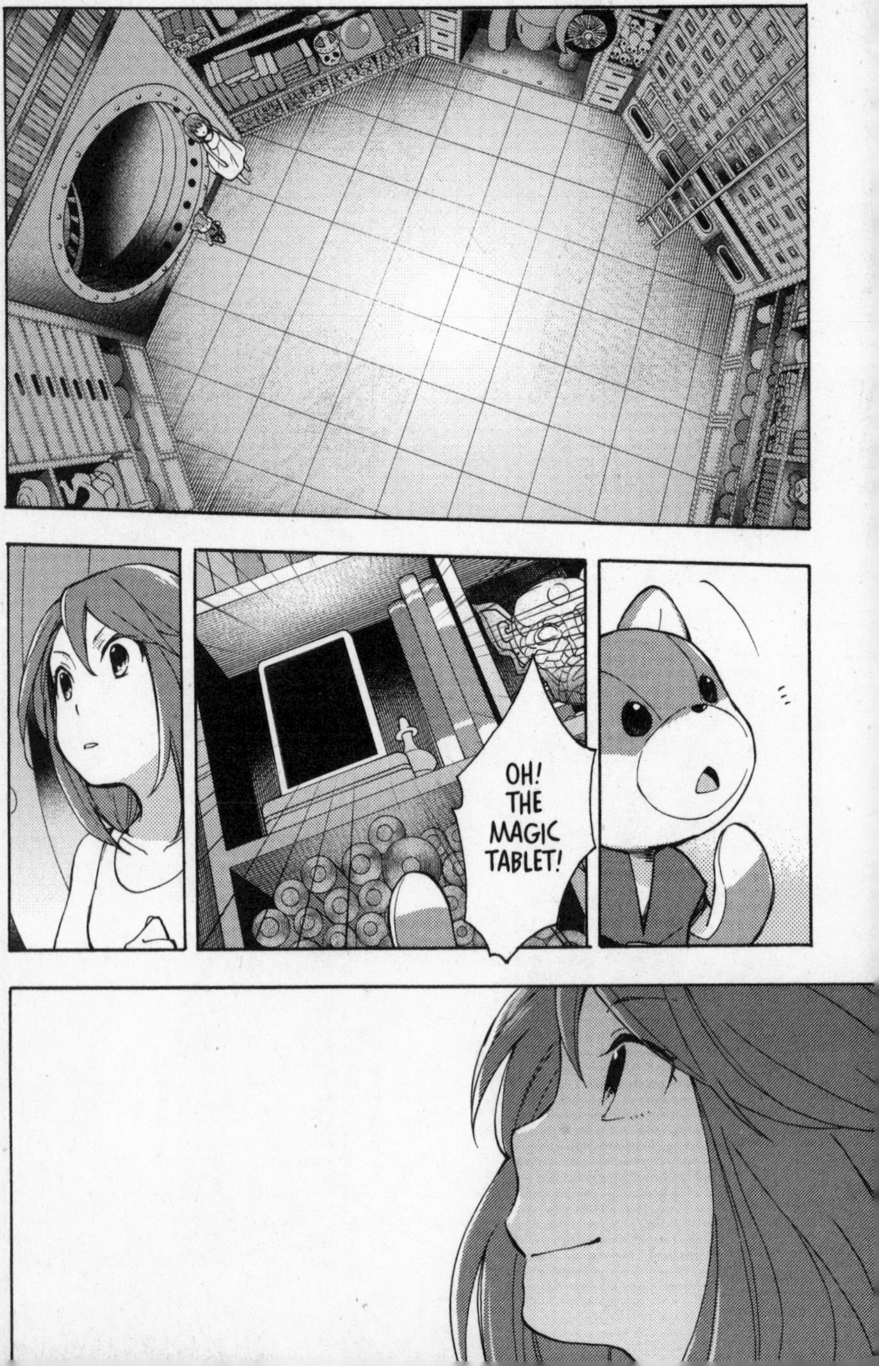
OH! THE MAGIC TABLET!

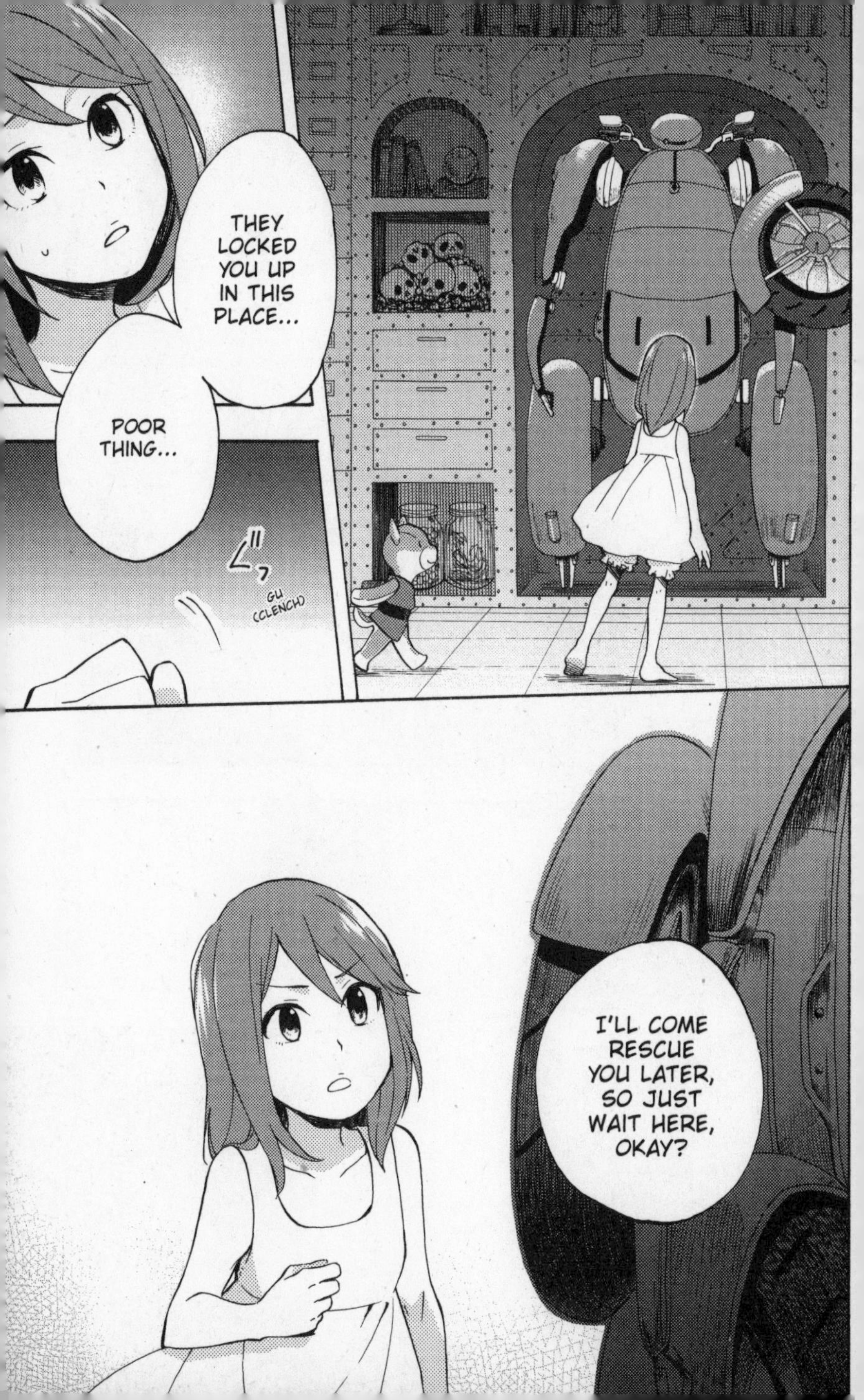
THEY LOCKED YOU UP IN THIS PLACE...
POOR THING...
GU (CLENCH)
I'LL COME RESCUE YOU LATER, SO JUST WAIT HERE, OKAY?

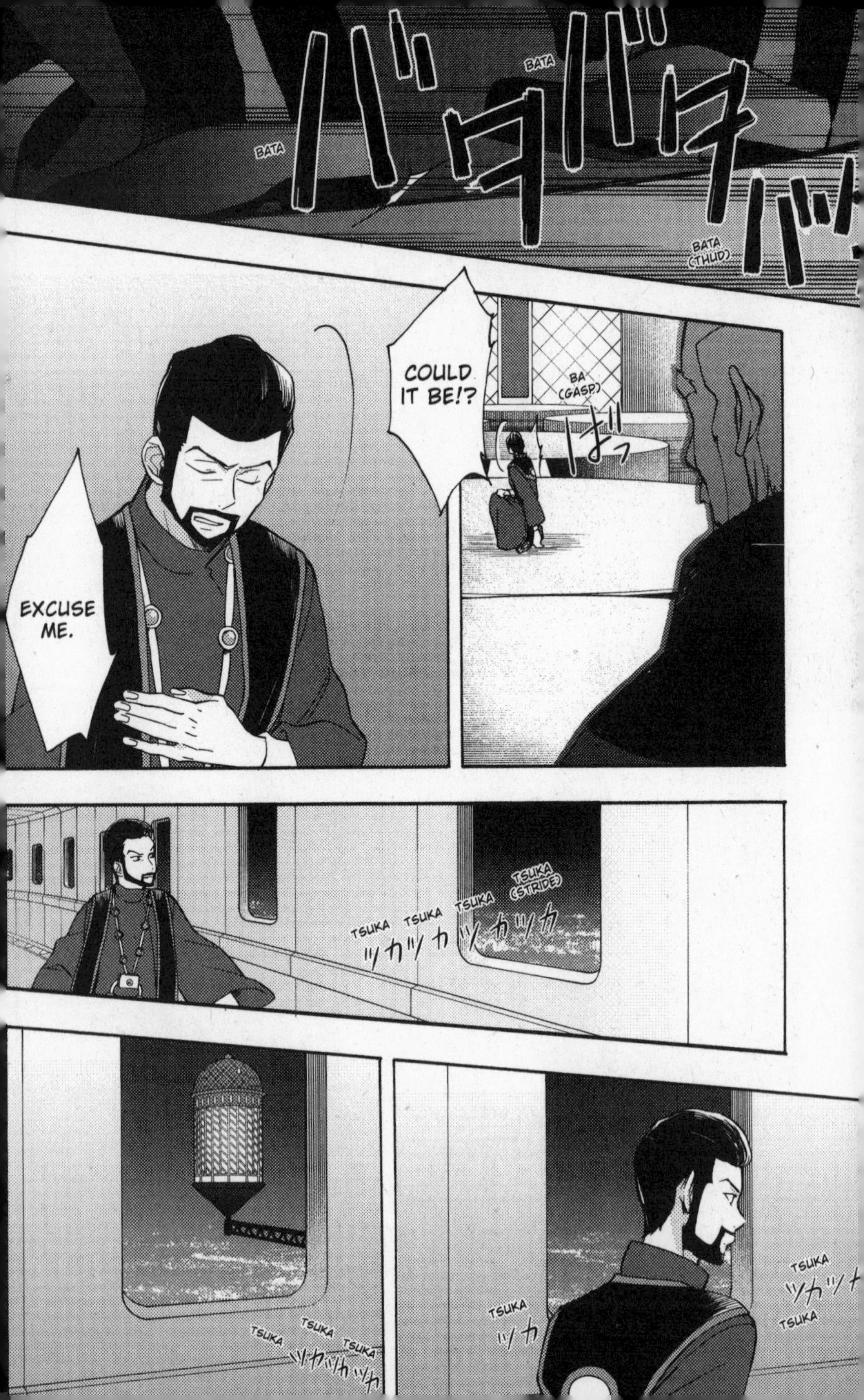
BATA
バタバタ
BATA (THUD)
バッ
BATA
COULD IT BE!?
BA (GASP)
ぱっ
EXCUSE ME.
TSUKA (STRIDE)
TSUKA
TSUKA
TSUKA
ツカツカツカ
TSUKA
TSUKA
TSUKA
TSUKA
ツカ
TSUKA
TSUKA
TSUKA
ツカツカツカ

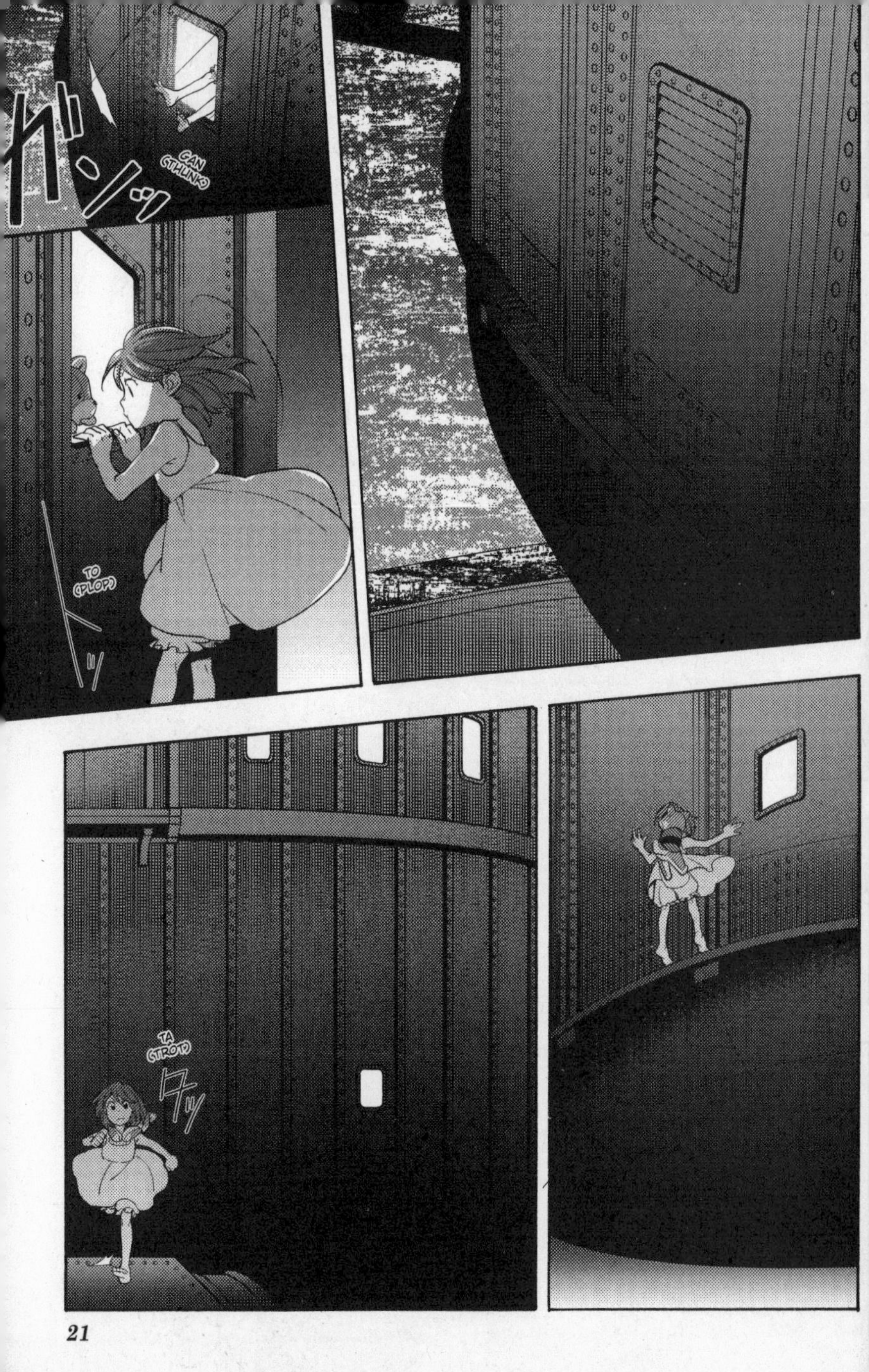
GAN
(THUNK)
TO
(PLOP)
TA
(TROT)

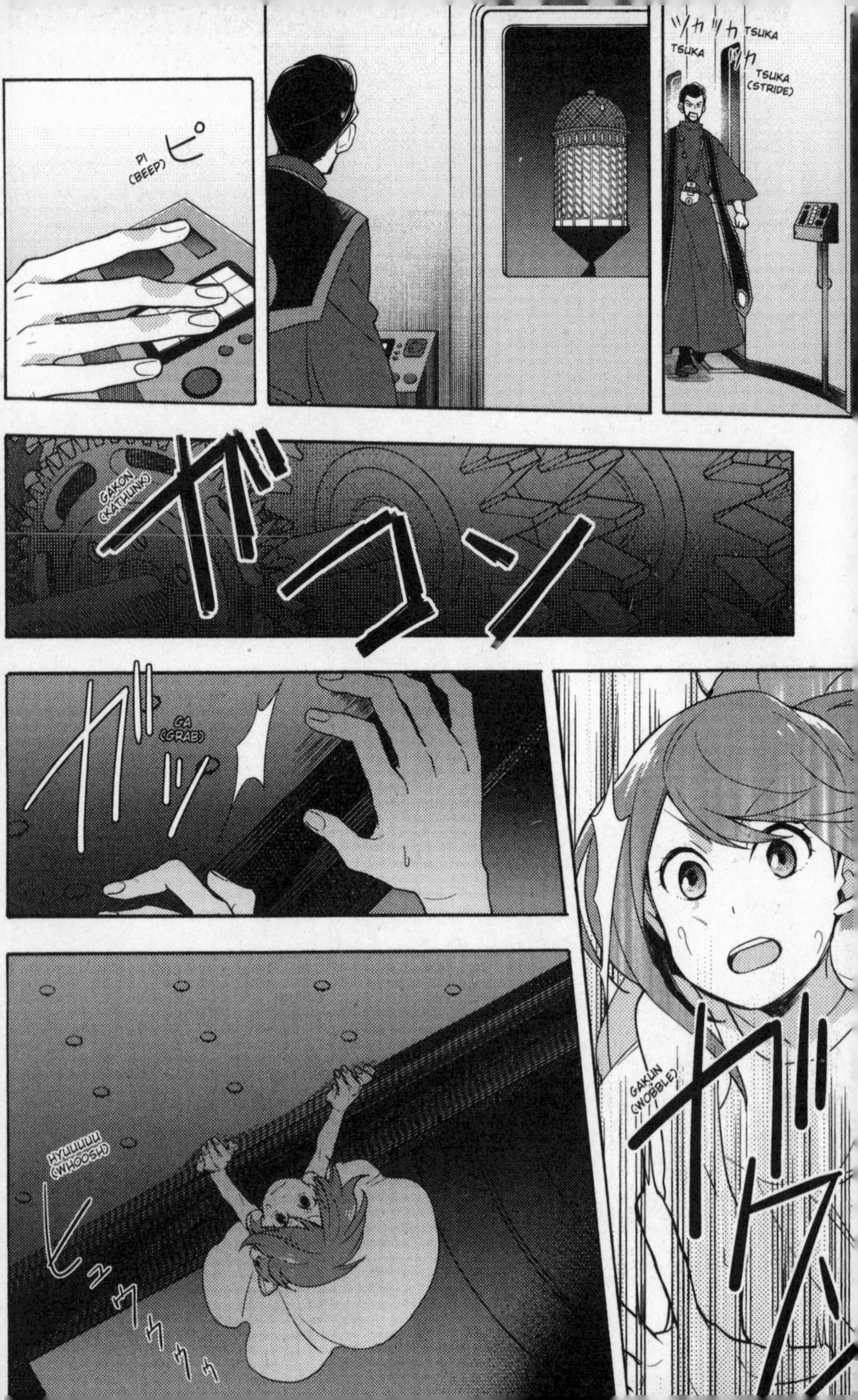
ツカツカ
TSUKA
TSUKA
ツカ
TSUKA (STRIDE)
PI (BEEP) ピ
GAKON (KATHUNK)
ガコン
GAKUN (WOBBLE)
ガクン
GA (GRAB)
ガッ
HYUUUUN (WHOOSH)
ヒュウウウウ

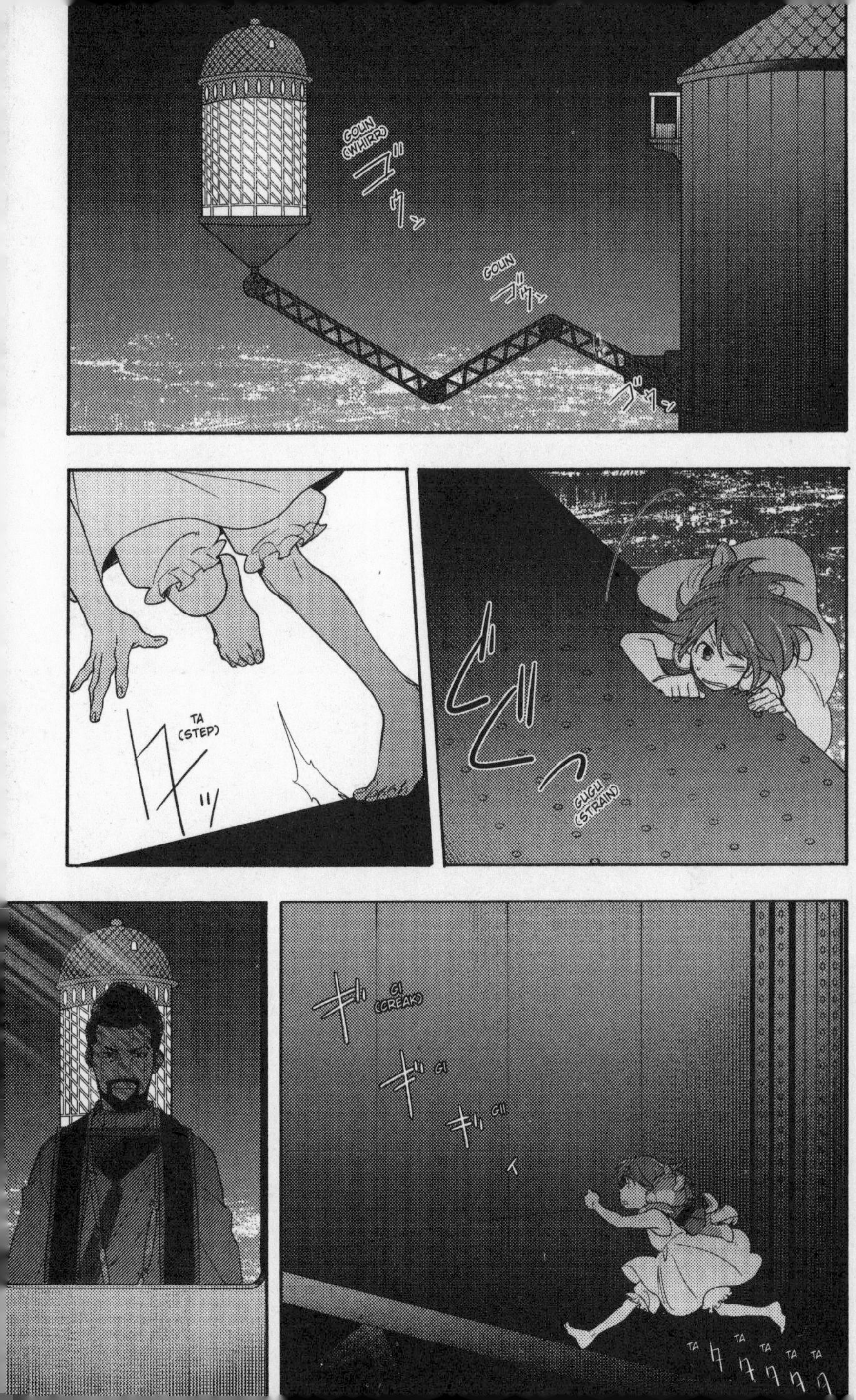
GOUN (WHIRR)
GOUN
GUGU (STRAIN)
TA (STEP)
GI (CREAK)
GI
GII
TA TA TA TA TA

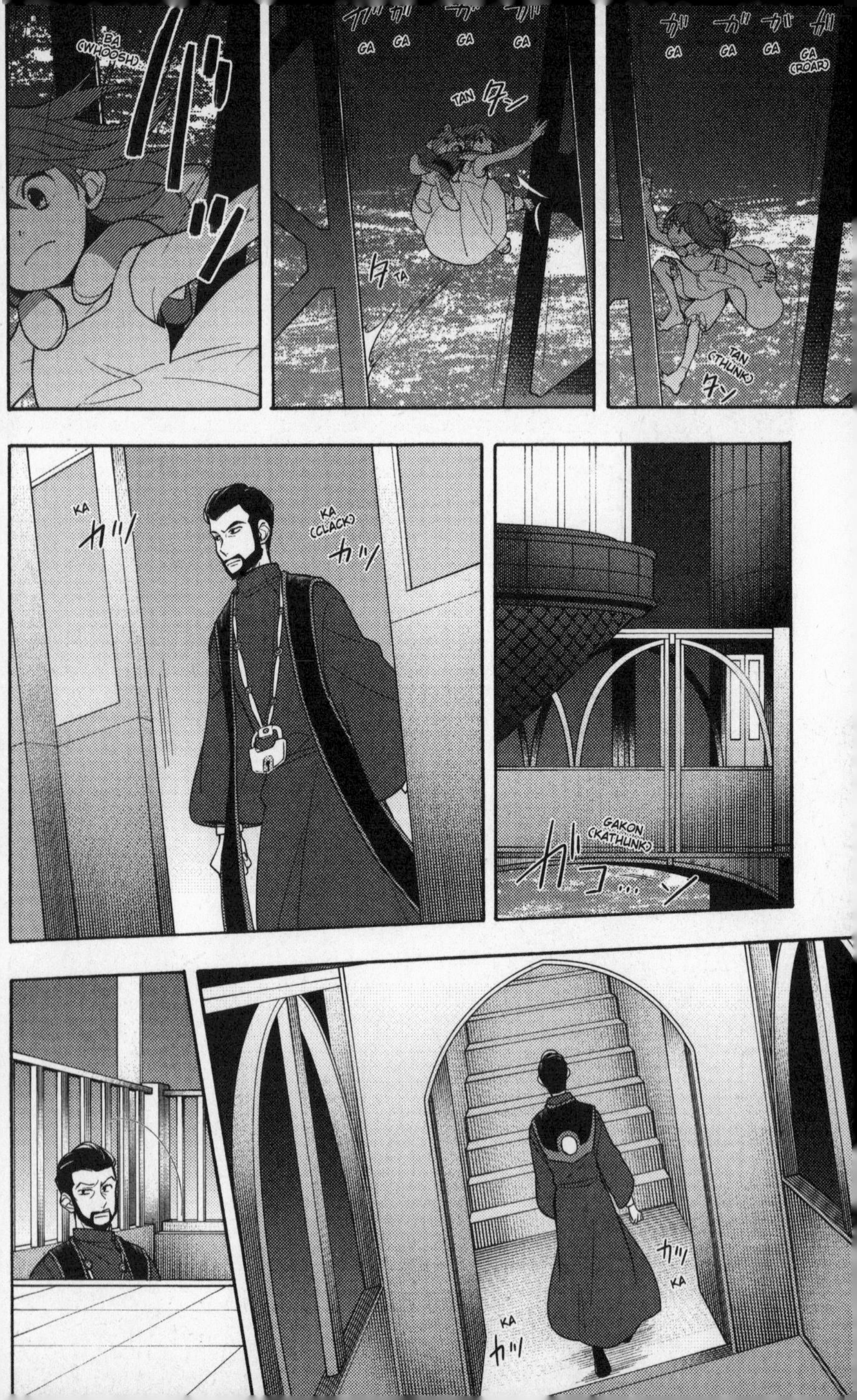

GA GA GA GA (ROAR)
TAN (THUNK)
GA GA GA GA
TAN
TA
BA (WHOOSH)
GAKON (KATHUNK)
KA (CLACK)
KA
KA
KA

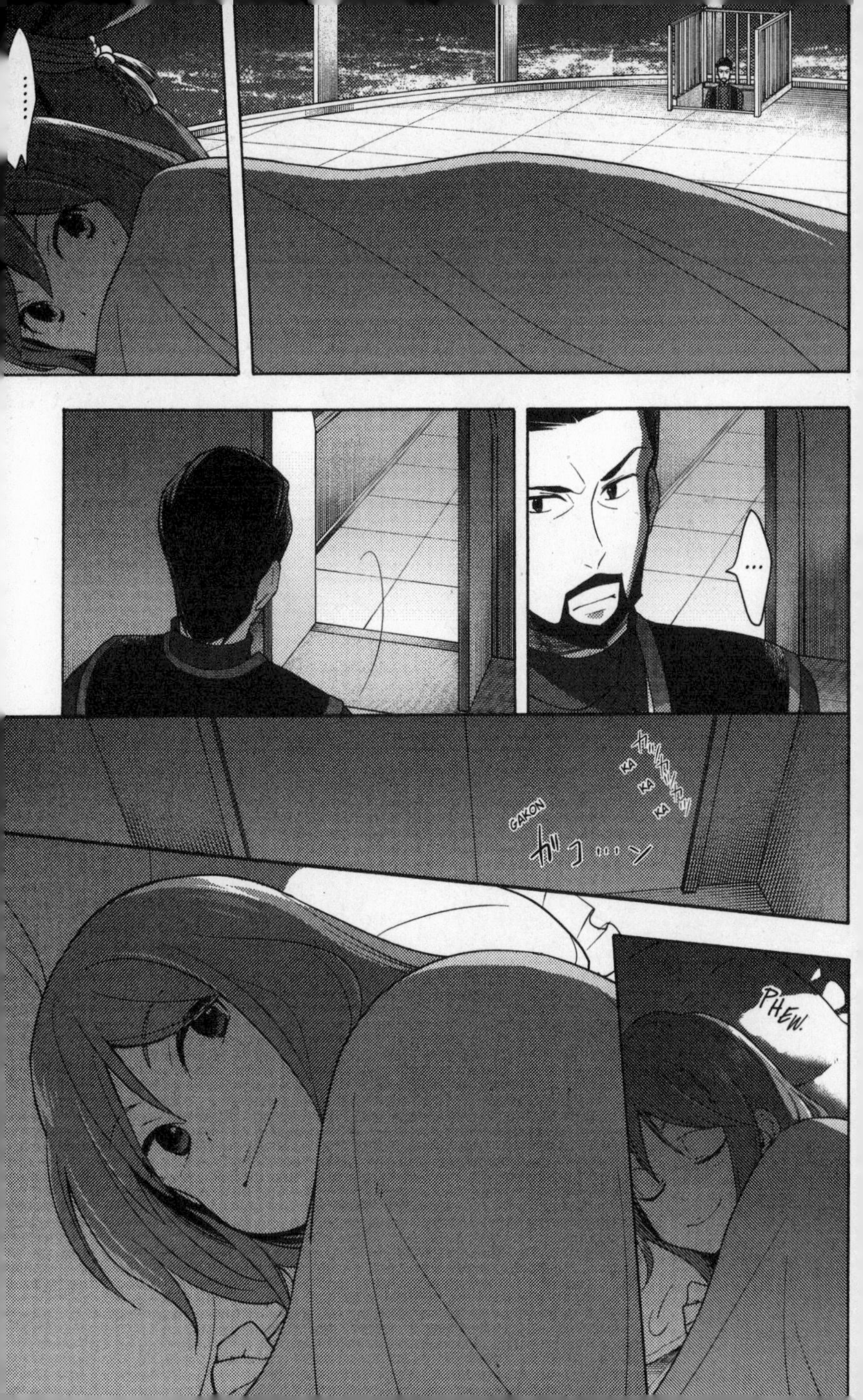
......
...
KA KA KA
GAKON
ガコ…ン
PHEW.

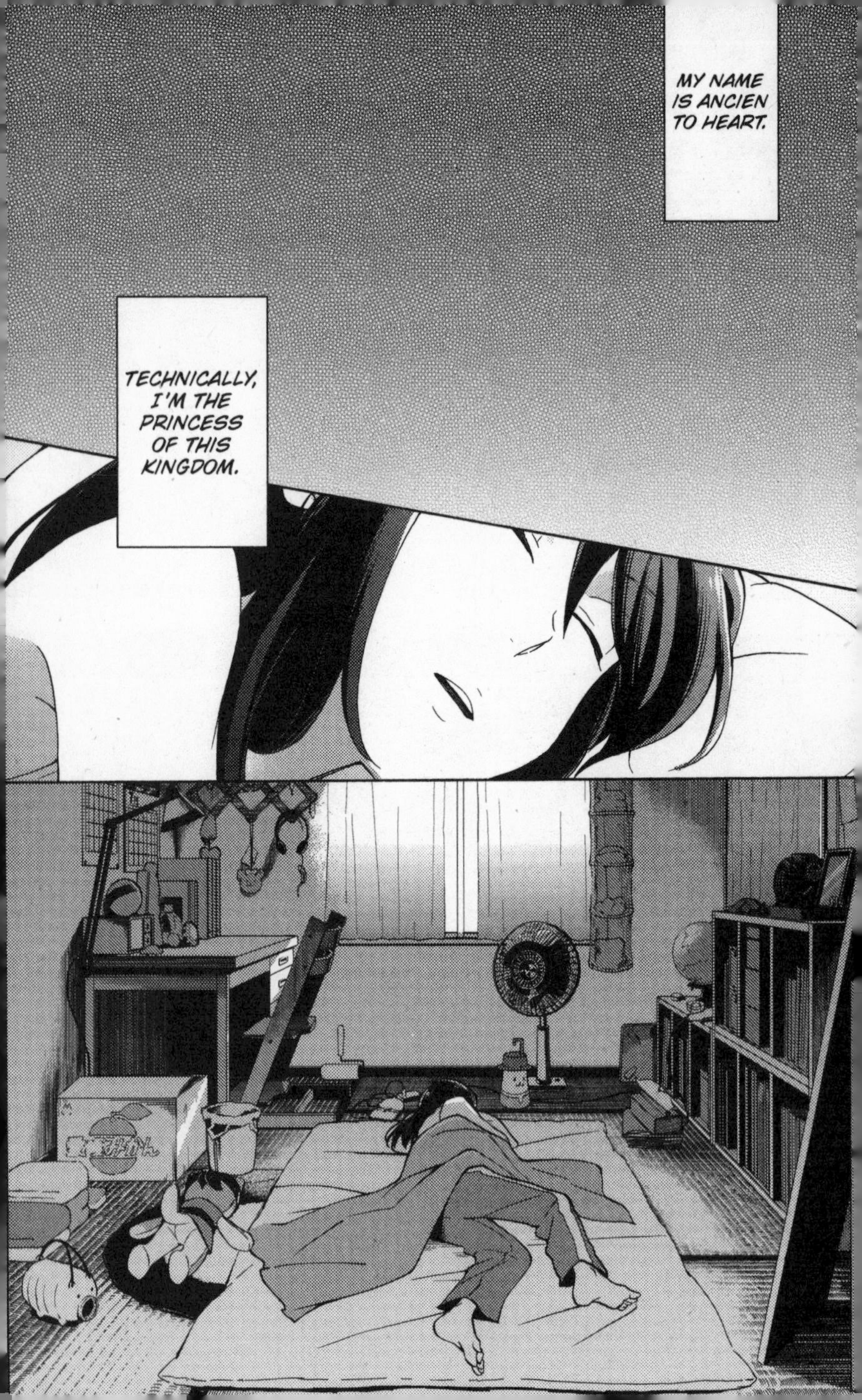
MY NAME IS ANCIEN TO HEART.
TECHNICALLY, I'M THE PRINCESS OF THIS KINGDOM.

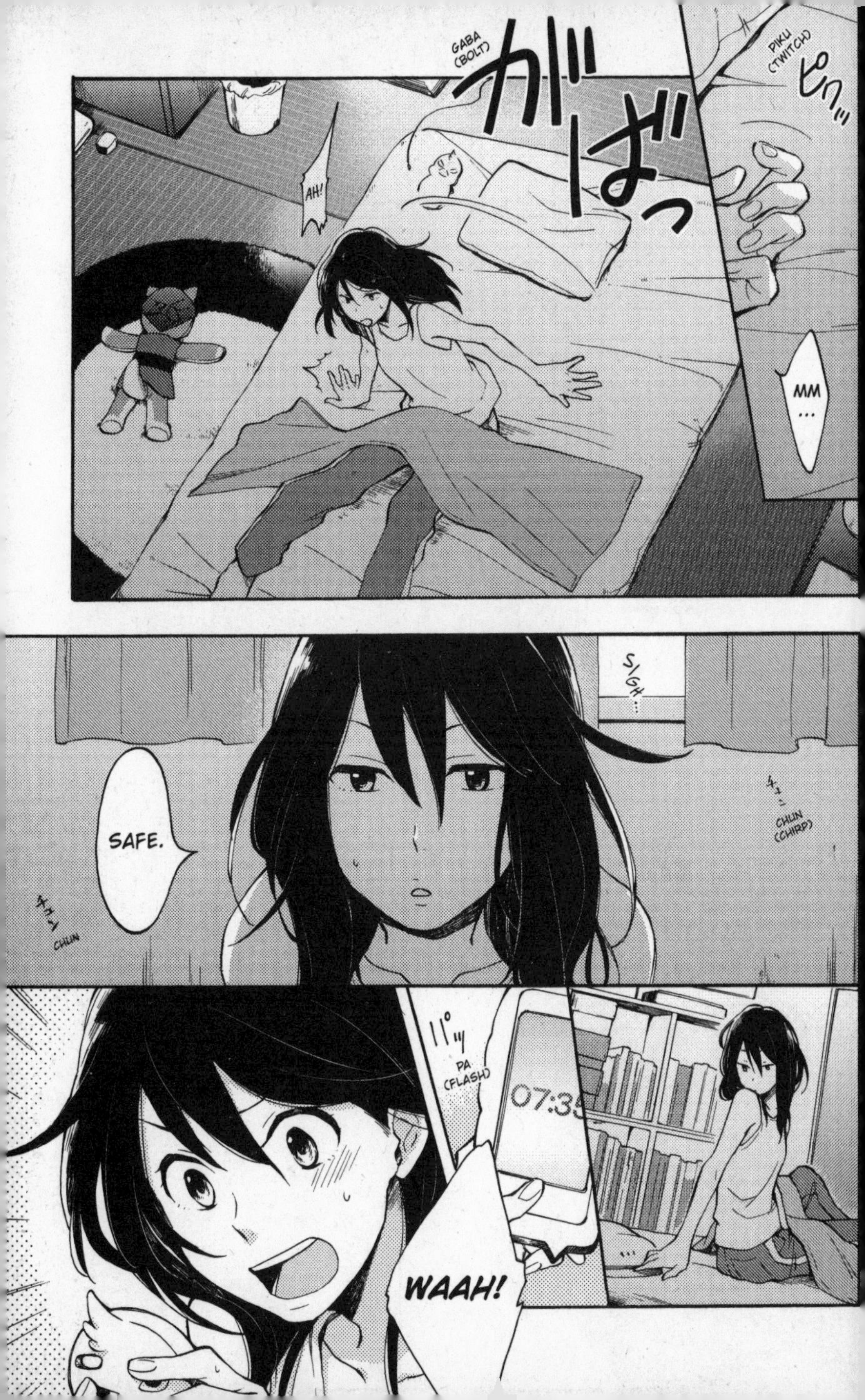
PIKU (TWITCH)
ピクッ
MM ...
GABA (BOLT)
がばっ
AH!
SIGH...
チュン
CHUN (CHIRP)
SAFE.
チュン
CHUN
...
パッ
PA (FLASH)
07:35
WAAH!

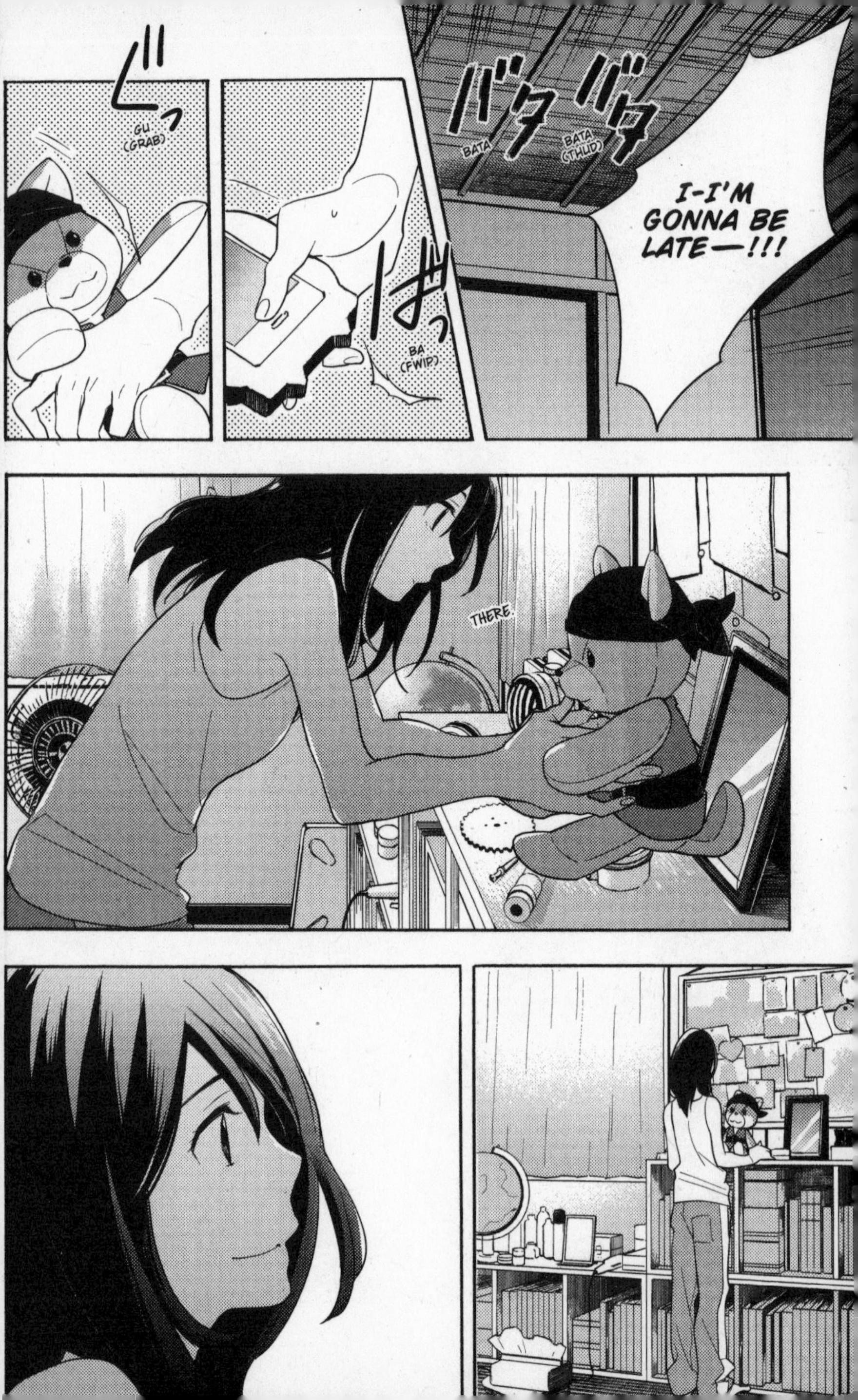
バタ
BATA
バタ
BATA (THUD)
I-I'M GONNA BE LATE—!!!
ばっ
BA (FWIP)
ぐっ
GU (GRAB)
THERE.

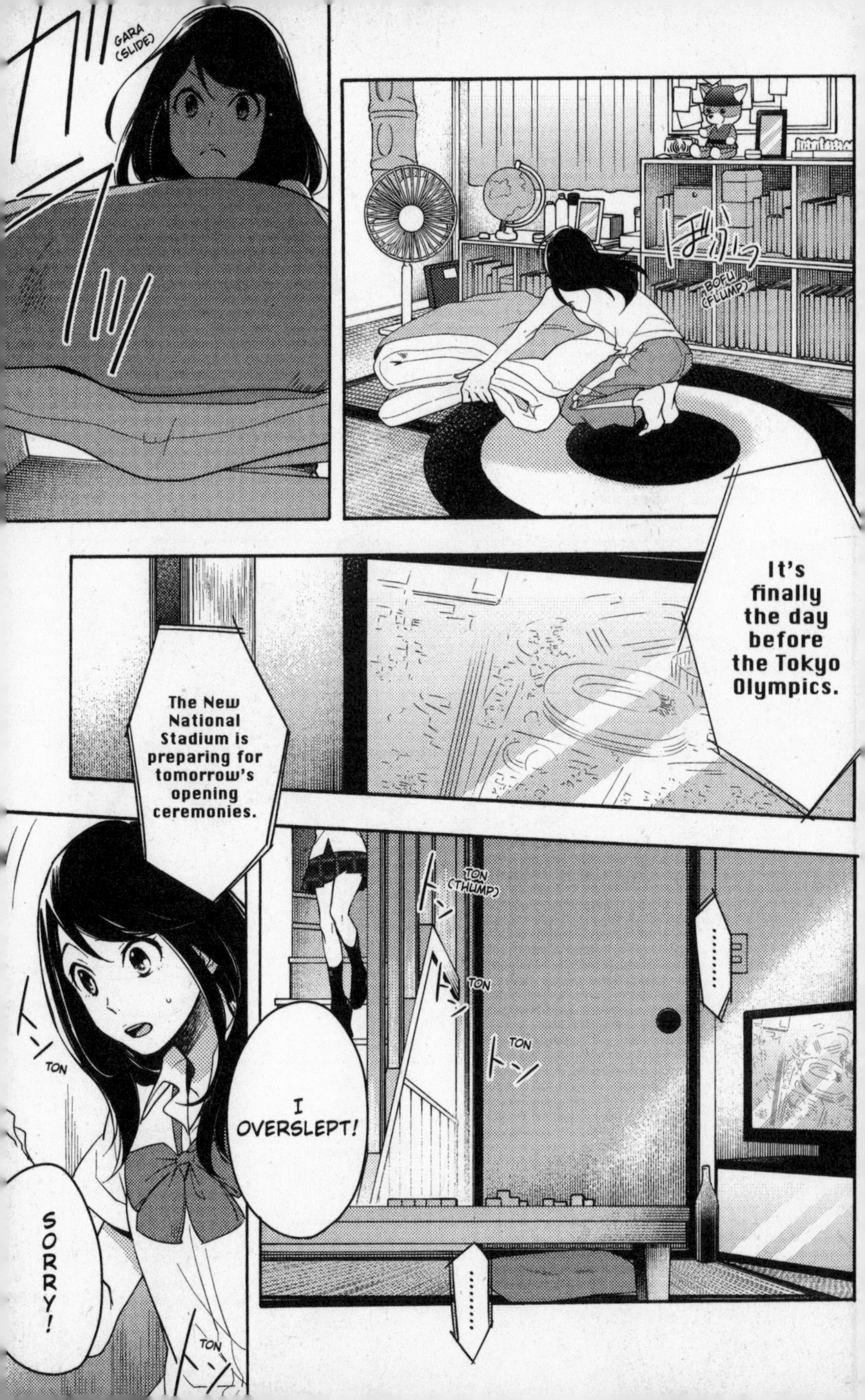

BOFU (FLUMP)
GARA (SLIDE)
It's finally the day before the Tokyo Olympics.
The New National Stadium is preparing for tomorrow's opening ceremonies.
......
TON (THUMP)
TON
TON
......
I OVERSLEPT!
TON
SORRY!
TON

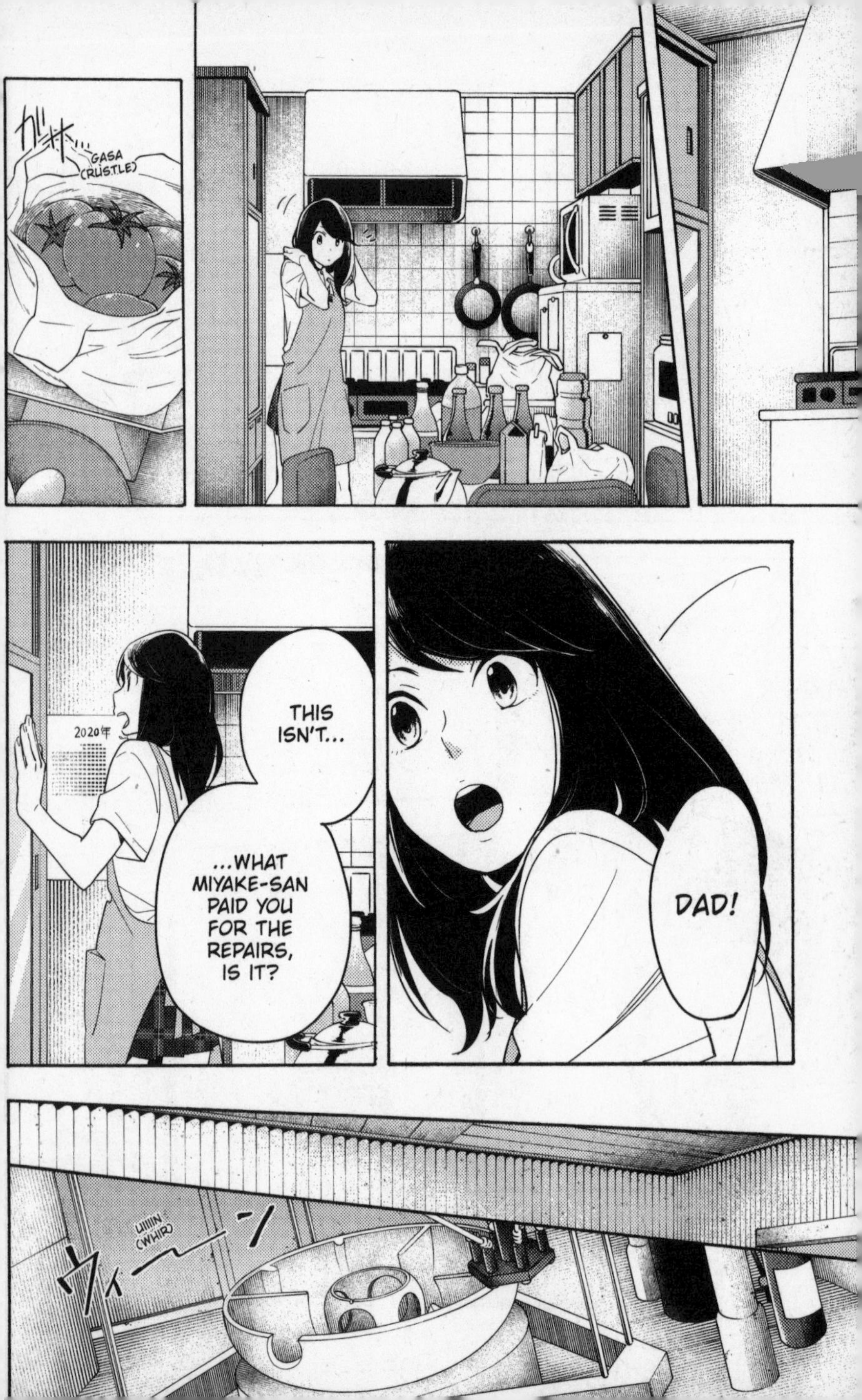
GASA
(RUSTLE)
DAD!
THIS ISN'T...
...WHAT MIYAKE-SAN PAID YOU FOR THE REPAIRS, IS IT?
UIIIIN
(WHIR)

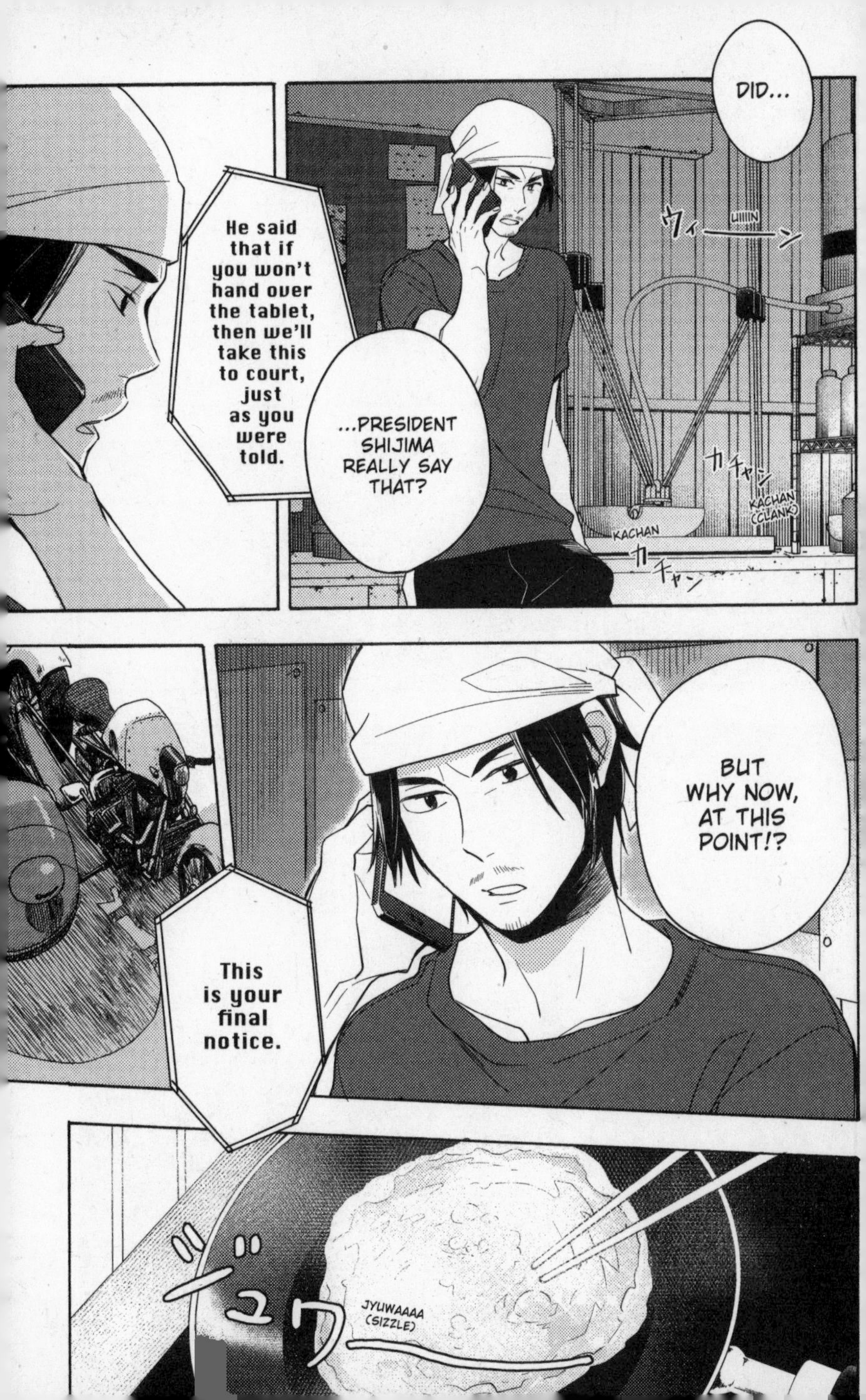
DID...
...PRESIDENT SHIJIMA REALLY SAY THAT?
ウィーン
UIIIIN
カチャン
KACHAN (CLANK)
カチャン
KACHAN
He said that if you won't hand over the tablet, then we'll take this to court, just as you were told.
BUT WHY NOW, AT THIS POINT!?
This is your final notice.
ジュワ
JYUWAAAA (SIZZLE)

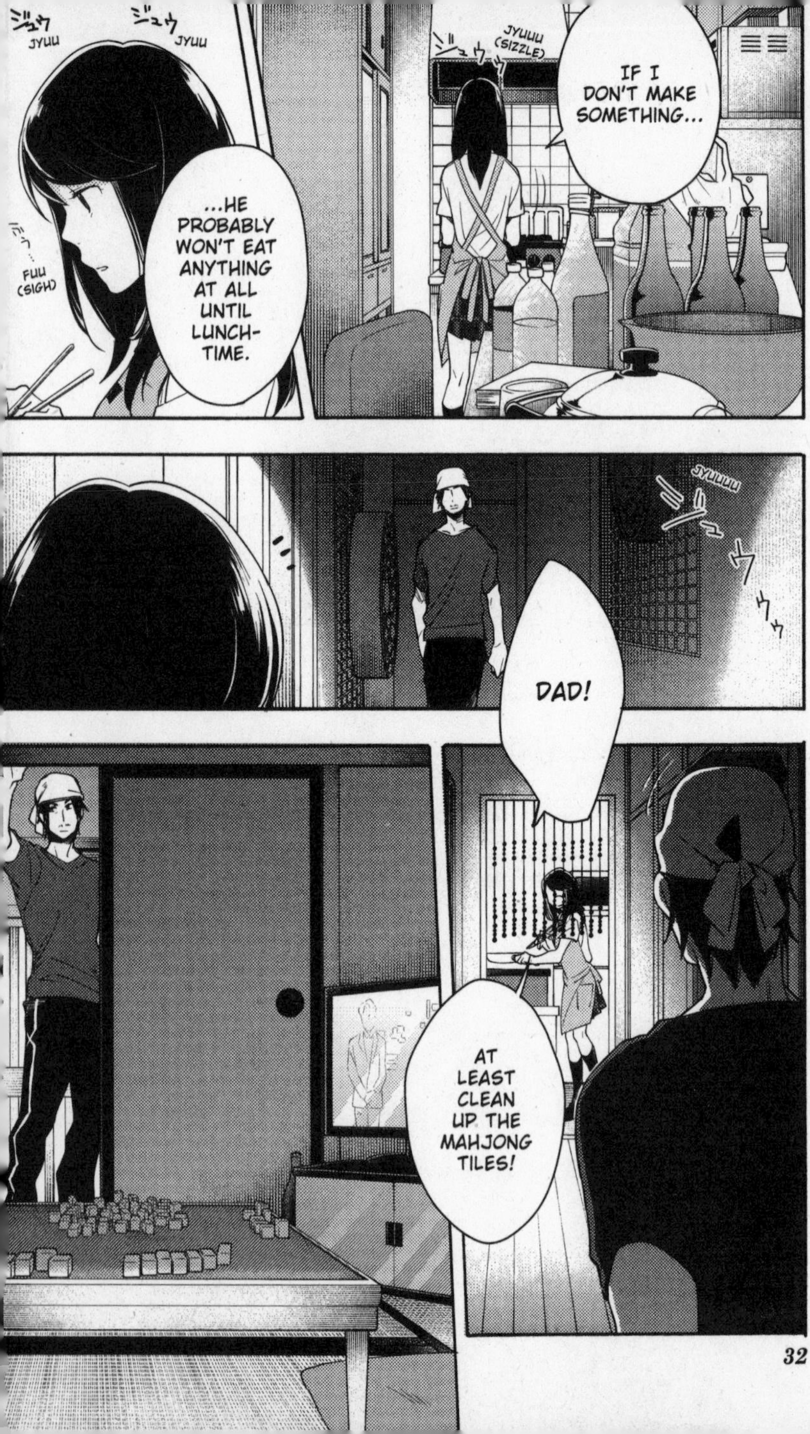
JYUUU (SIZZLE)
IF I DON'T MAKE SOMETHING...
JYUU
JYUU
FUU (SIGH)
...HE PROBABLY WON'T EAT ANYTHING AT ALL UNTIL LUNCH-TIME.
JYUUUU
DAD!
AT LEAST CLEAN UP THE MAHJONG TILES!

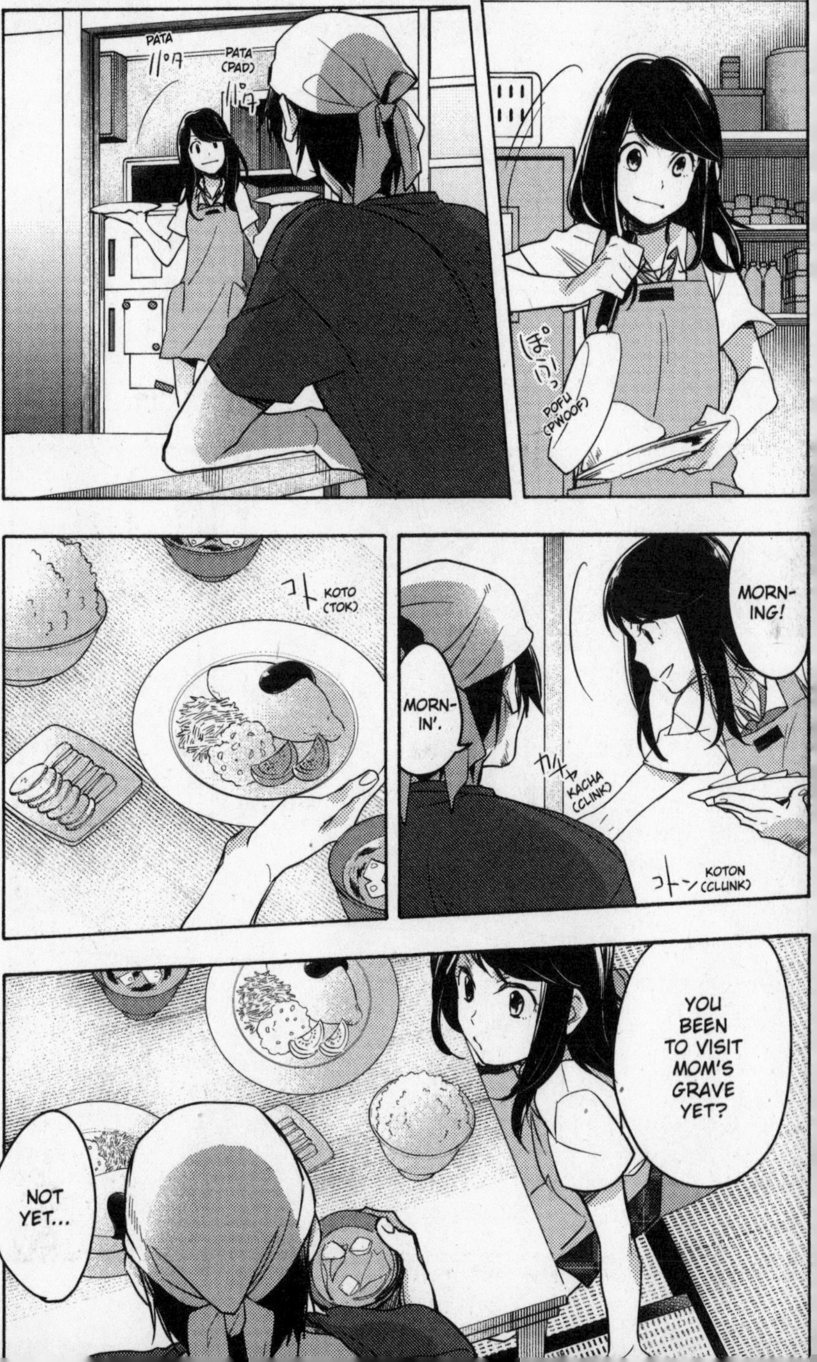
ぽふっ
POFU (PWOOF)
パタ
PATA
パタ
PATA (PAD)
MORNING!
MORNIN'.
カチャ
KACHA (CLINK)
コトン
KOTON (CLUNK)
コト
KOTO (TOK)
YOU BEEN TO VISIT MOM'S GRAVE YET?
NOT YET...

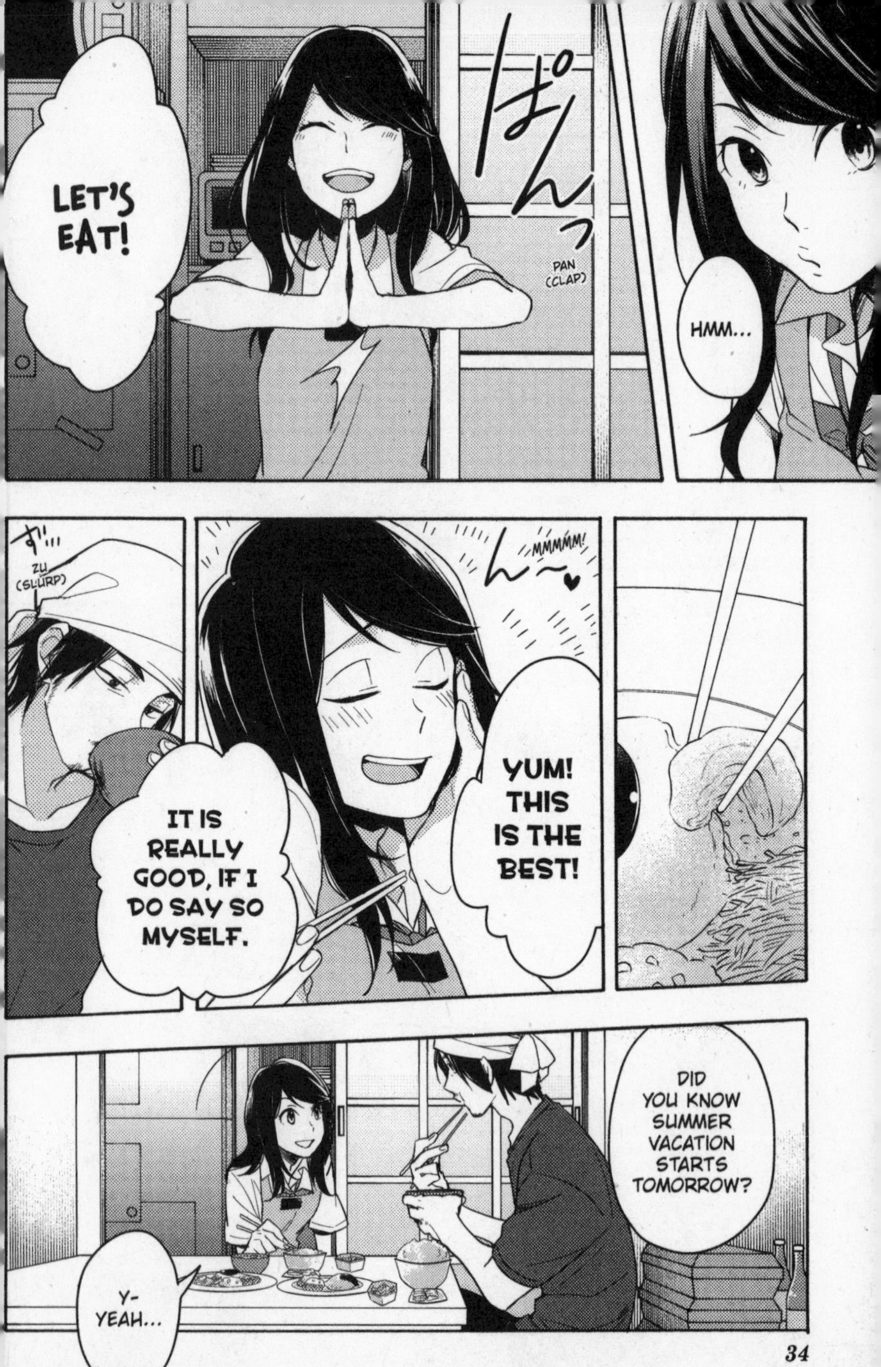
HMM...
ぱんっ
PAN (CLAP)
LET'S EAT!
ん〜♥
MMMMM!
YUM! THIS IS THE BEST!
ZU (SLURP)
IT IS REALLY GOOD, IF I DO SAY SO MYSELF.
DID YOU KNOW SUMMER VACATION STARTS TOMORROW?
Y-YEAH...

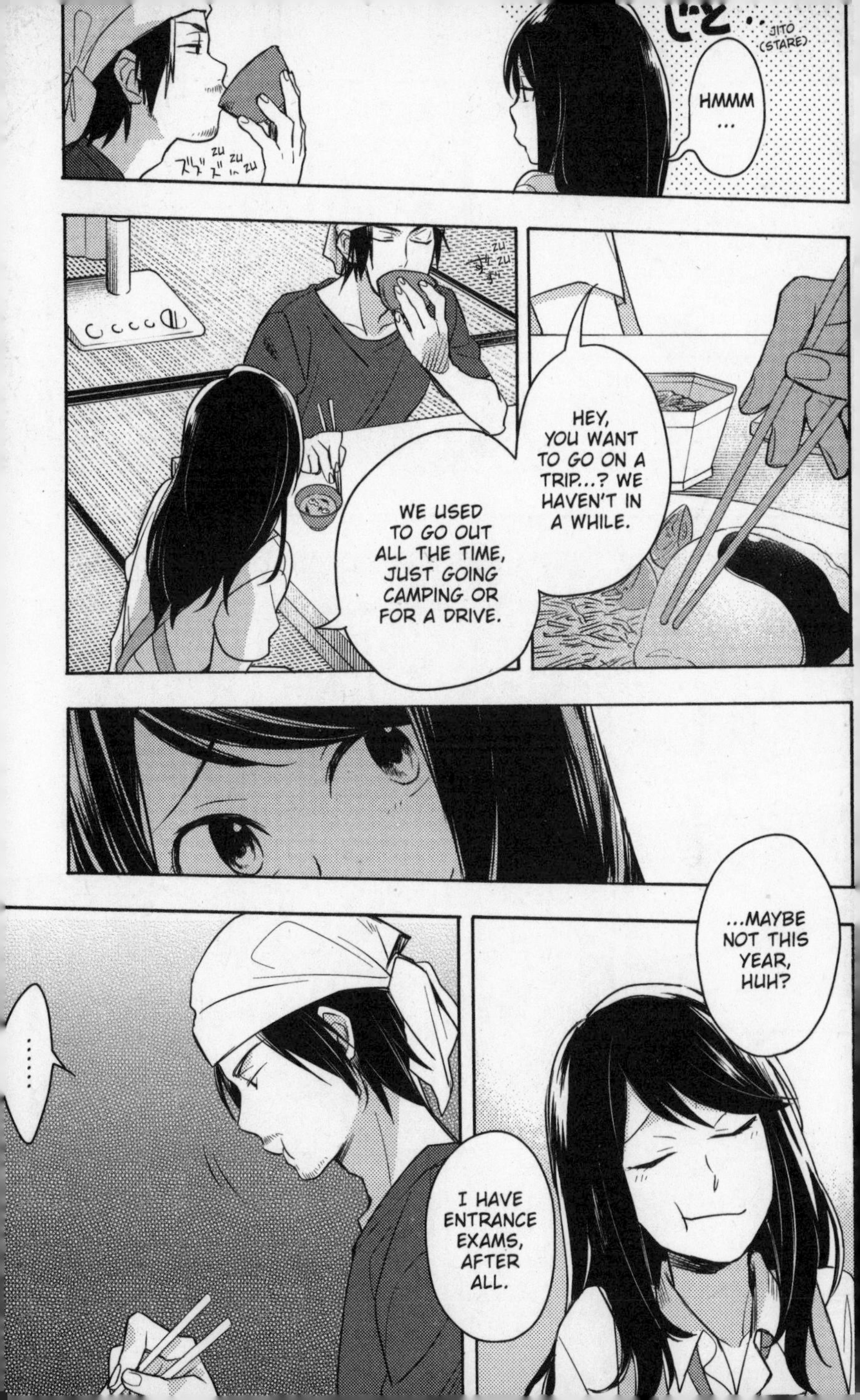
JITO (STARE)
HMMM ...
ZU ZU ZU
HEY, YOU WANT TO GO ON A TRIP...? WE HAVEN'T IN A WHILE.
ZU ZU
WE USED TO GO OUT ALL THE TIME, JUST GOING CAMPING OR FOR A DRIVE.
...MAYBE NOT THIS YEAR, HUH?
I HAVE ENTRANCE EXAMS, AFTER ALL.
......

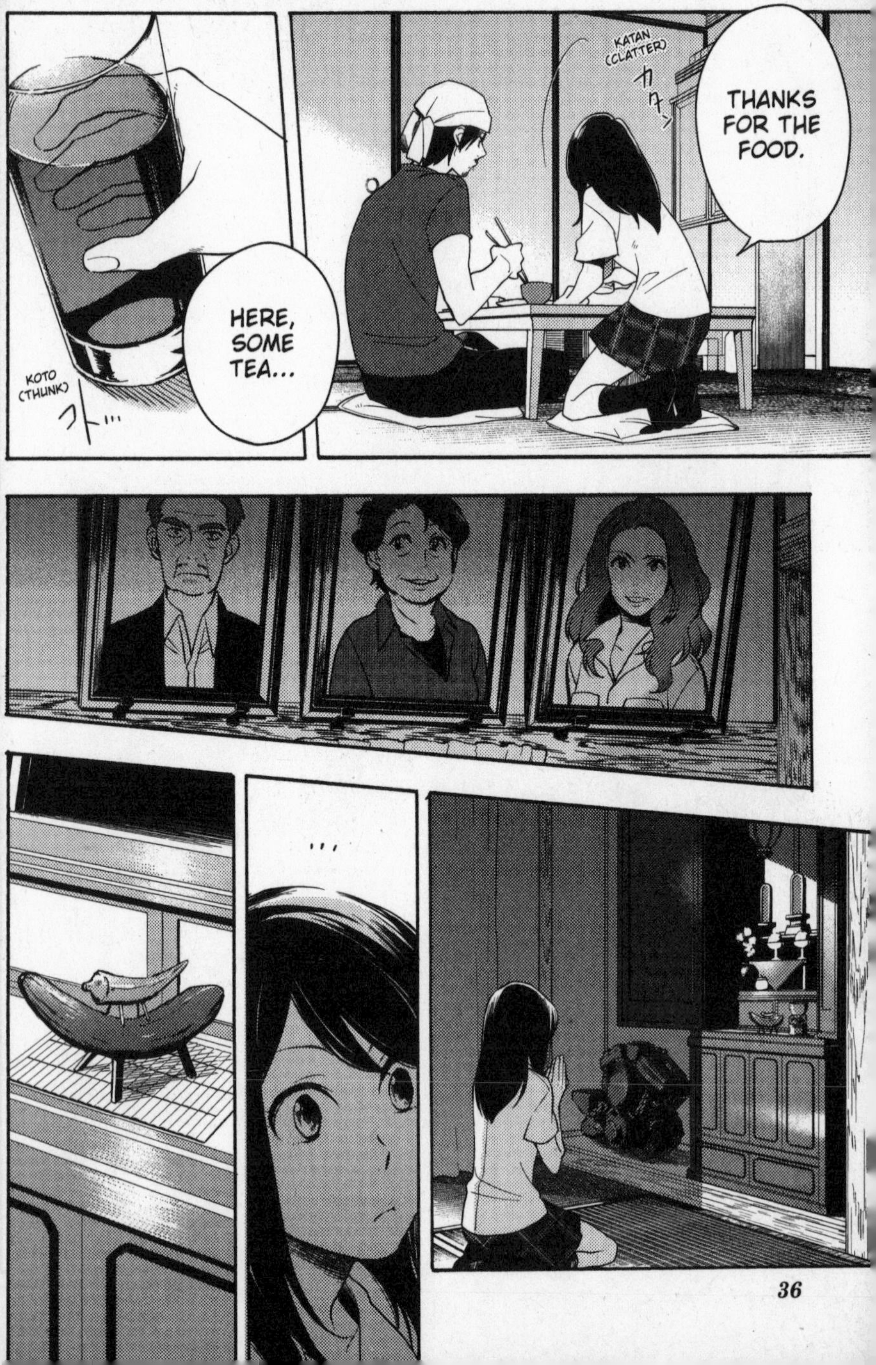
KATAN (CLATTER)
THANKS FOR THE FOOD.
HERE, SOME TEA...
KOTO (THUNK)
...

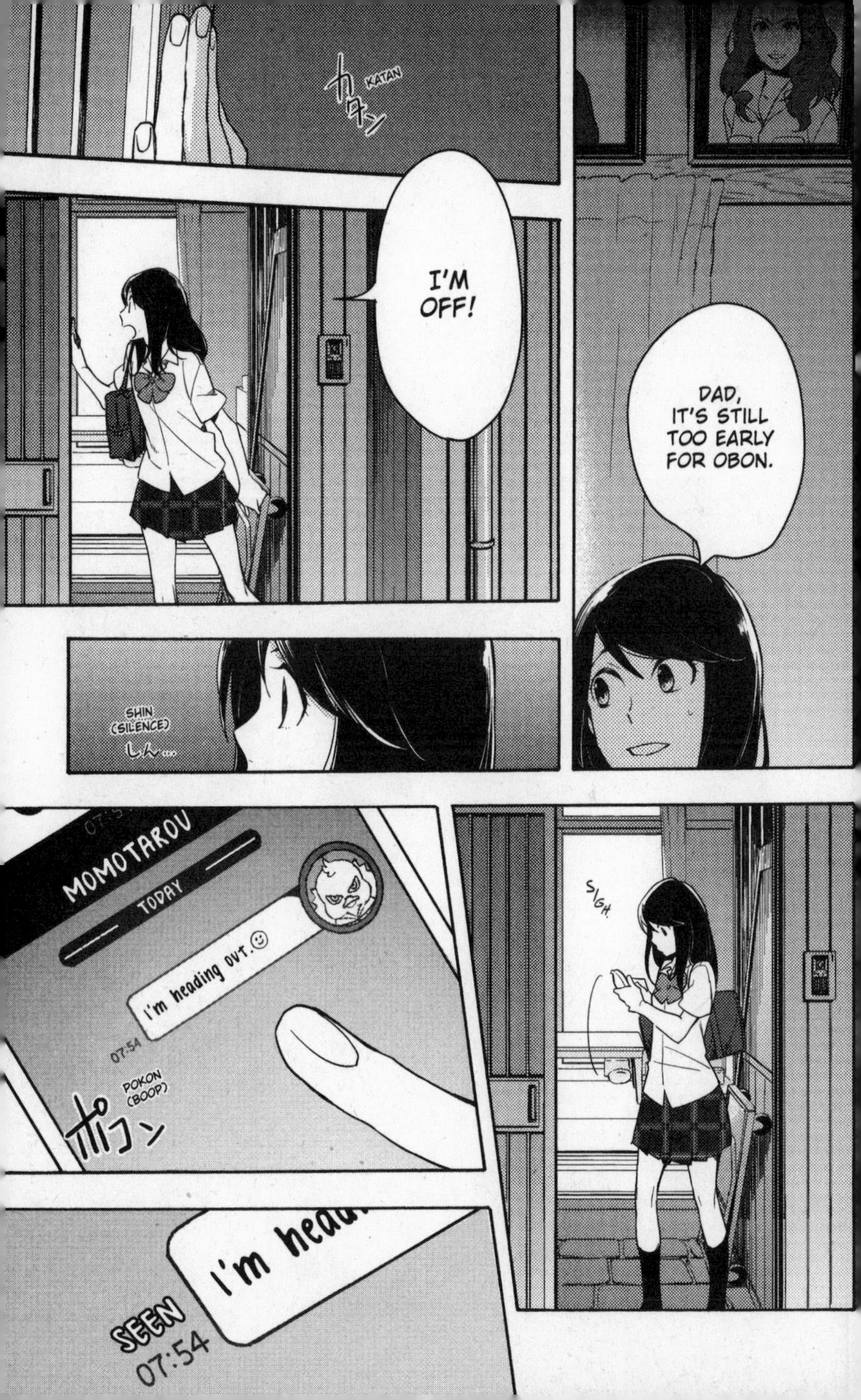
DAD, IT'S STILL TOO EARLY FOR OBON.
カタン
KATAN
I'M OFF!
SHIN (SILENCE)
しん…
SIGH.
MOMOTAROU
TODAY
i'm heading out. ☺
07:54
POKON (BOOP)
ポコン
i'm head
SEEN
07:54

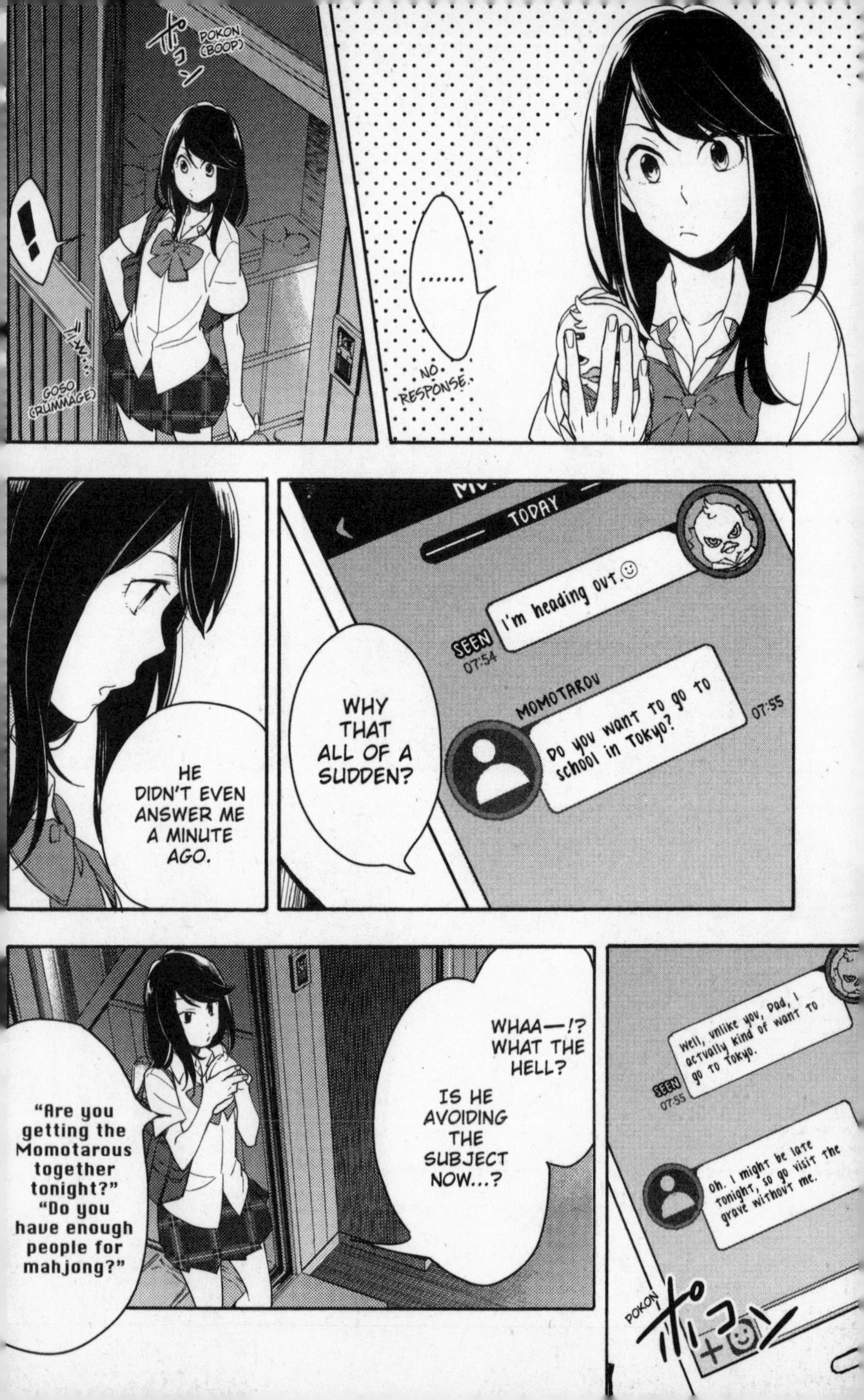
......
NO RESPONSE.
POKON (BOOP)
!
GOSO (RUMMAGE)
TODAY
I'm heading out. ☺
SEEN 07:54
MOMOTAROU
Do you want to go to school in Tokyo?
07:55
WHY THAT ALL OF A SUDDEN?
HE DIDN'T EVEN ANSWER ME A MINUTE AGO.
Well, unlike you, Dad, I actually kind of want to go to Tokyo.
SEEN 07:55
Oh. I might be late tonight, so go visit the grave without me.
POKON
WHAA—!? WHAT THE HELL?
IS HE AVOIDING THE SUBJECT NOW...?
"Are you getting the Momotarous together tonight?" "Do you have enough people for mahjong?"

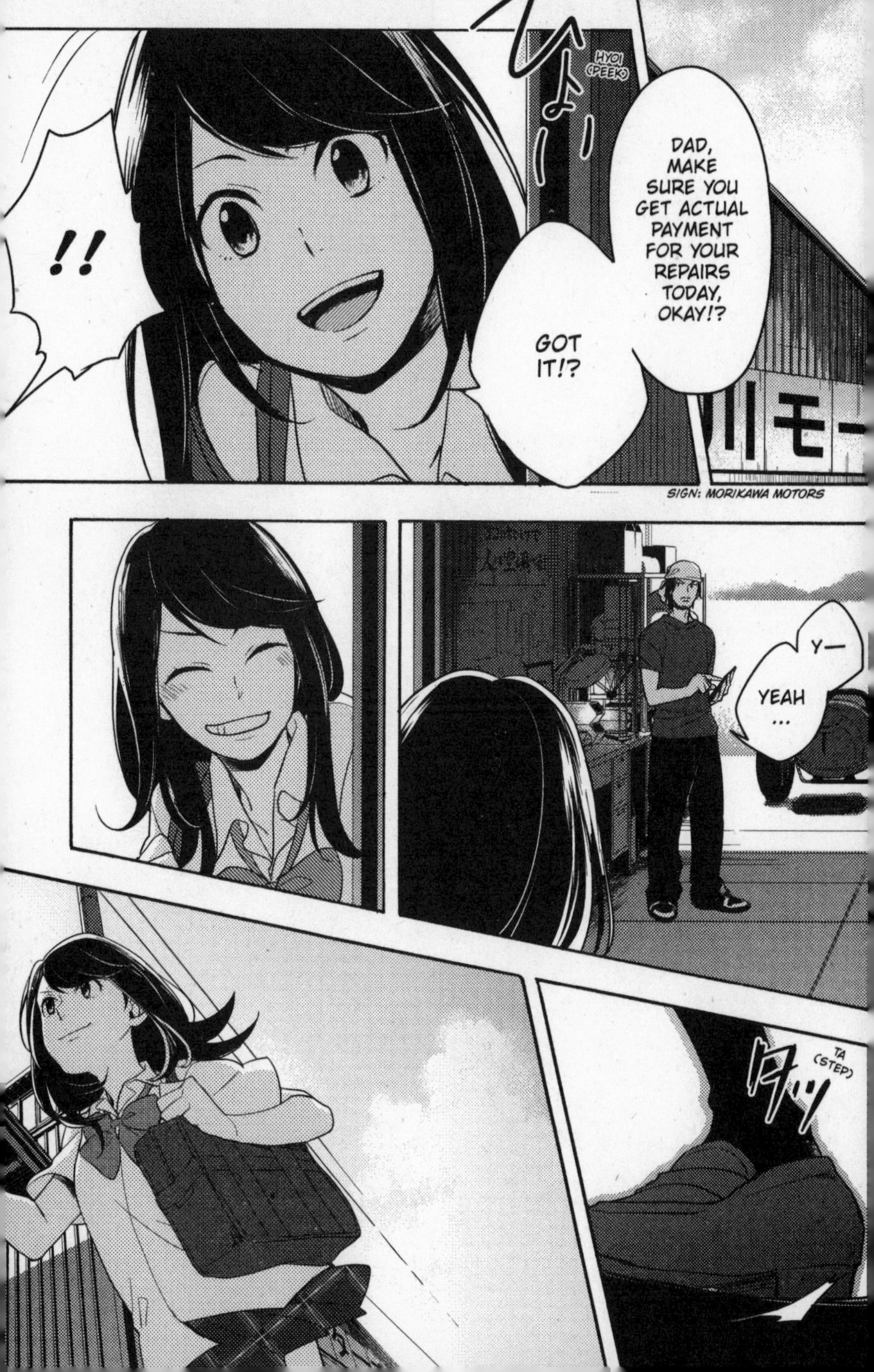
HYOI (PEEK)
DAD, MAKE SURE YOU GET ACTUAL PAYMENT FOR YOUR REPAIRS TODAY, OKAY!?
GOT IT!?
!!
SIGN: MORIKAWA MOTORS
Y— YEAH ...
TA (STEP)

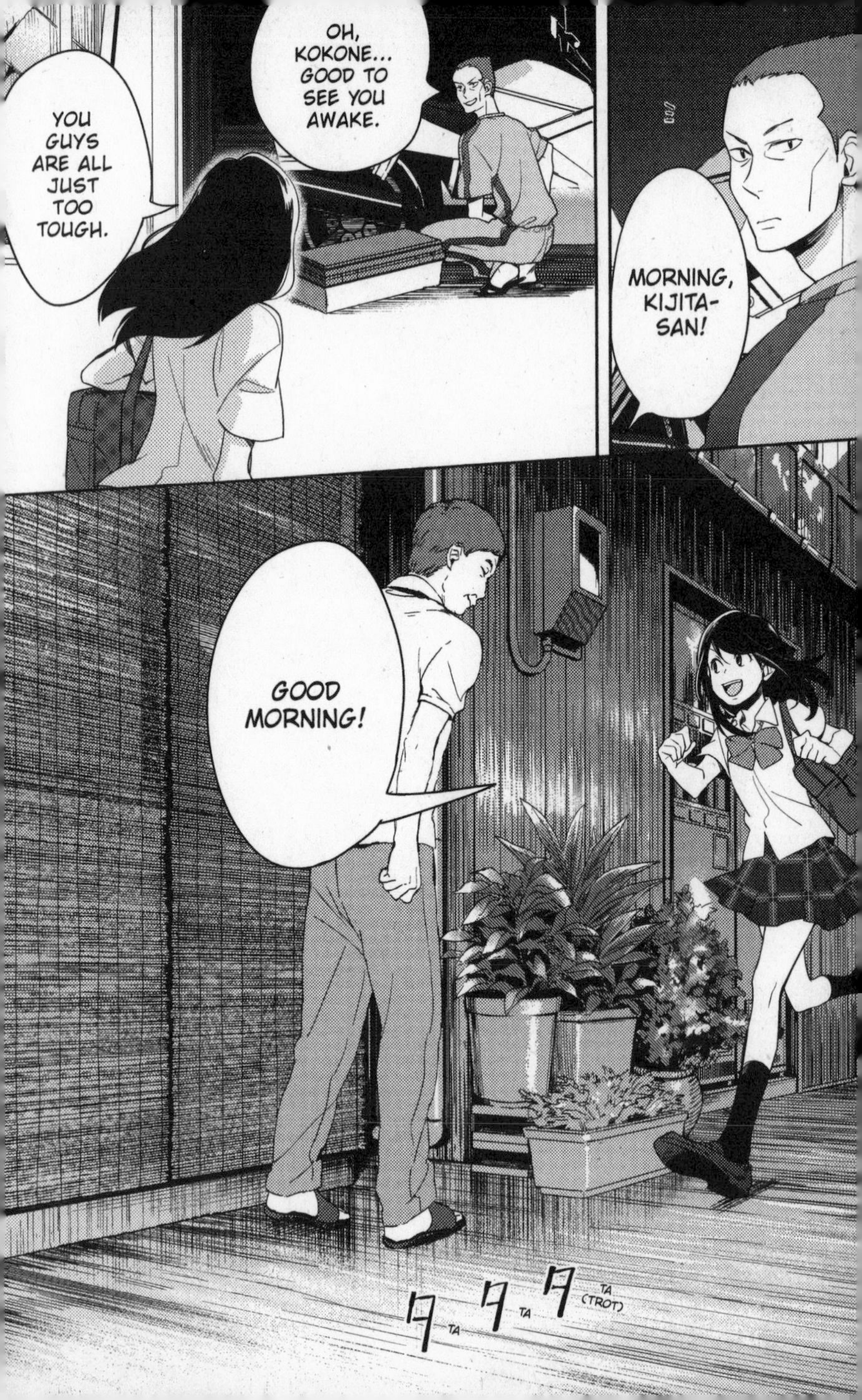
MORNING, KIJITA-SAN!
OH, KOKONE... GOOD TO SEE YOU AWAKE.
YOU GUYS ARE ALL JUST TOO TOUGH.
GOOD MORNING!
タ TA タ TA タ TA (TROT)

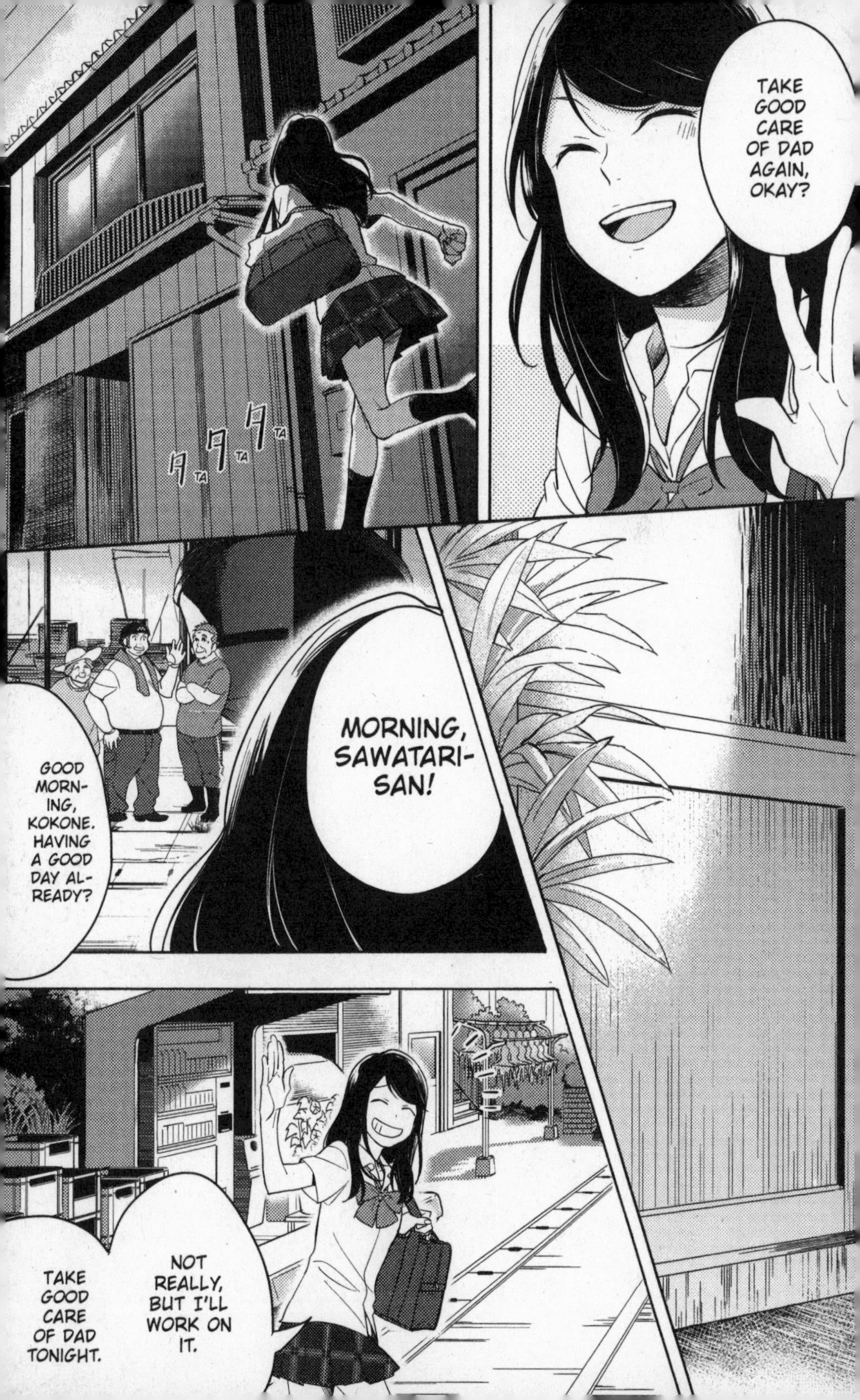
TAKE GOOD CARE OF DAD AGAIN, OKAY?
TA TA TA
MORNING, SAWATARI-SAN!
GOOD MORN-ING, KOKONE. HAVING A GOOD DAY AL-READY?
NOT REALLY, BUT I'LL WORK ON IT.
TAKE GOOD CARE OF DAD TONIGHT.

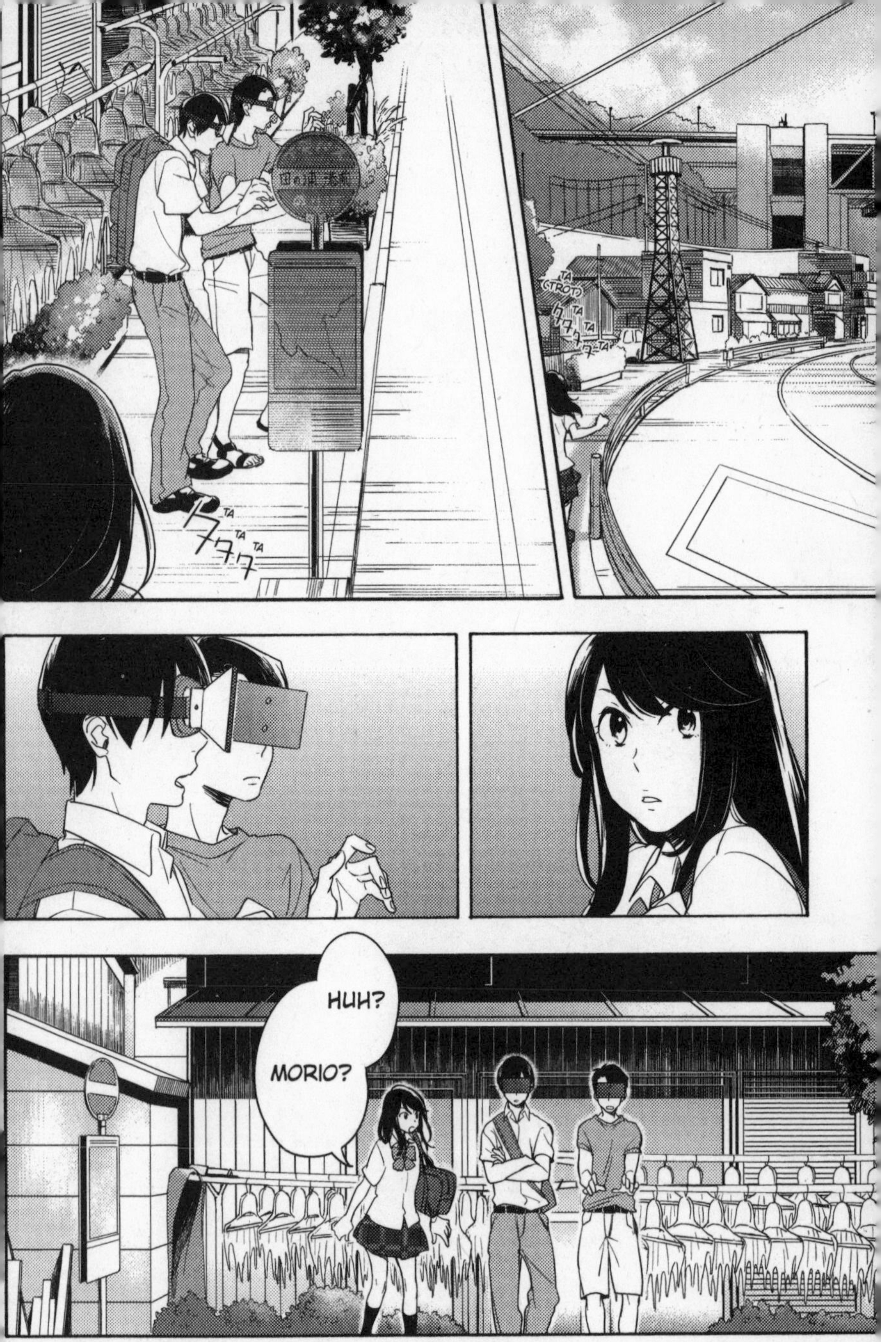
TA (TROT) TA TA TA
TA TA TA
HUH?
MORIO?

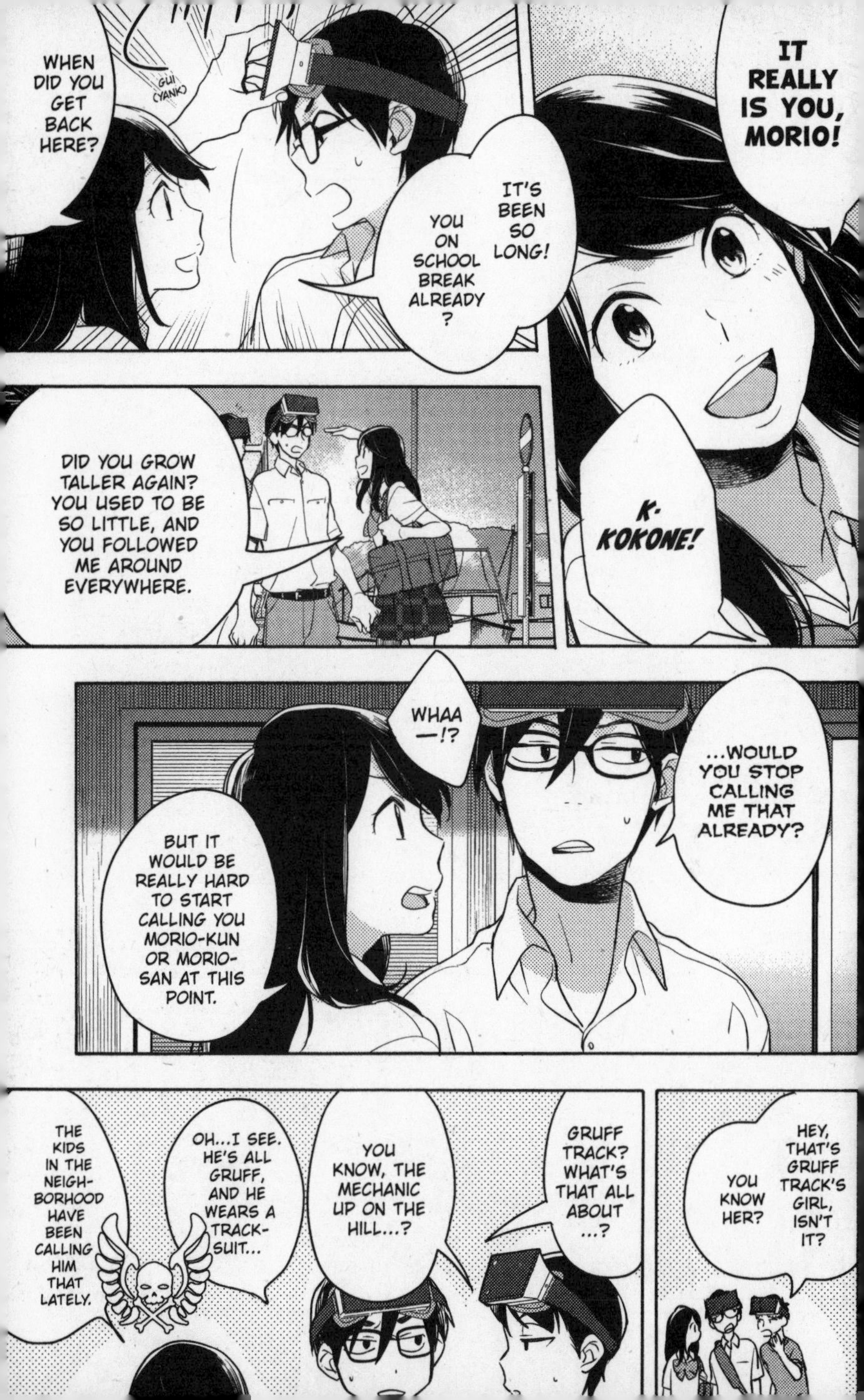
IT REALLY IS YOU, MORIO!
K-KOKONE!
IT'S BEEN SO LONG!
YOU ON SCHOOL BREAK ALREADY?
WHEN DID YOU GET BACK HERE?
GUI (YANK)
DID YOU GROW TALLER AGAIN? YOU USED TO BE SO LITTLE, AND YOU FOLLOWED ME AROUND EVERYWHERE.
...WOULD YOU STOP CALLING ME THAT ALREADY?
WHAA—!?
BUT IT WOULD BE REALLY HARD TO START CALLING YOU MORIO-KUN OR MORIO-SAN AT THIS POINT.
HEY, THAT'S GRUFF TRACK'S GIRL, ISN'T IT?
YOU KNOW HER?
GRUFF TRACK? WHAT'S THAT ALL ABOUT...?
YOU KNOW, THE MECHANIC UP ON THE HILL...?
OH...I SEE. HE'S ALL GRUFF, AND HE WEARS A TRACK-SUIT...
THE KIDS IN THE NEIGHBORHOOD HAVE BEEN CALLING HIM THAT LATELY.

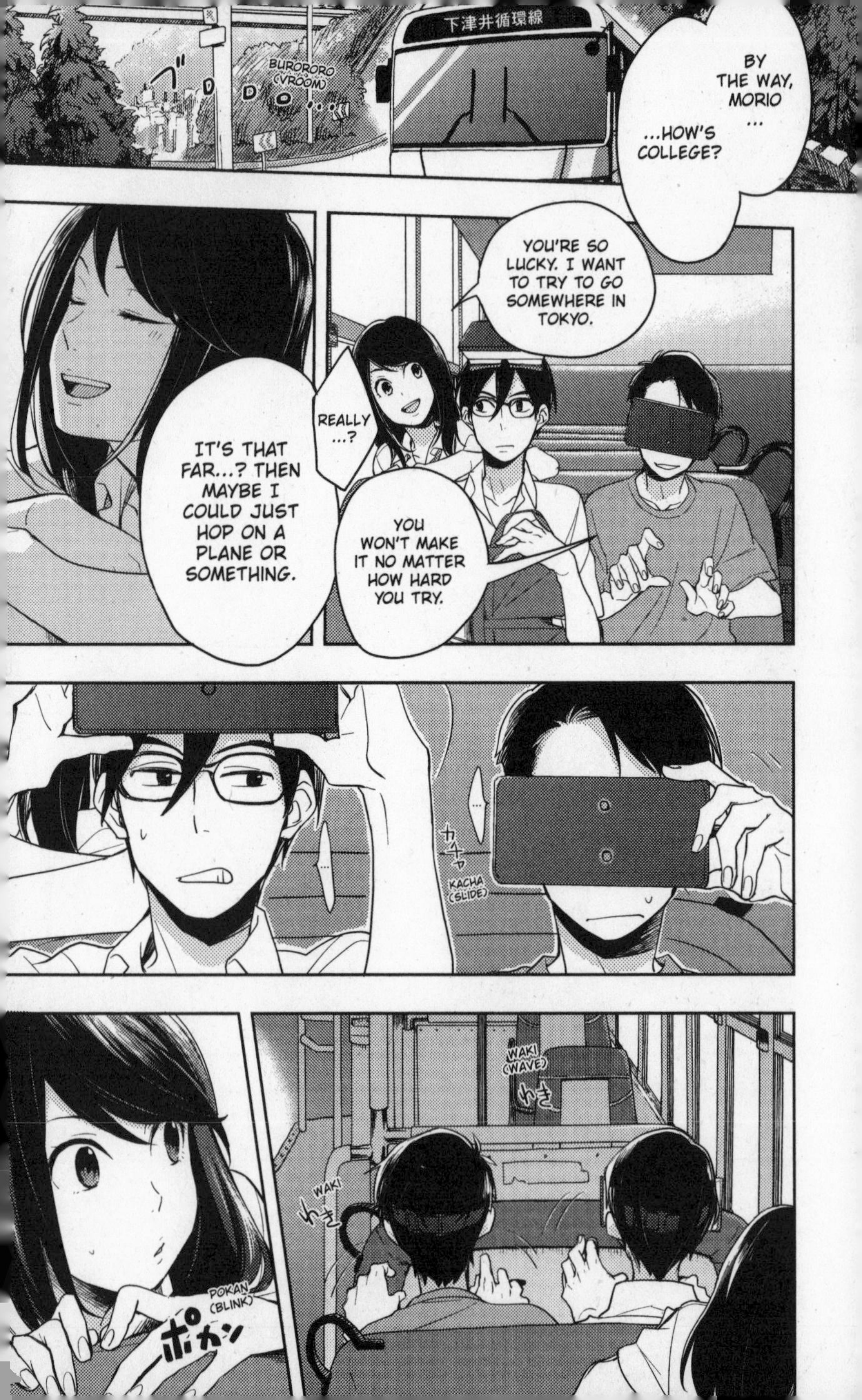
下津井循環線
BURORORO (VROOM)
BY THE WAY, MORIO ...
...HOW'S COLLEGE?
YOU'RE SO LUCKY. I WANT TO TRY TO GO SOMEWHERE IN TOKYO.
REALLY ...?
YOU WON'T MAKE IT NO MATTER HOW HARD YOU TRY.
IT'S THAT FAR...? THEN MAYBE I COULD JUST HOP ON A PLANE OR SOMETHING.
...
KACHA (SLIDE)
...
WAKI (WAVE)
WAKI
POKAN (BLINK)

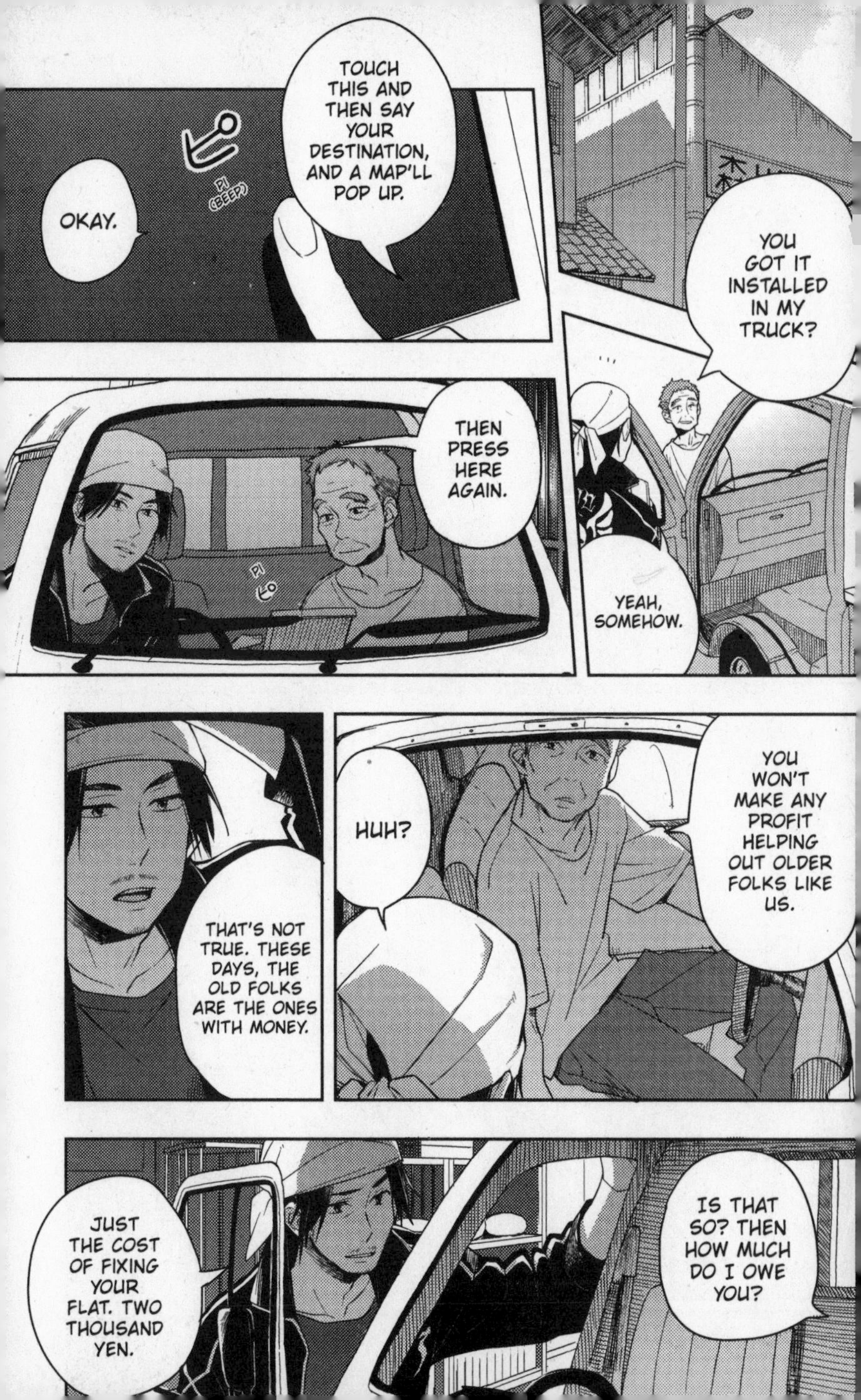
YOU GOT IT INSTALLED IN MY TRUCK?
...
YEAH, SOMEHOW.
TOUCH THIS AND THEN SAY YOUR DESTINATION, AND A MAP'LL POP UP.
ピ
PI (BEEP)
OKAY.
THEN PRESS HERE AGAIN.
PI
ピ
YOU WON'T MAKE ANY PROFIT HELPING OUT OLDER FOLKS LIKE US.
HUH?
THAT'S NOT TRUE. THESE DAYS, THE OLD FOLKS ARE THE ONES WITH MONEY.
IS THAT SO? THEN HOW MUCH DO I OWE YOU?
JUST THE COST OF FIXING YOUR FLAT. TWO THOUSAND YEN.

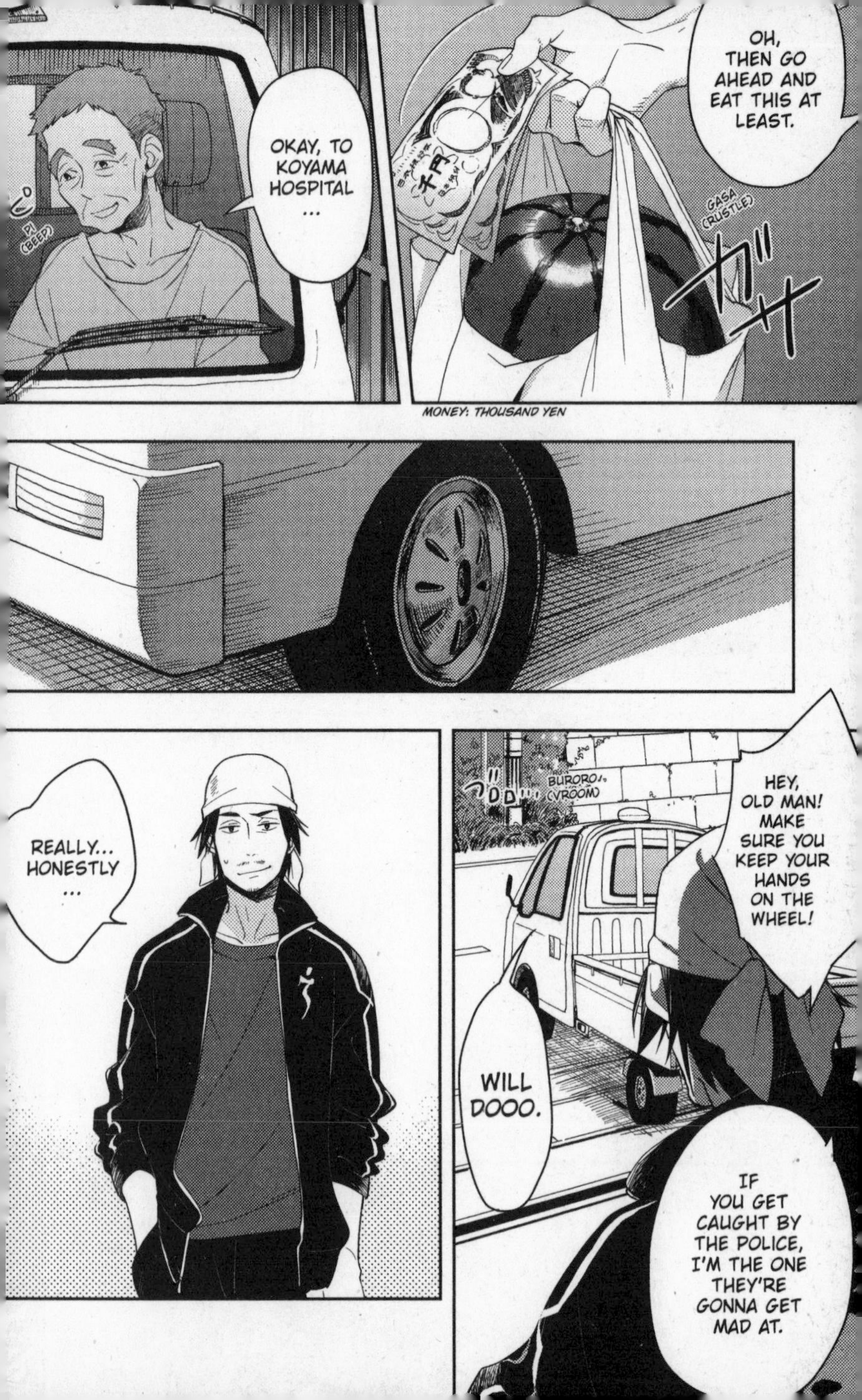
OH, THEN GO AHEAD AND EAT THIS AT LEAST.
GASA (RUSTLE)
MONEY: THOUSAND YEN
PI (BEEP)
OKAY, TO KOYAMA HOSPITAL ...
BURORO (VROOM)
HEY, OLD MAN! MAKE SURE YOU KEEP YOUR HANDS ON THE WHEEL!
WILL DOOO.
IF YOU GET CAUGHT BY THE POLICE, I'M THE ONE THEY'RE GONNA GET MAD AT.
REALLY... HONESTLY ...

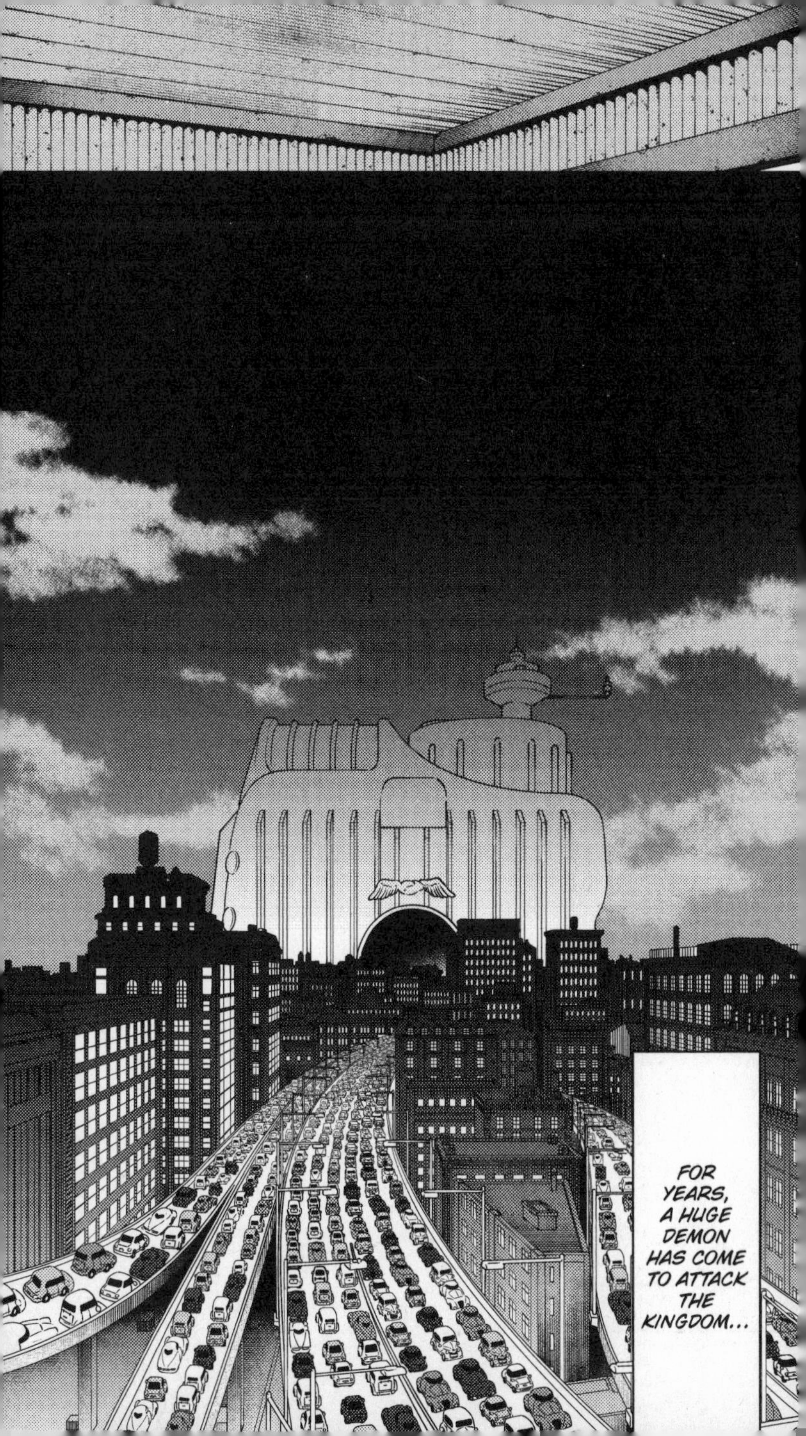
FOR YEARS, A HUGE DEMON HAS COME TO ATTACK THE KINGDOM...

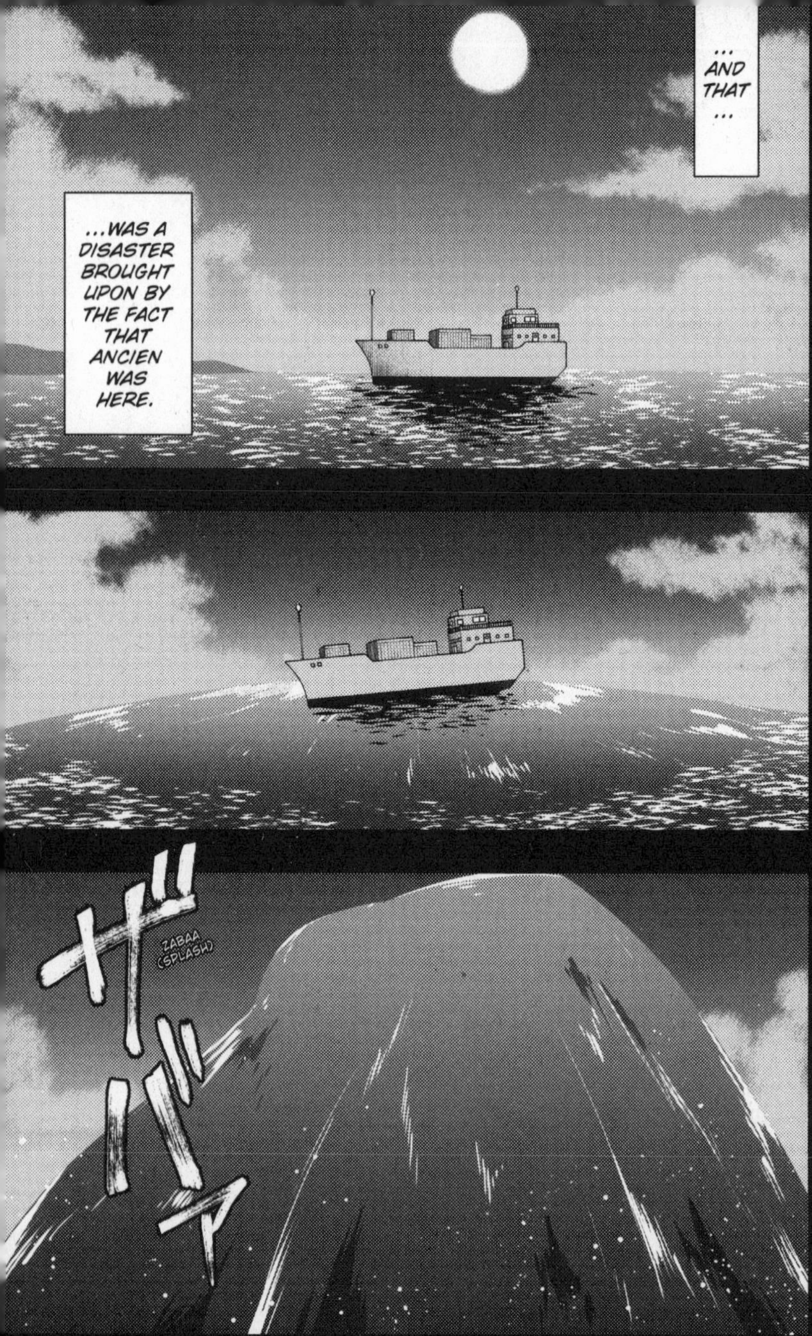
...AND THAT...
...WAS A DISASTER BROUGHT UPON BY THE FACT THAT ANCIEN WAS HERE.
ザバァ
ZABAA (SPLASH)

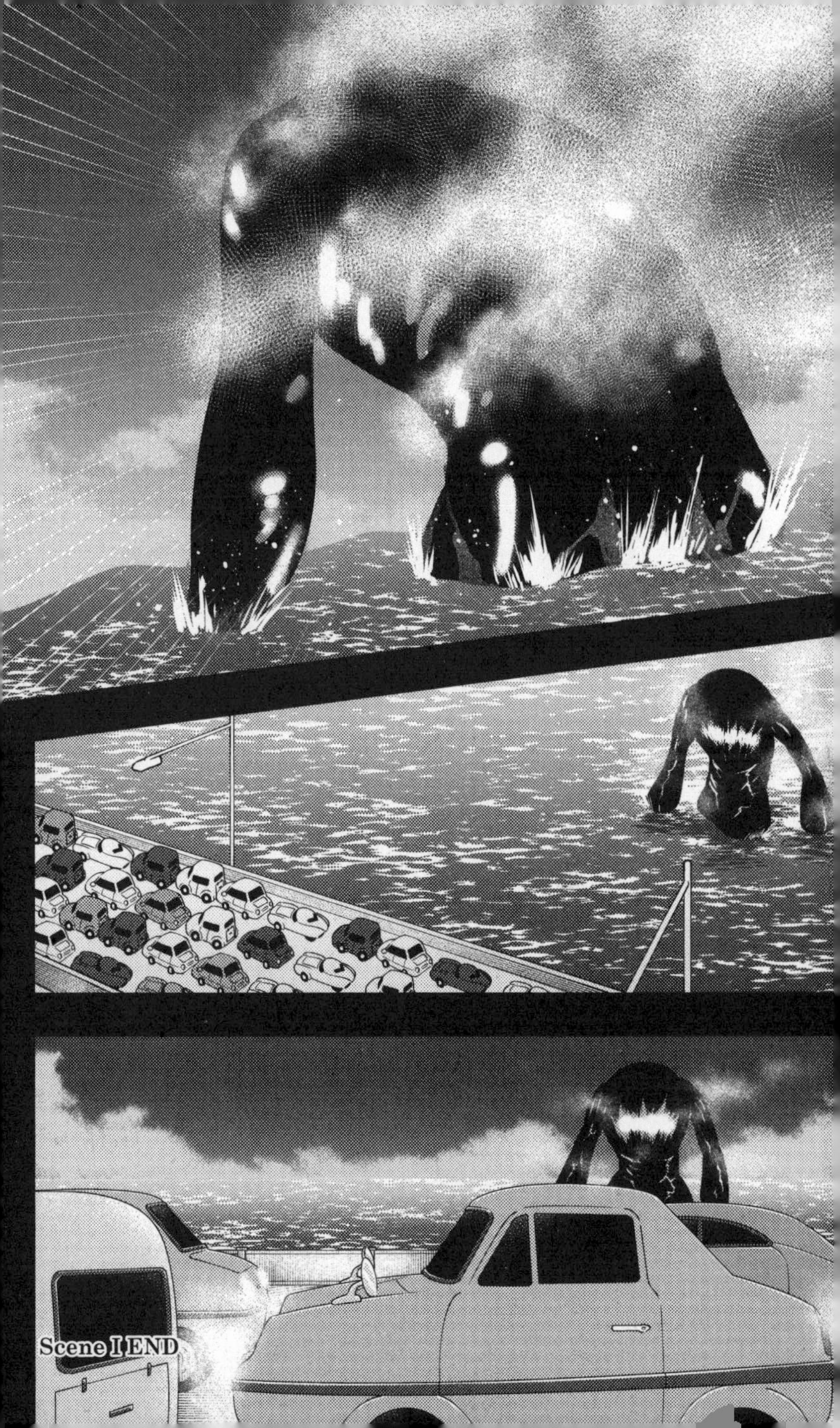
Scene I END

# Napping Princess
### The Story of the Unknown Me

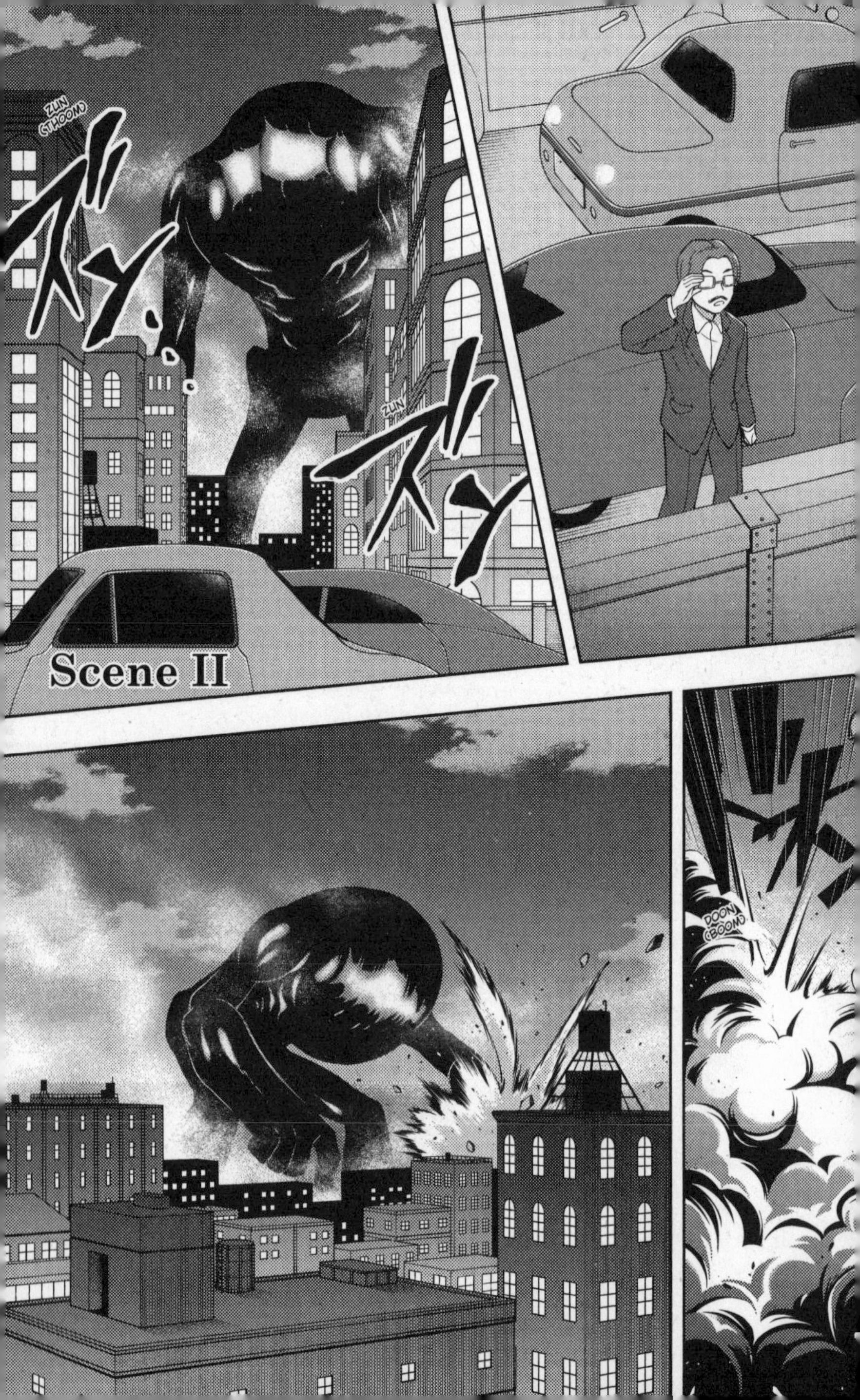
ZUN (THOOM)
ZUN
Scene II
DOON (BOOM)

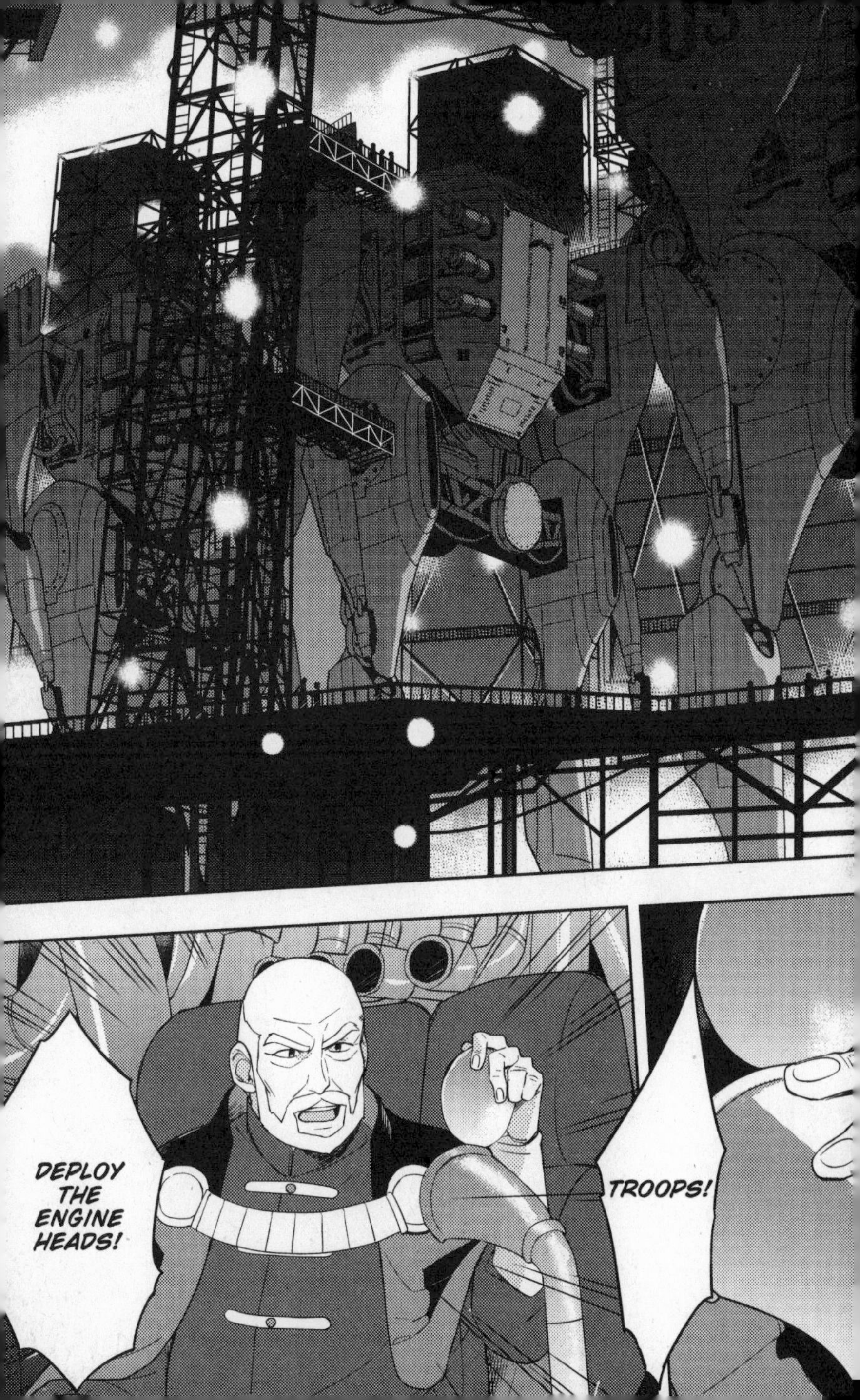
TROOPS!
DEPLOY THE ENGINE HEADS!

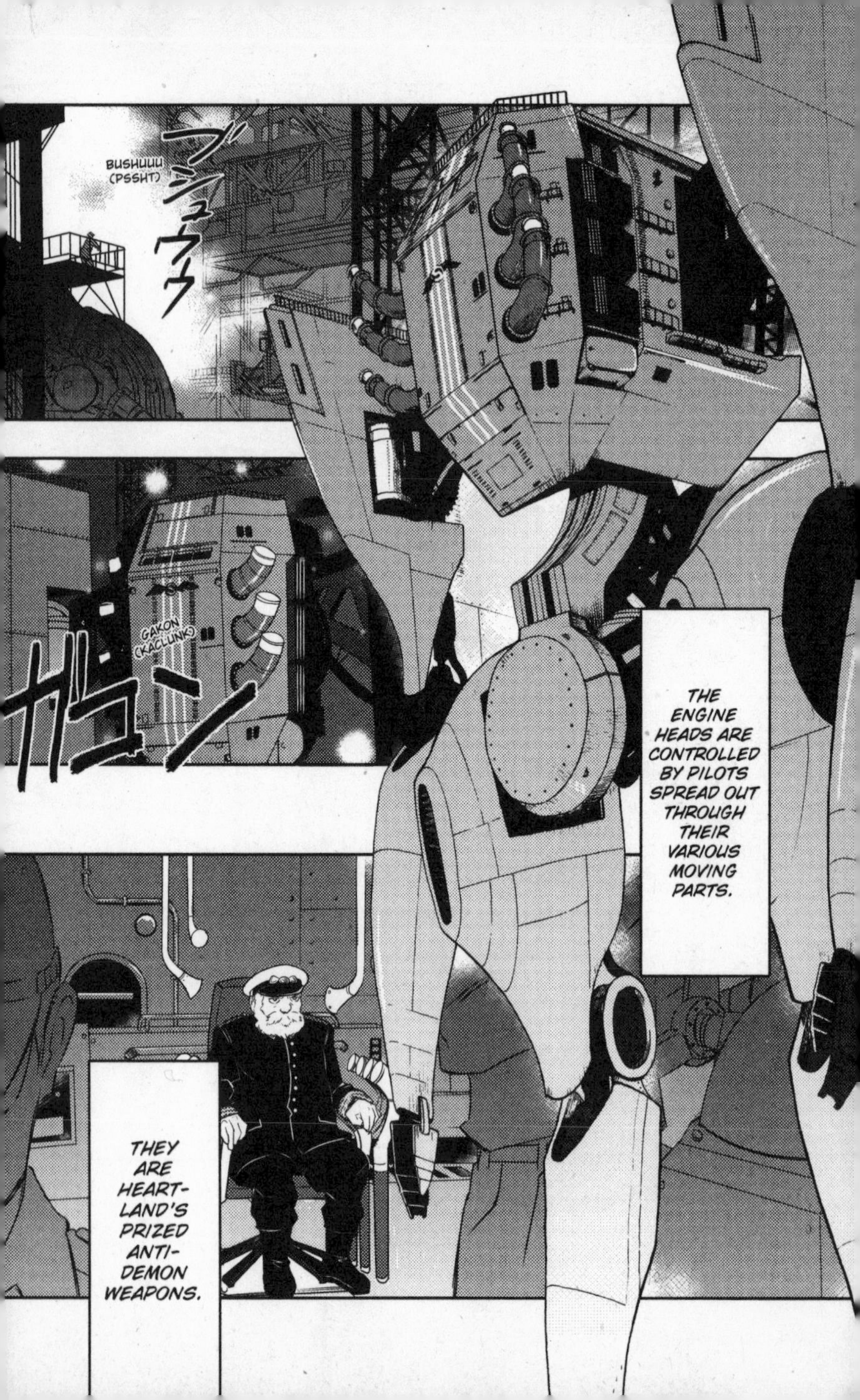
ブシュウウ
BUSHUUU (PSSHT)
ガコン
GAKON (KACLUNK)
THE ENGINE HEADS ARE CONTROLLED BY PILOTS SPREAD OUT THROUGH THEIR VARIOUS MOVING PARTS.
THEY ARE HEART-LAND'S PRIZED ANTI-DEMON WEAPONS.

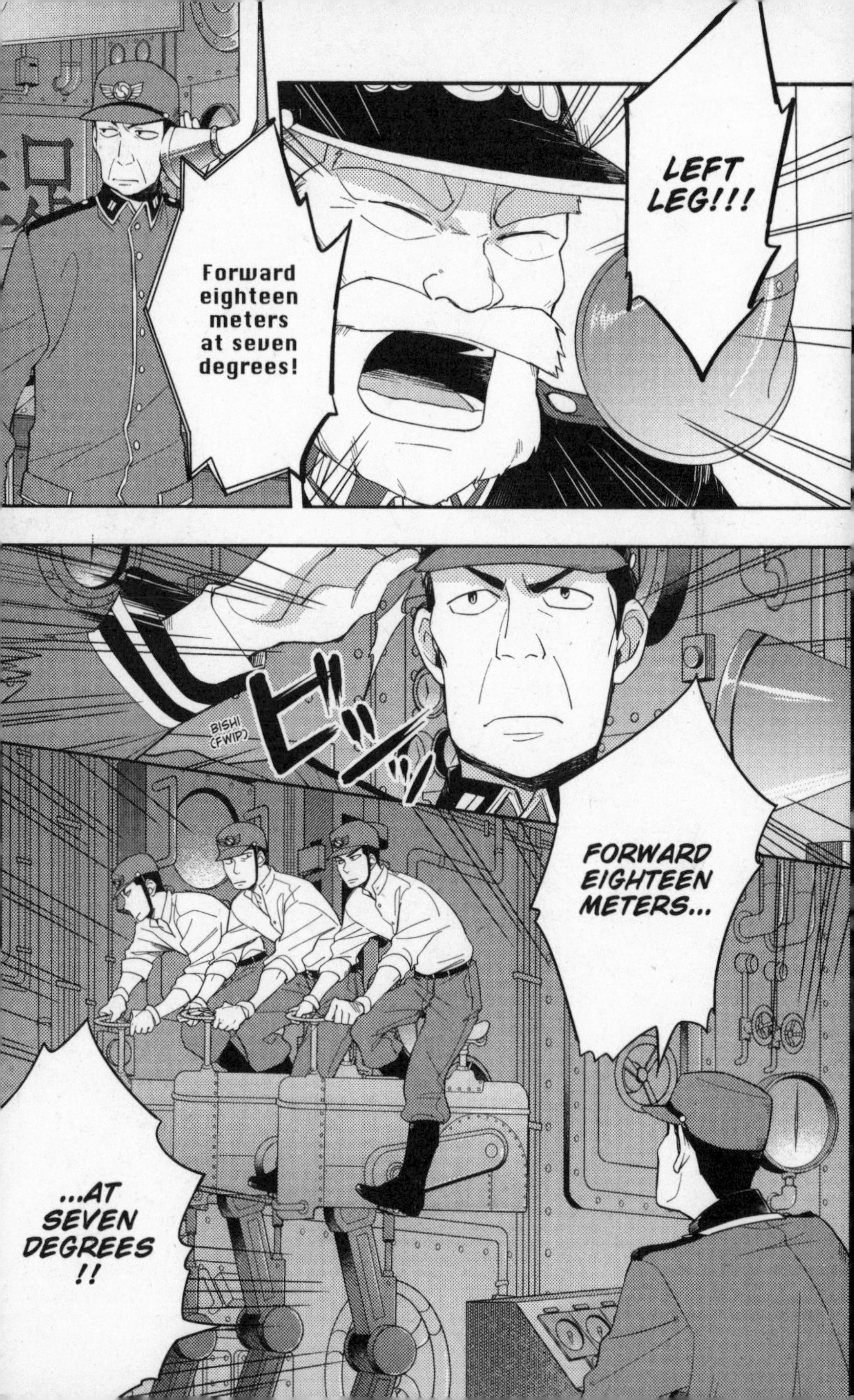
LEFT LEG!!!
Forward eighteen meters at seven degrees!
BISHI (FWIP)
FORWARD EIGHTEEN METERS...
...AT SEVEN DEGREES!!

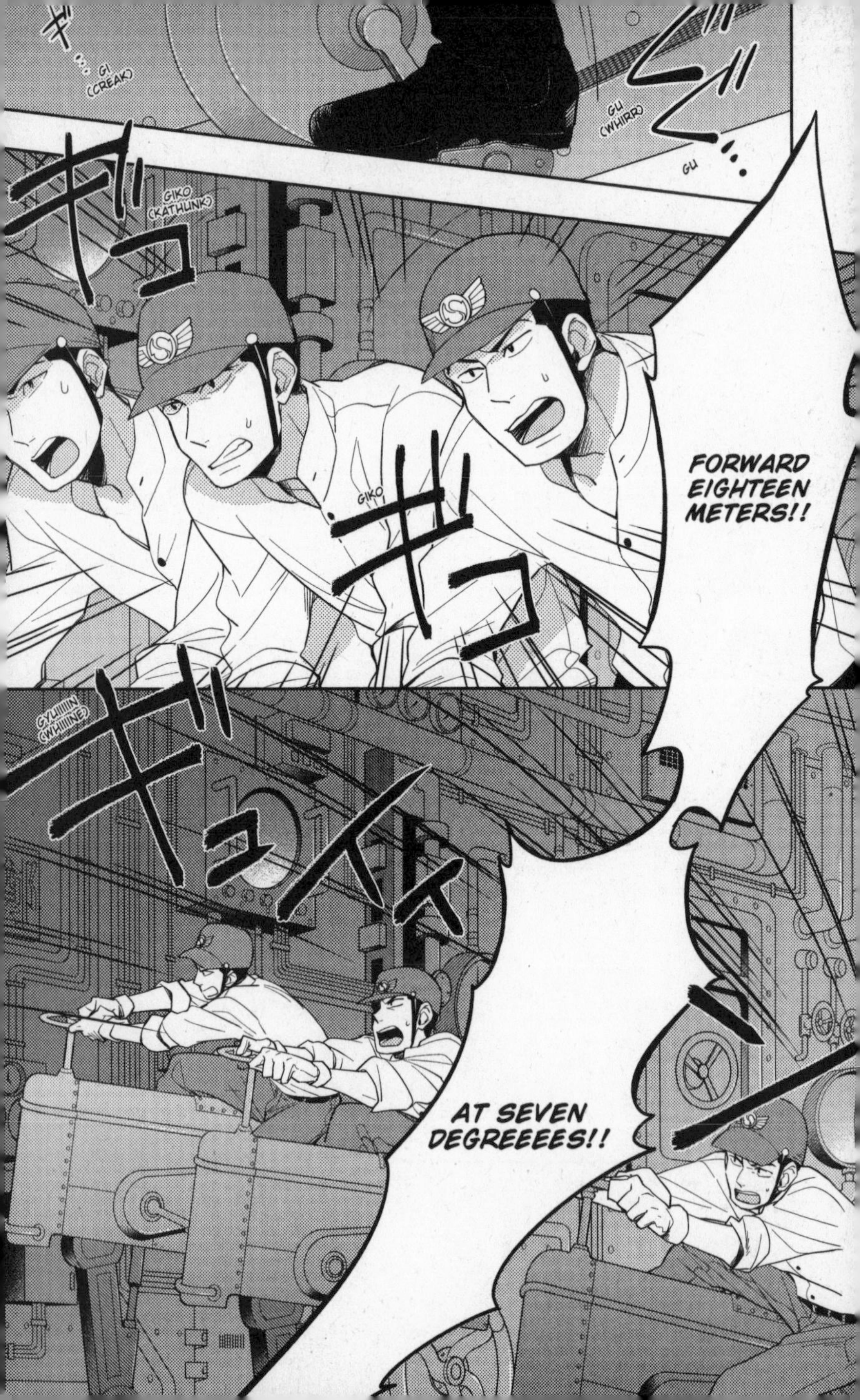
GU (WHIRR)
GU
GI (CREAK)
FORWARD EIGHTEEN METERS!!
GIKO (KATHUNK)
GIKO
AT SEVEN DEGREEEES!!
GYUIIIIN (WHIIINE)

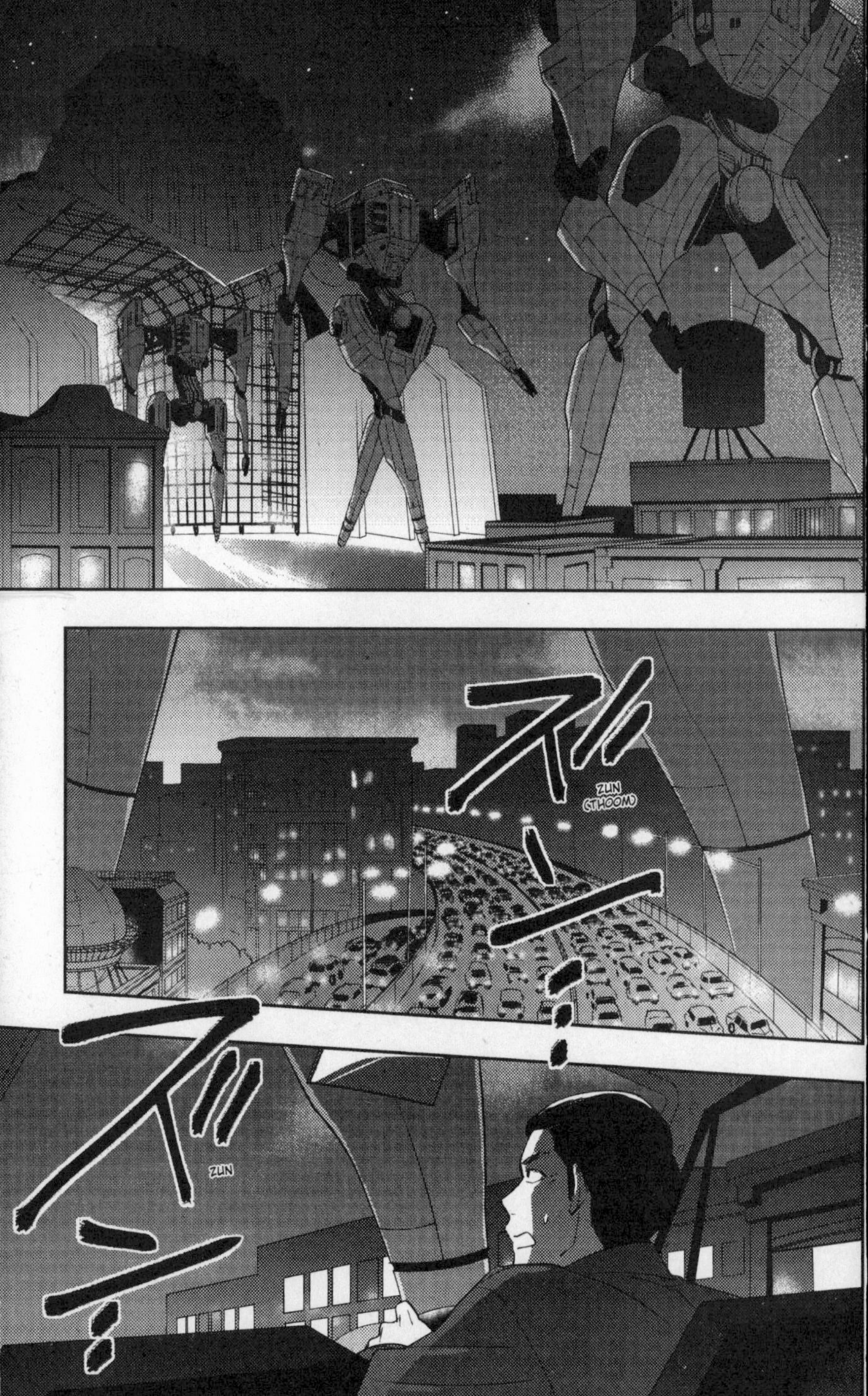
ZUN
(THOOM)
ZUN

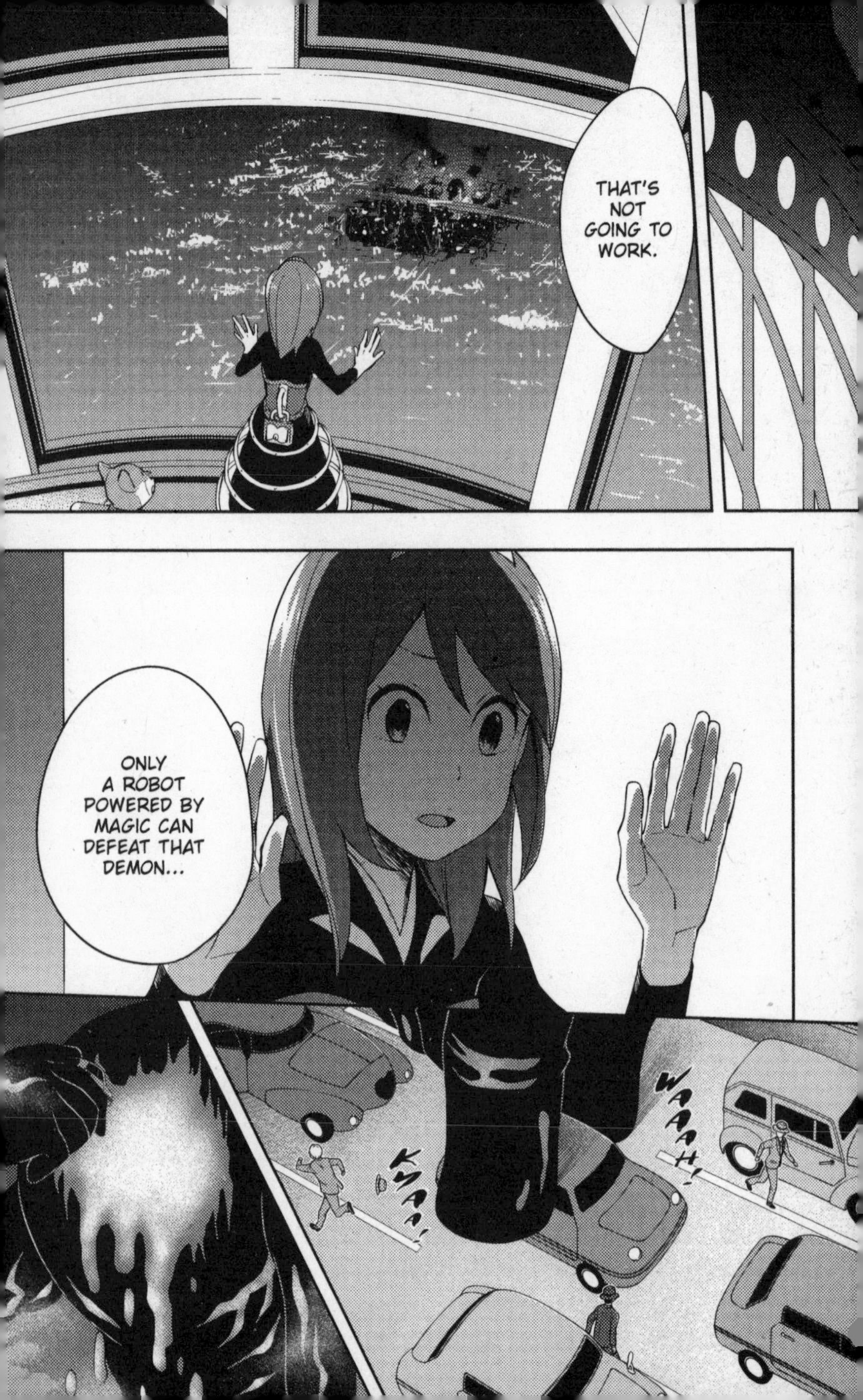
THAT'S NOT GOING TO WORK.
ONLY A ROBOT POWERED BY MAGIC CAN DEFEAT THAT DEMON...
WAAAH!
KYAAA!

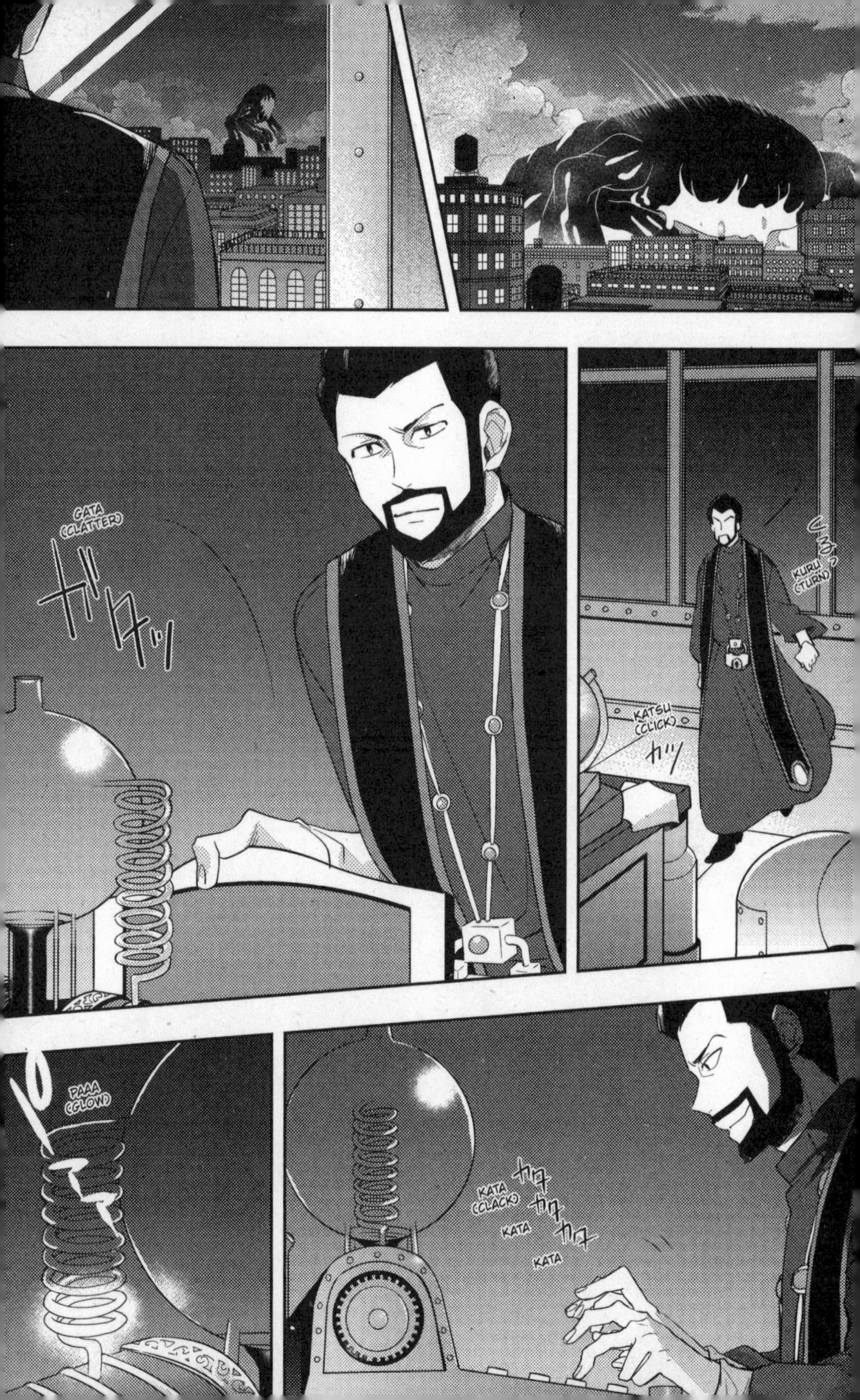

くるっ
KURU (TURN)
KATSU (CLICK)
カッ
GATA (CLATTER)
ガタッ
カタ カタ カタ
KATA (CLACK)
KATA
KATA
PAAA (GLOW)

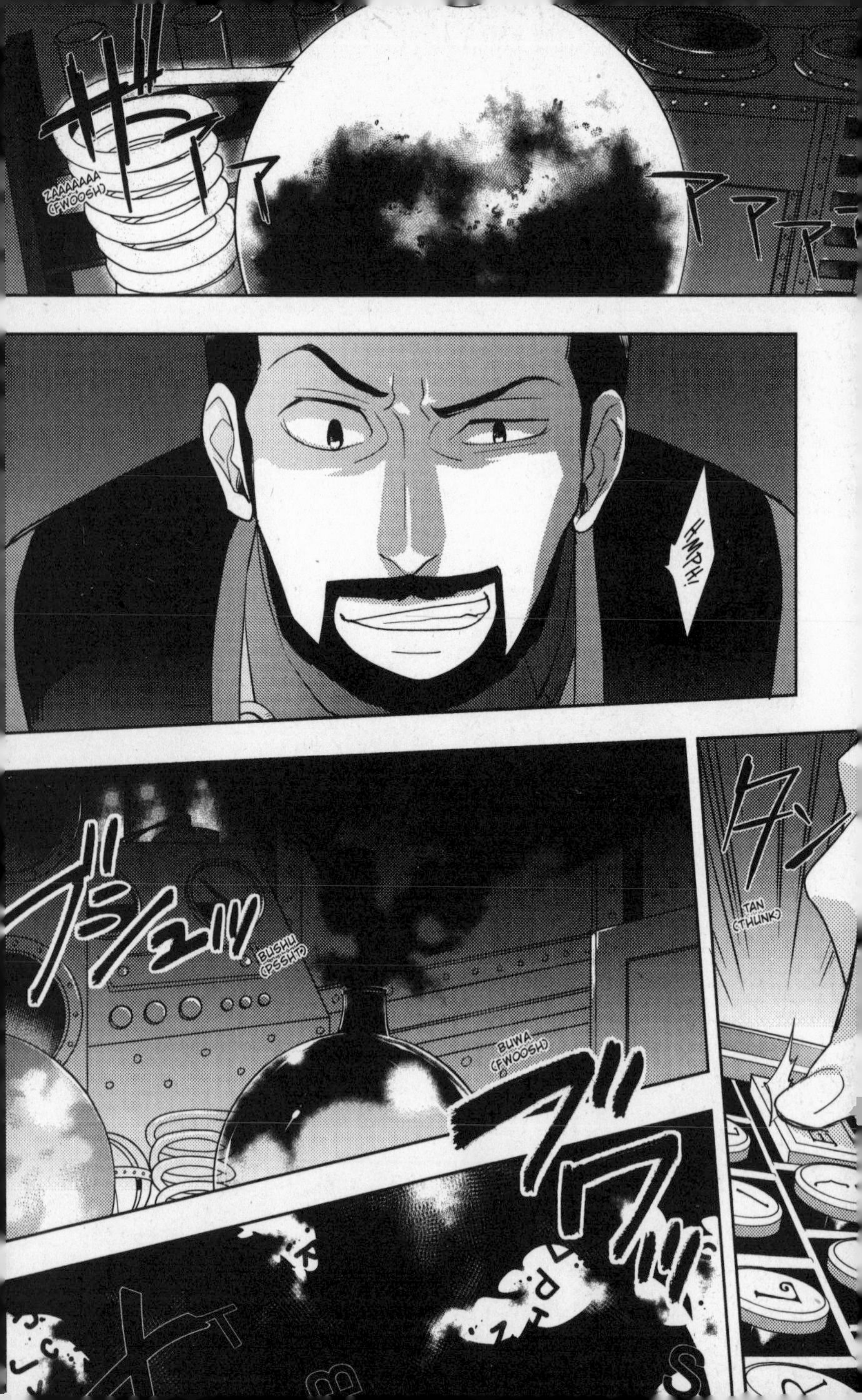
ZAAAAAAA (FWOOSH)
HMPH!
TAN (THUNK)
BUSHU (PSSHT)
BUWA (FWOOSH)

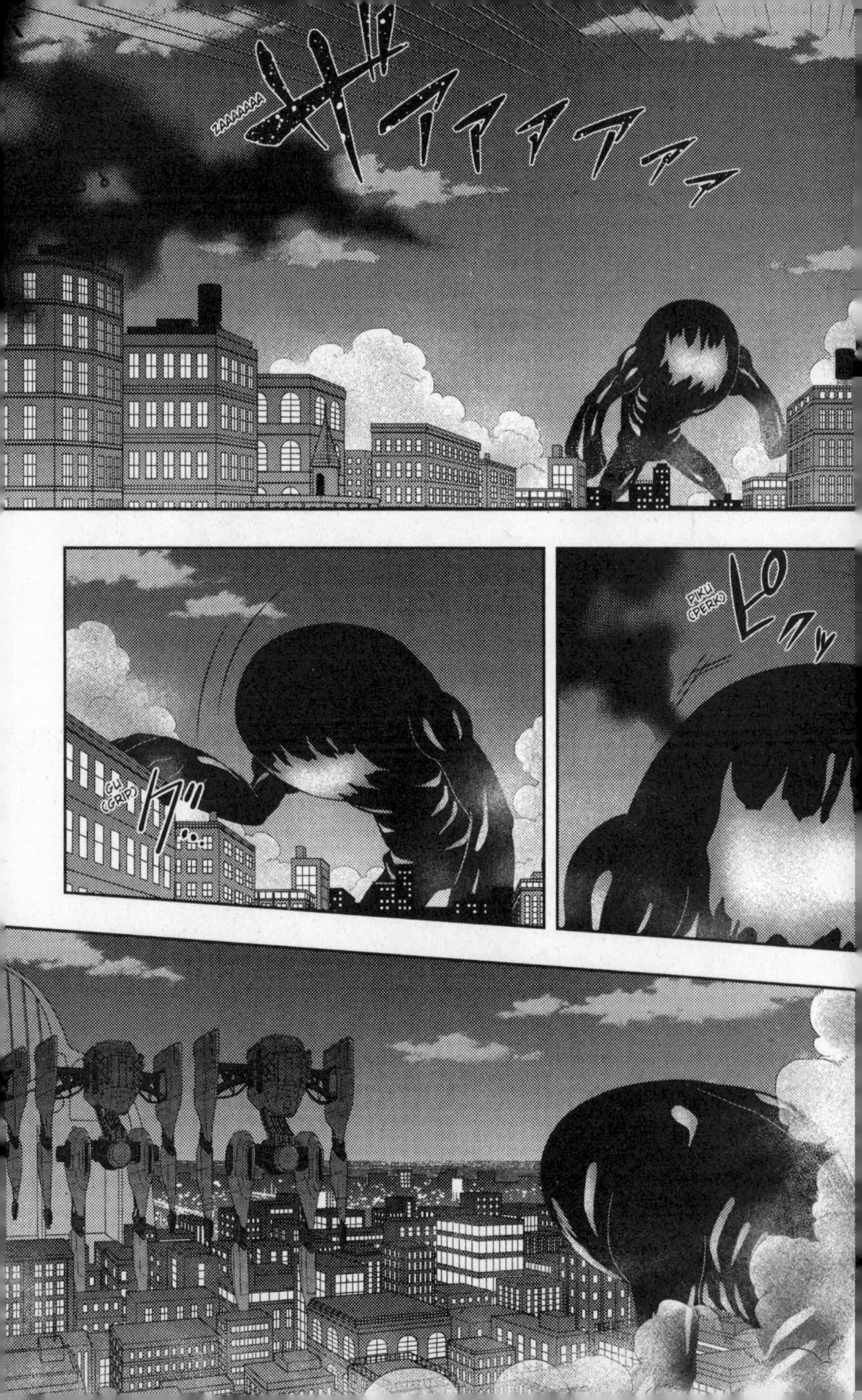
ZAAAAAAA
PIKU (PERK)
ピクッ
GU (GRIP)
グッ

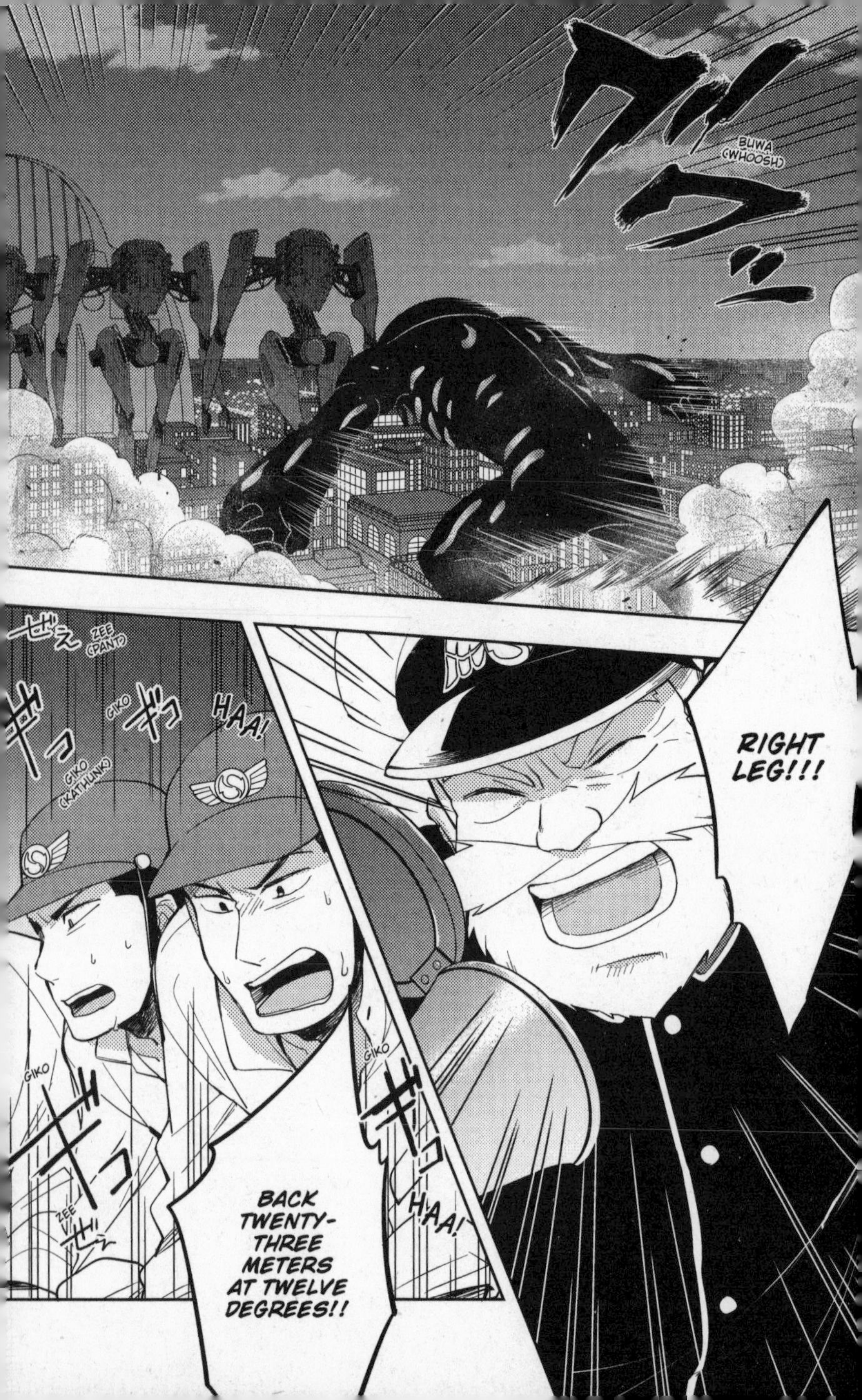
BUWA
(WHOOSH)
RIGHT LEG!!!
GIKO
HAA!
ZEE
(PANT)
GIKO
HAA!
GIKO
(KATHUNK)
GIKO
BACK TWENTY-THREE METERS AT TWELVE DEGREES!!
ZEE

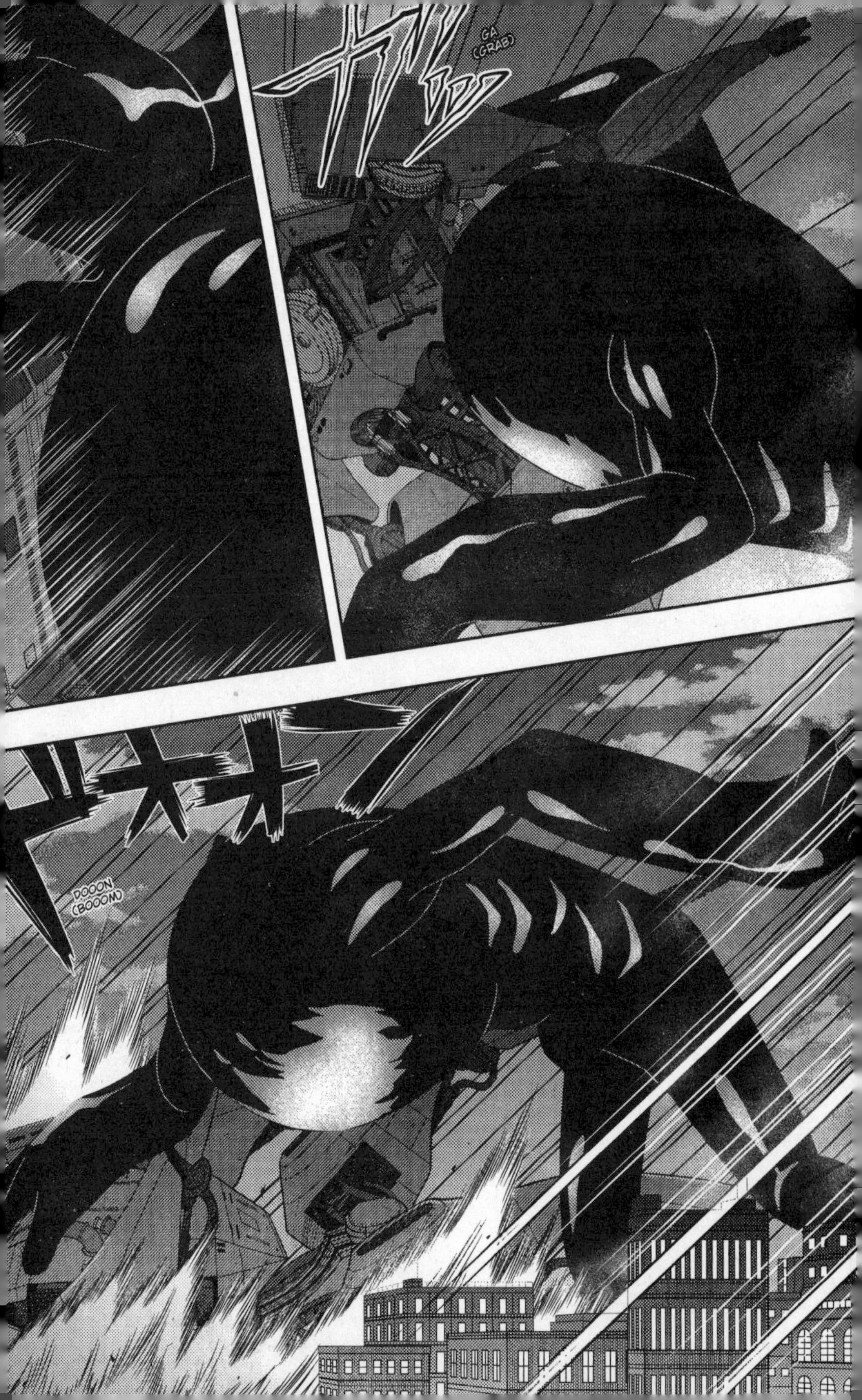
GA
(GRAB)
DOOON
(BOOOM)

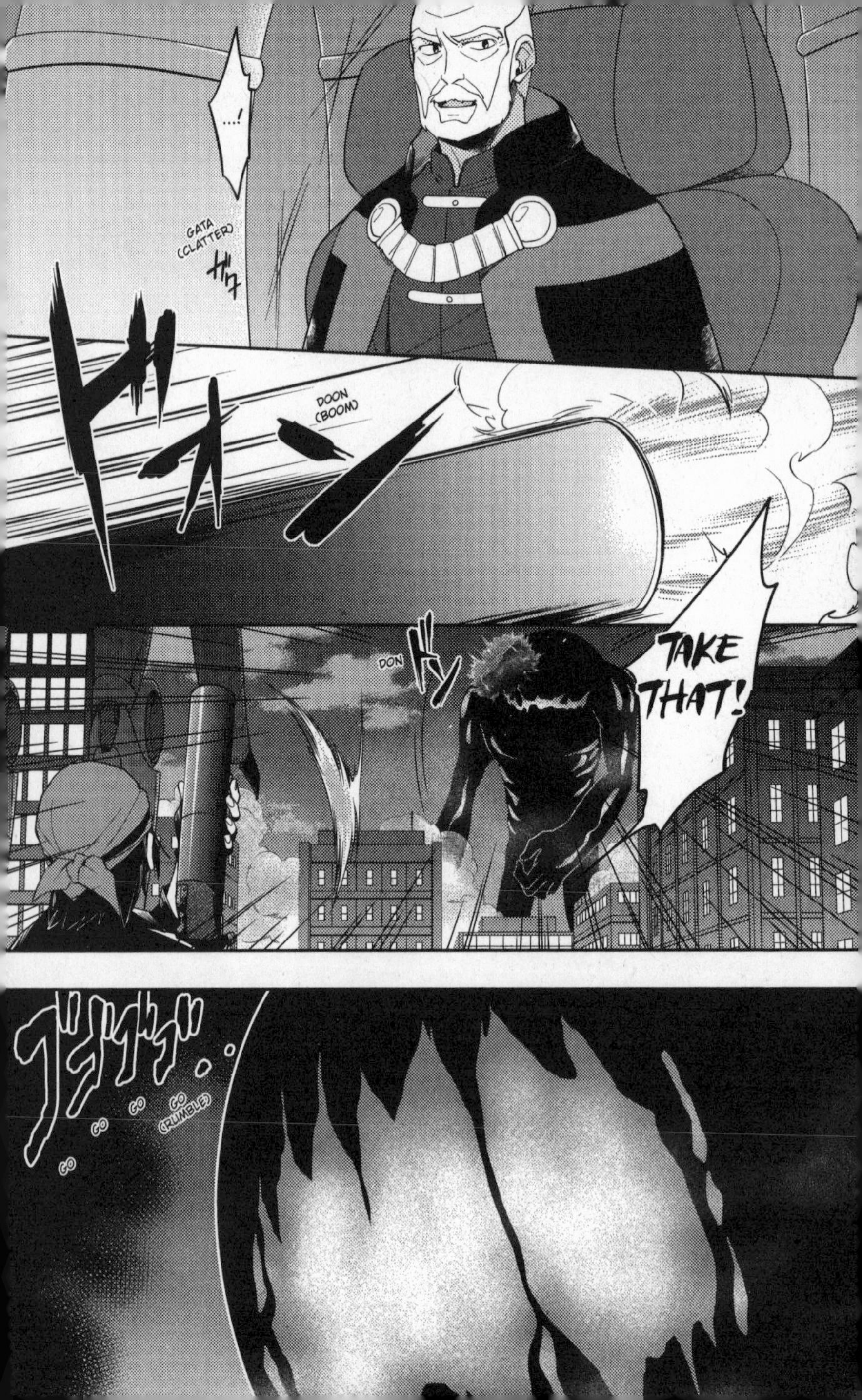

...!
GATA (CLATTER)
ガタ
DOON (BOOM)
ドオン
TAKE THAT!
DON
ドン
GO GO GO GO (RUMBLE)
ゴゴゴゴ

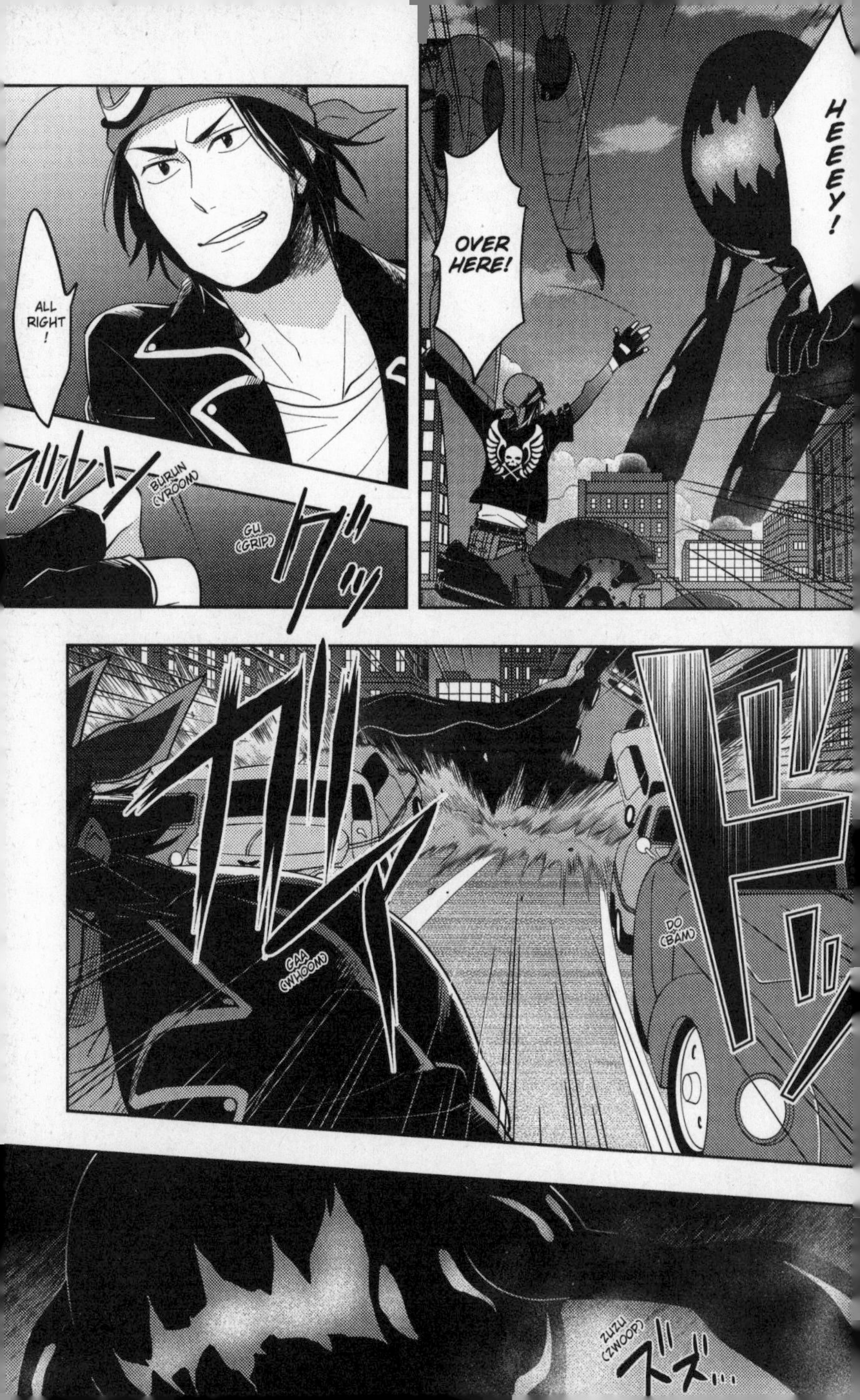
HEEEY!
OVER HERE!
ALL RIGHT!
BURUN (VROOM)
GU (GRIP)
DO (BAM)
GAA (WHOOM)
ZUZU (ZWOOP)

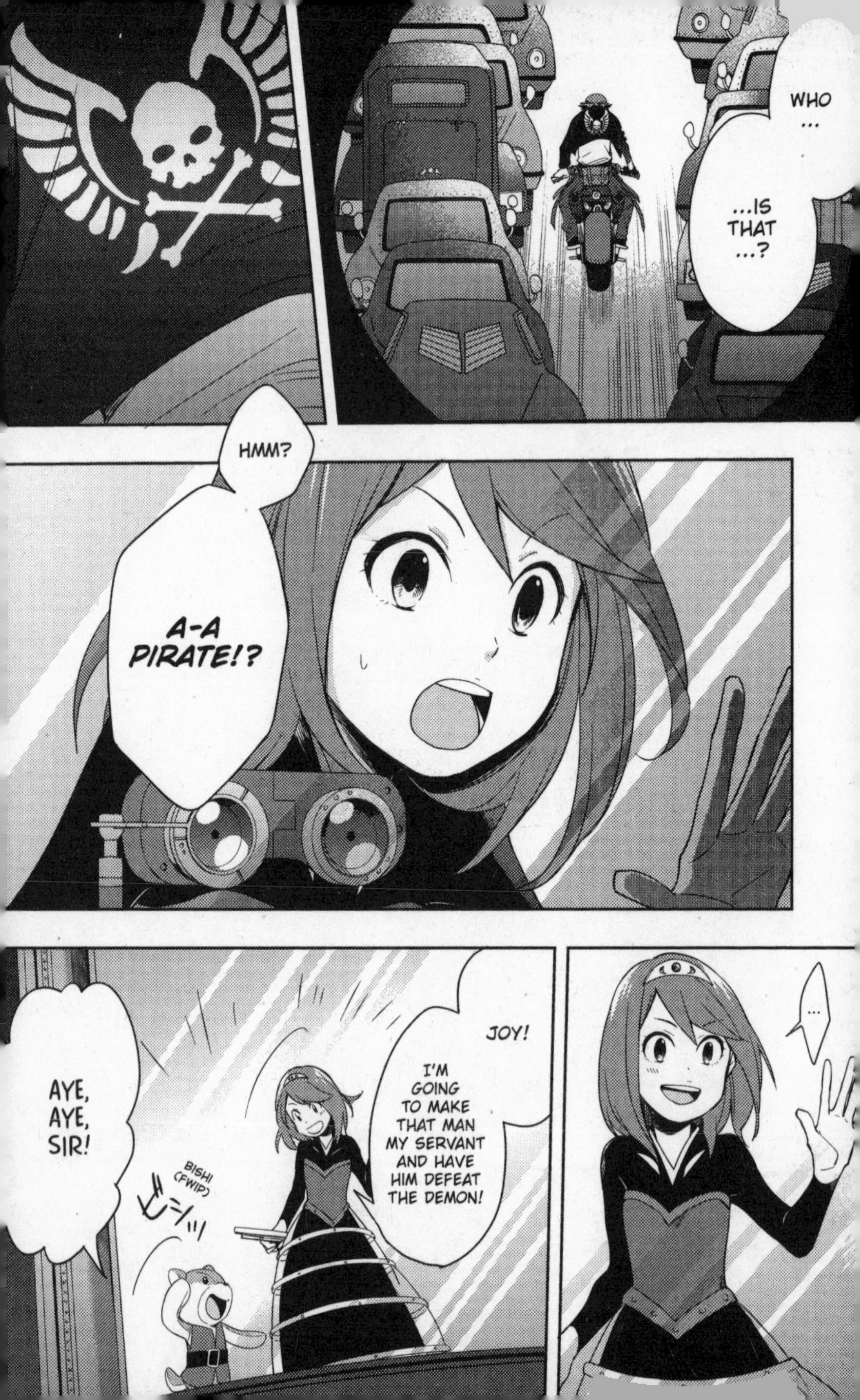
WHO ...
...IS THAT ...?
HMM?
A-A PIRATE!?
...
JOY!
I'M GOING TO MAKE THAT MAN MY SERVANT AND HAVE HIM DEFEAT THE DEMON!
AYE, AYE, SIR!
BISHI (FWIP)

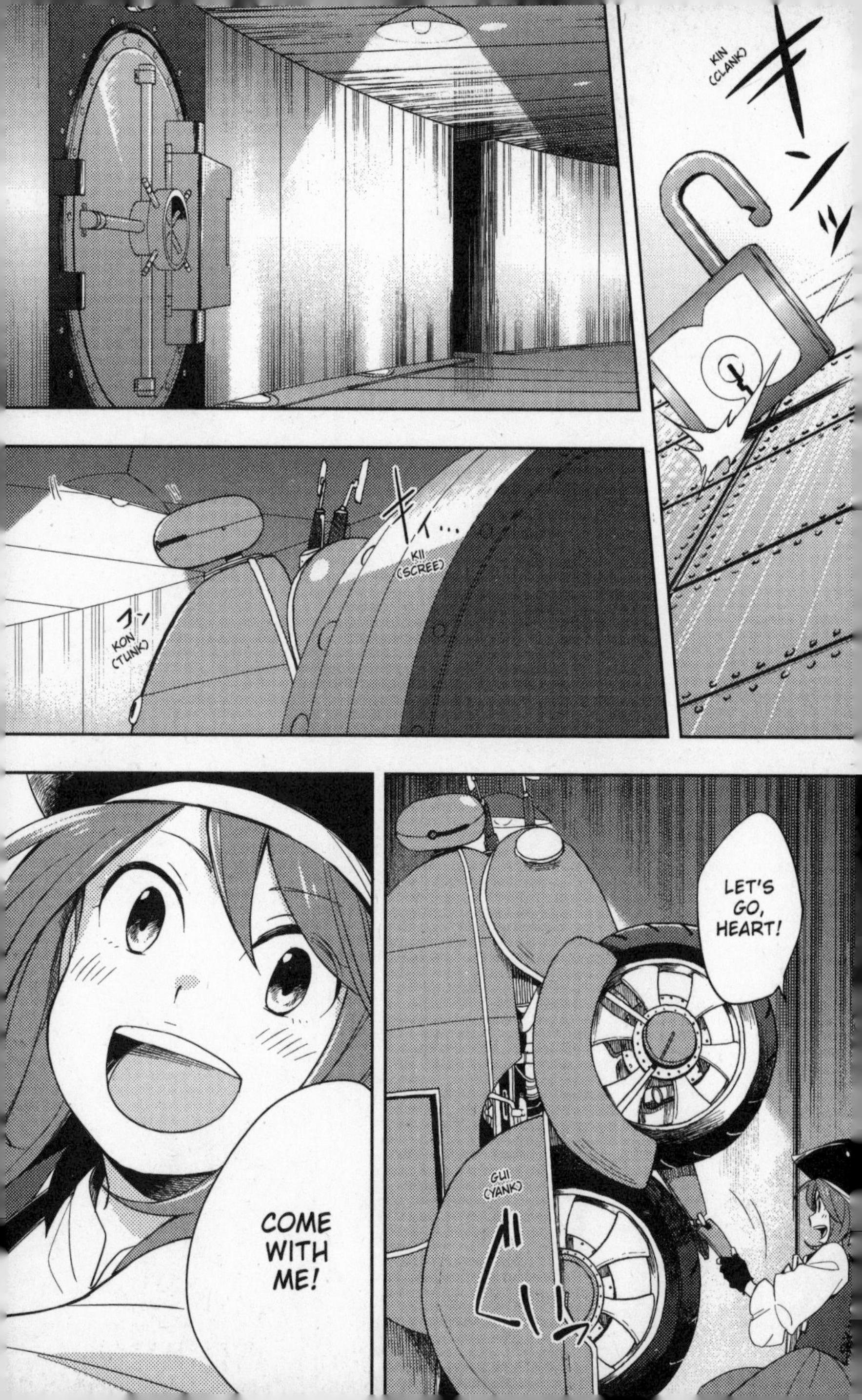
KIN (CLANK)
KII (SCREE)
KON (TUNK)
LET'S GO, HEART!
GUI (YANK)
COME WITH ME!

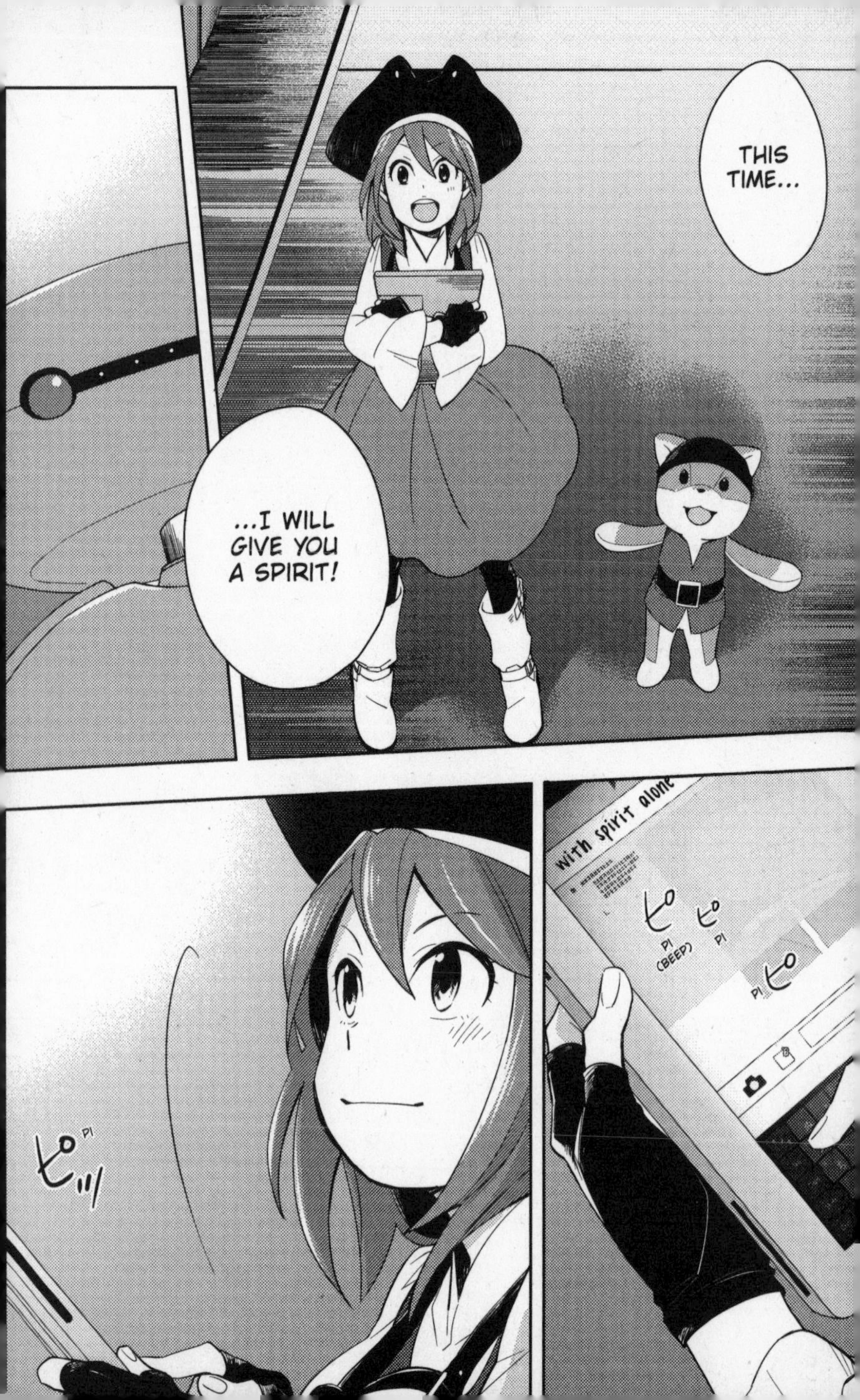
THIS TIME...
...I WILL GIVE YOU A SPIRIT!
with spirit alone
ピ PI (BEEP)
ピ PI
ピ PI
ピッ PI

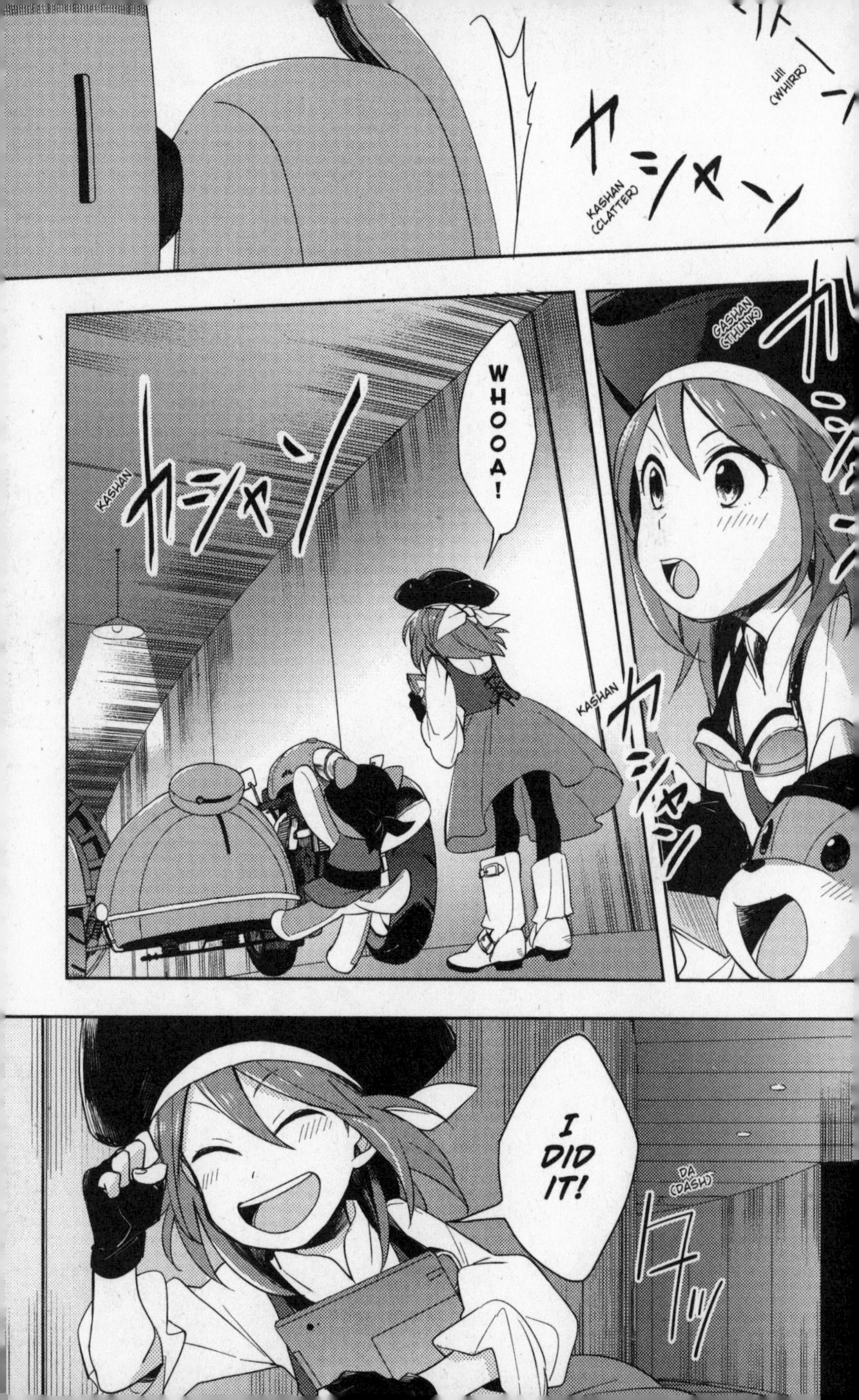
UII (WHIRR)
KASHAN (CLATTER)
GASHAN (THUNK)
KASHAN
WHOOA!
KASHAN
I DID IT!
DA (DASH)

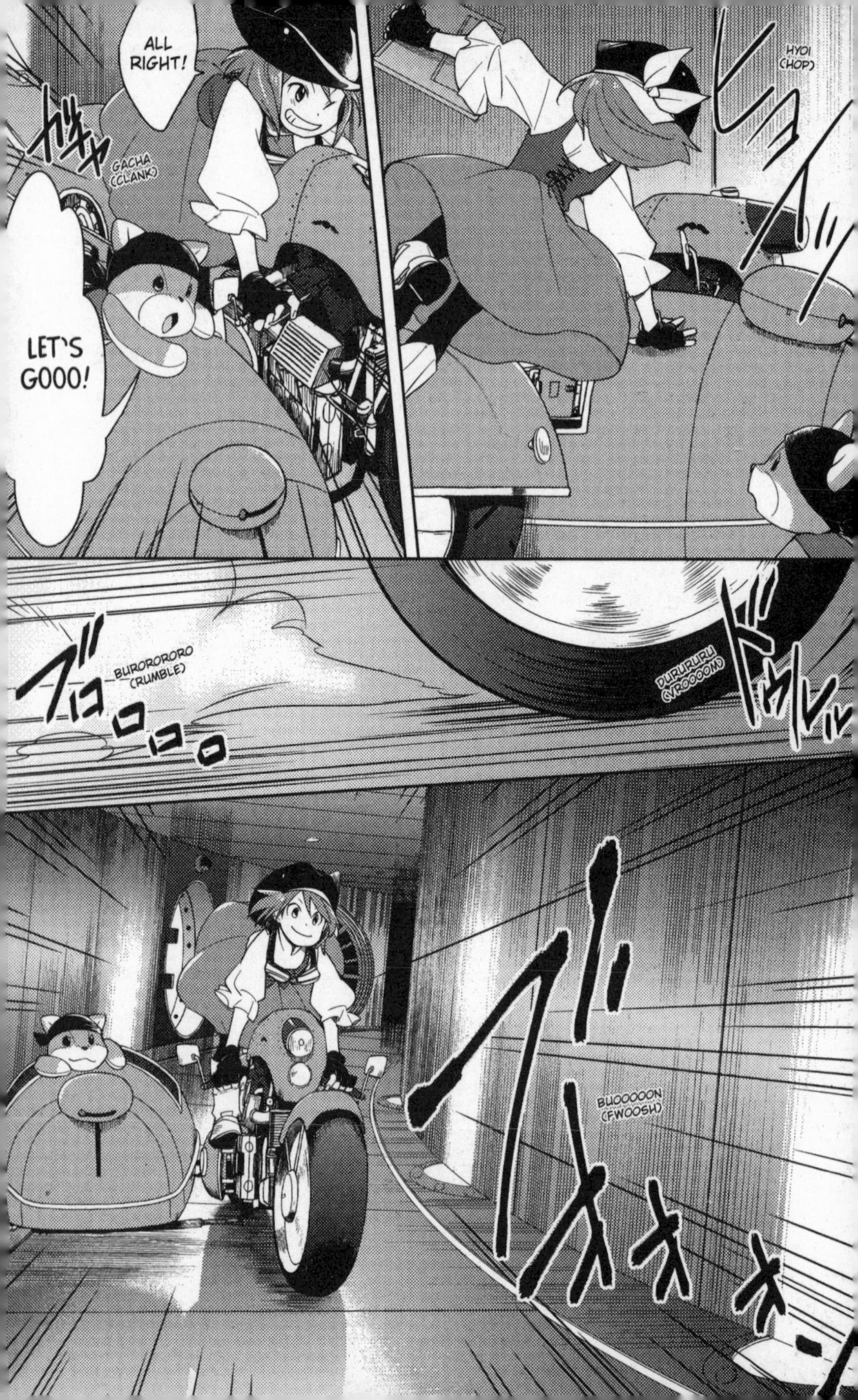
HYOI (HOP)
ALL RIGHT!
GACHA (CLANK)
LET'S GOOO!
DURURURU (VROOOOM)
BURORORORO (RUMBLE)
BUOOOOON (FWOOSH)

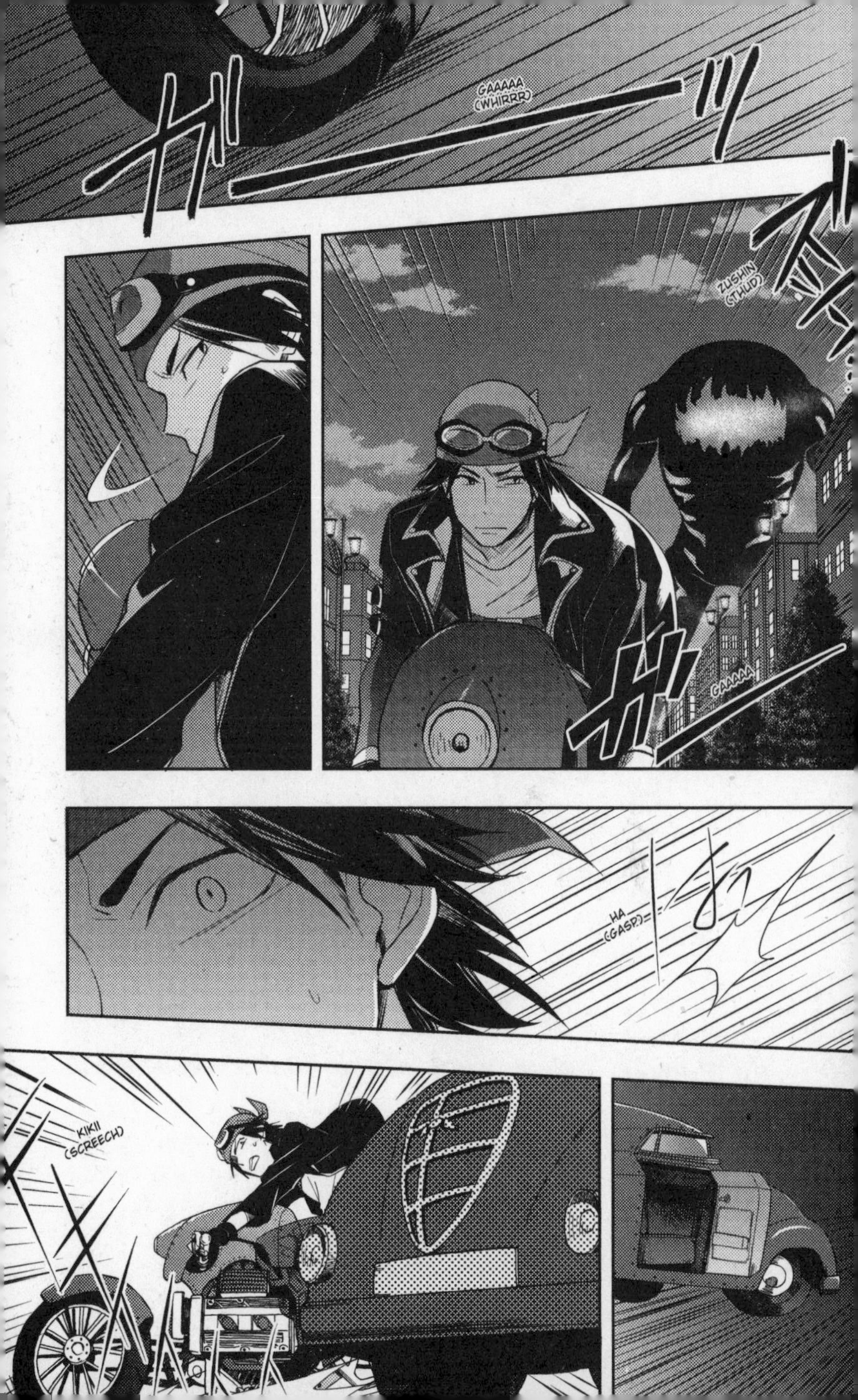
GAAAAA (WHIRRR)
ZUSHIN (THUD)
GAAAAA
HA (GASP)
KIKII (SCREECH)

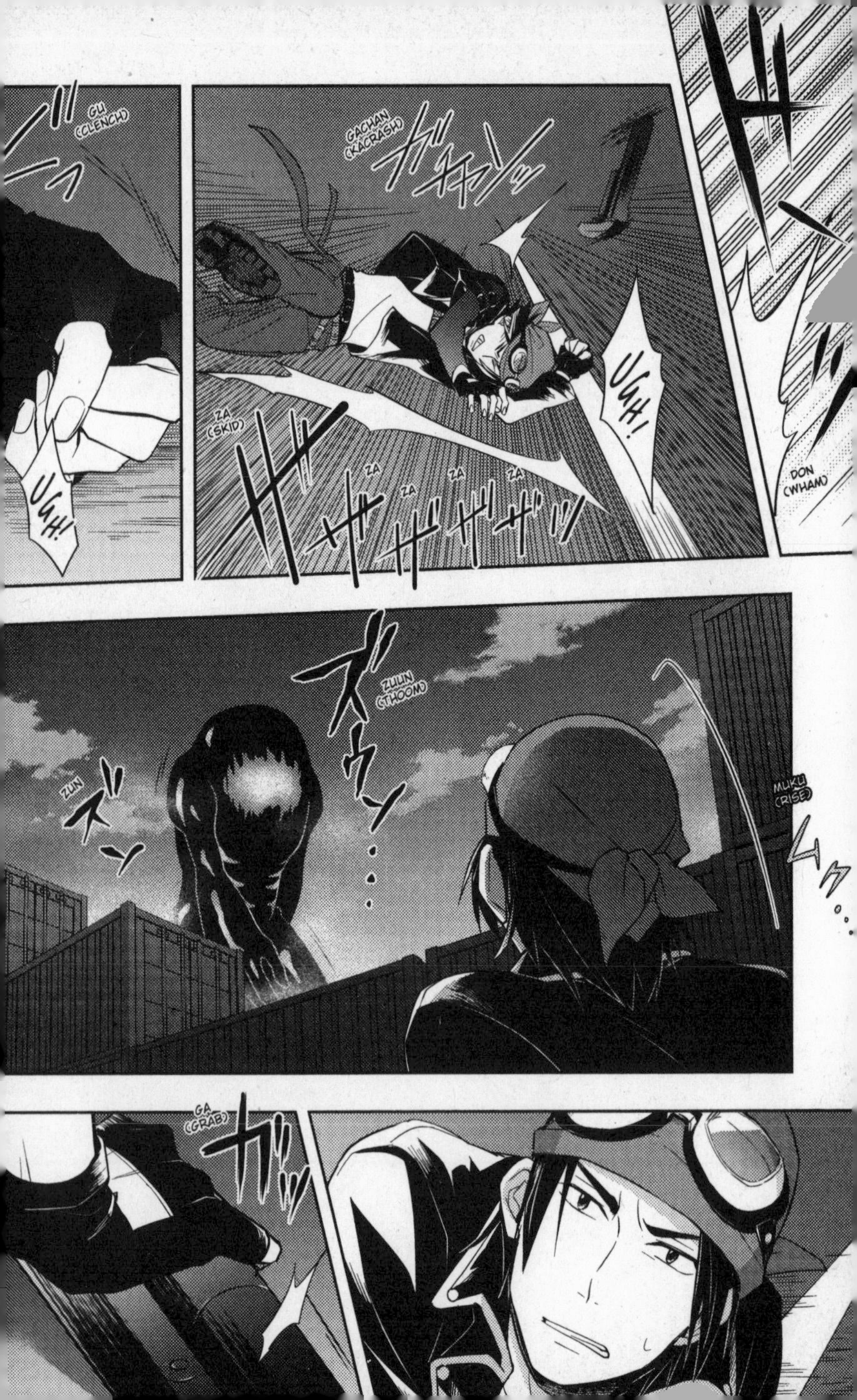
DON (WHAM)
GACHAN (KACRASH)
UGH!
ZA (SKID)
ZA
ZA
ZA
ZA
GU (CLENCH)
UGH!
MUKU (RISE)
ZUUN (THOOM)
ZUN
GA (GRAB)

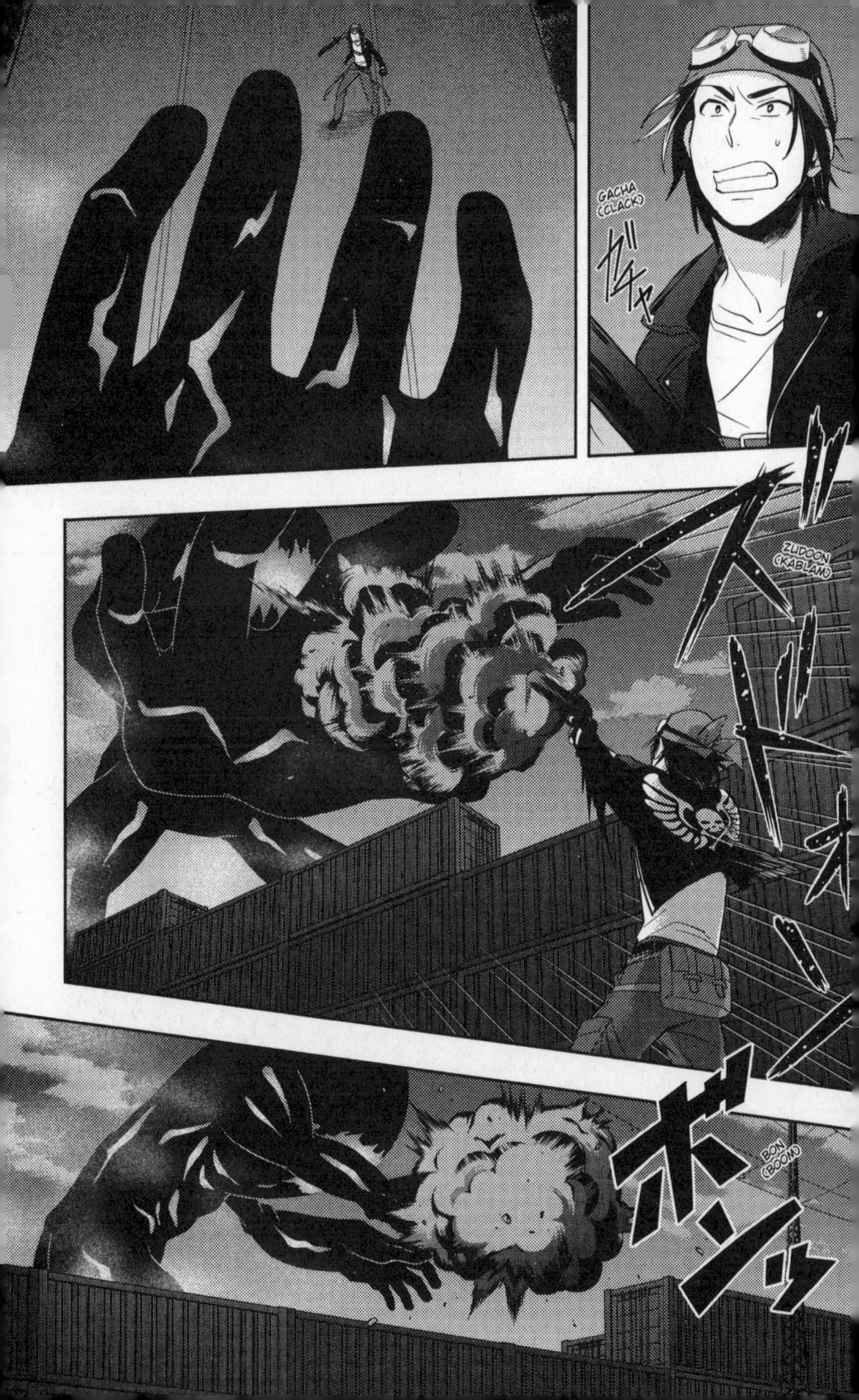
GACHA (CLACK)
ZUDOON (KABLAM)
BON (BOOM)

ﾋｭｩｩｩ
SHUUU
(STEAM)

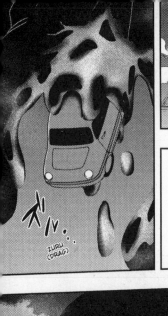

ズ゛ル...
ZURU
(DRAG)

!!?

ズ゛
ZUZU
(CHOOP)

ドシャン
DOSHAN
(CRASH)

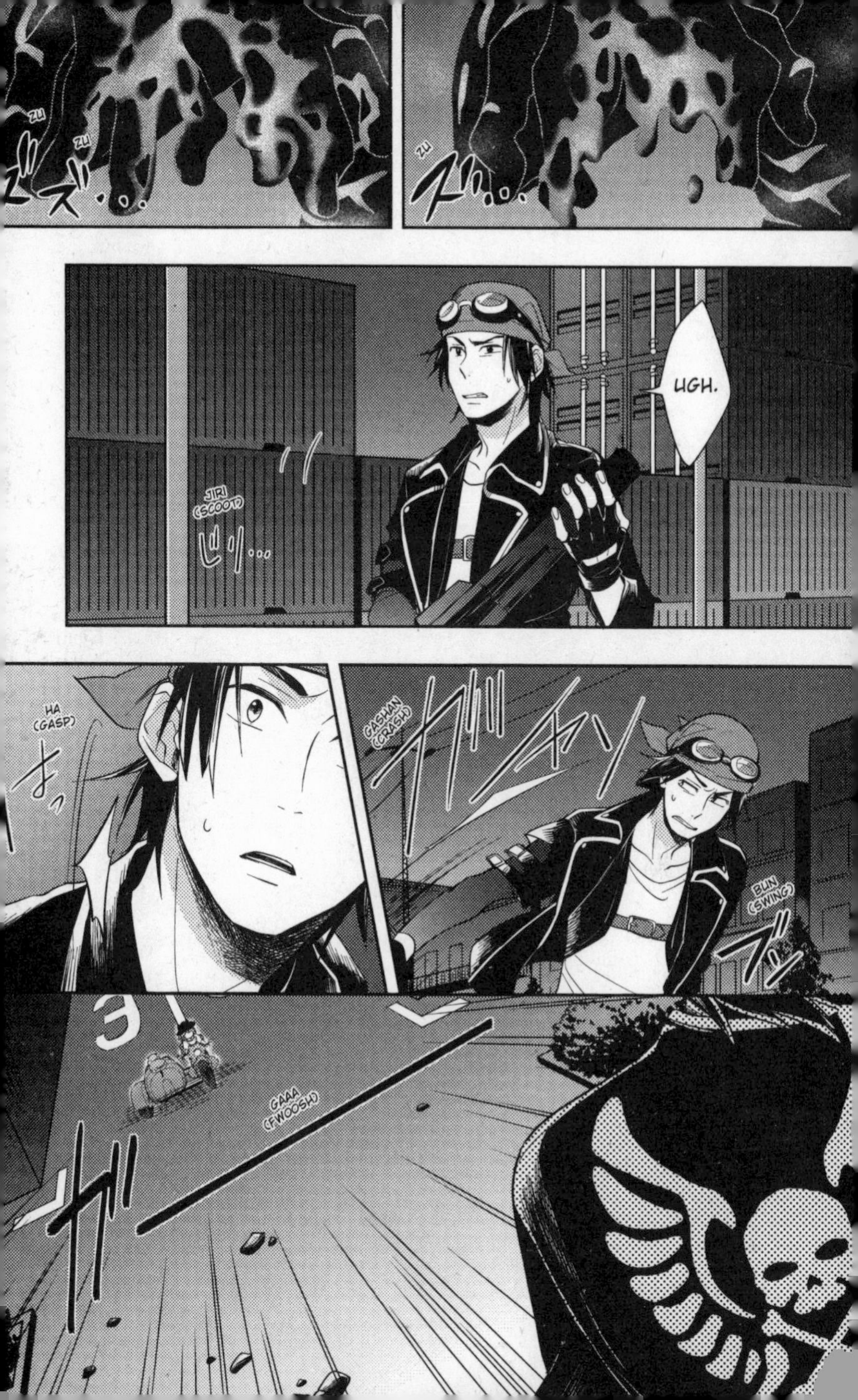
ZU
ZU
ZU
UGH.
JIRI (SCOOT)
GASHAN (CRASH)
BUN (SWING)
HA (GASP)
GAAA (FWOOSH)

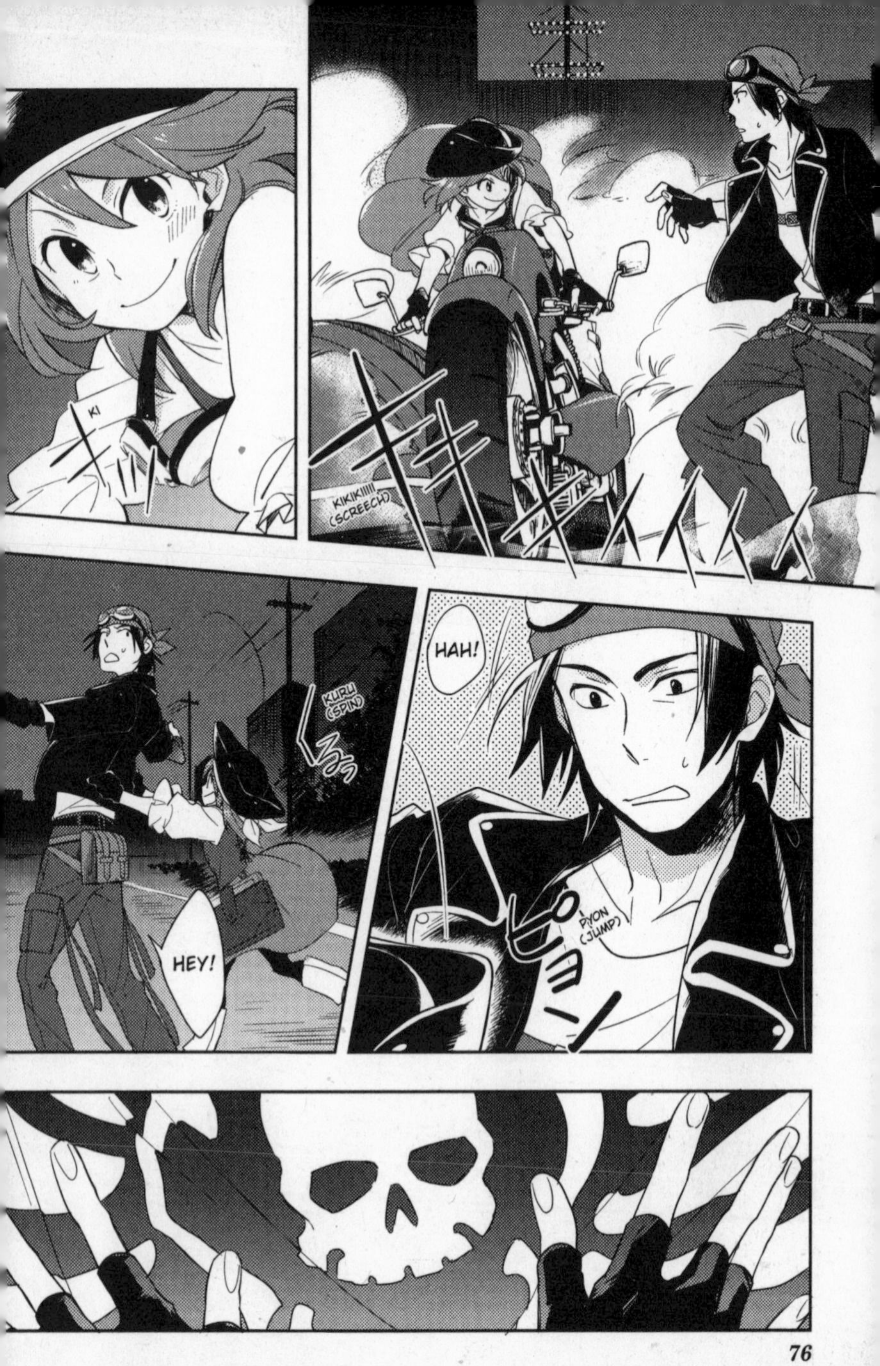
KIKIKIIIIII (SCREECH)
KI
HAH!
PYON (JUMP)
KURU (SPIN)
HEY!

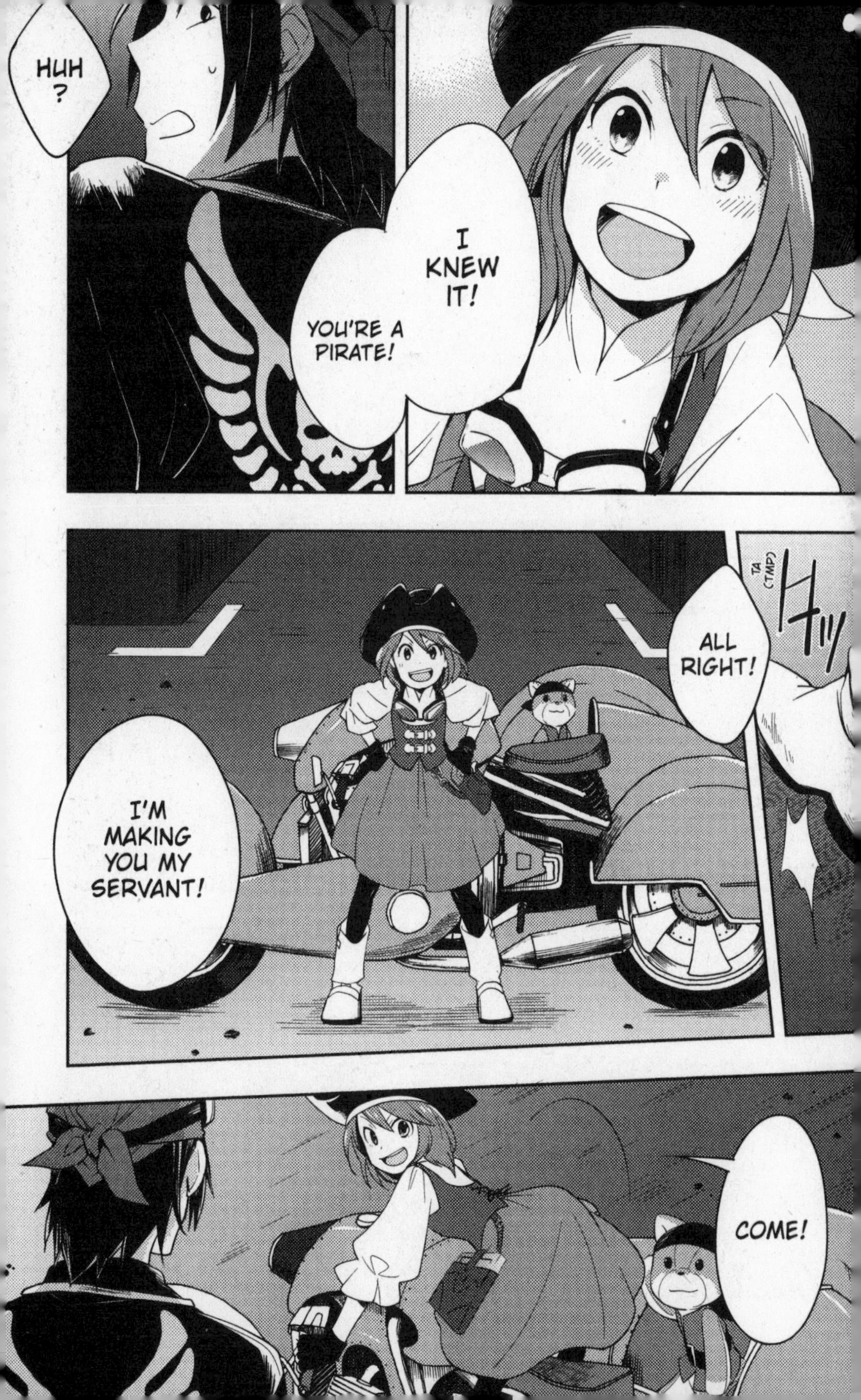
I KNEW IT!
YOU'RE A PIRATE!
HUH?
TA (TMP)
ALL RIGHT!
I'M MAKING YOU MY SERVANT!
COME!

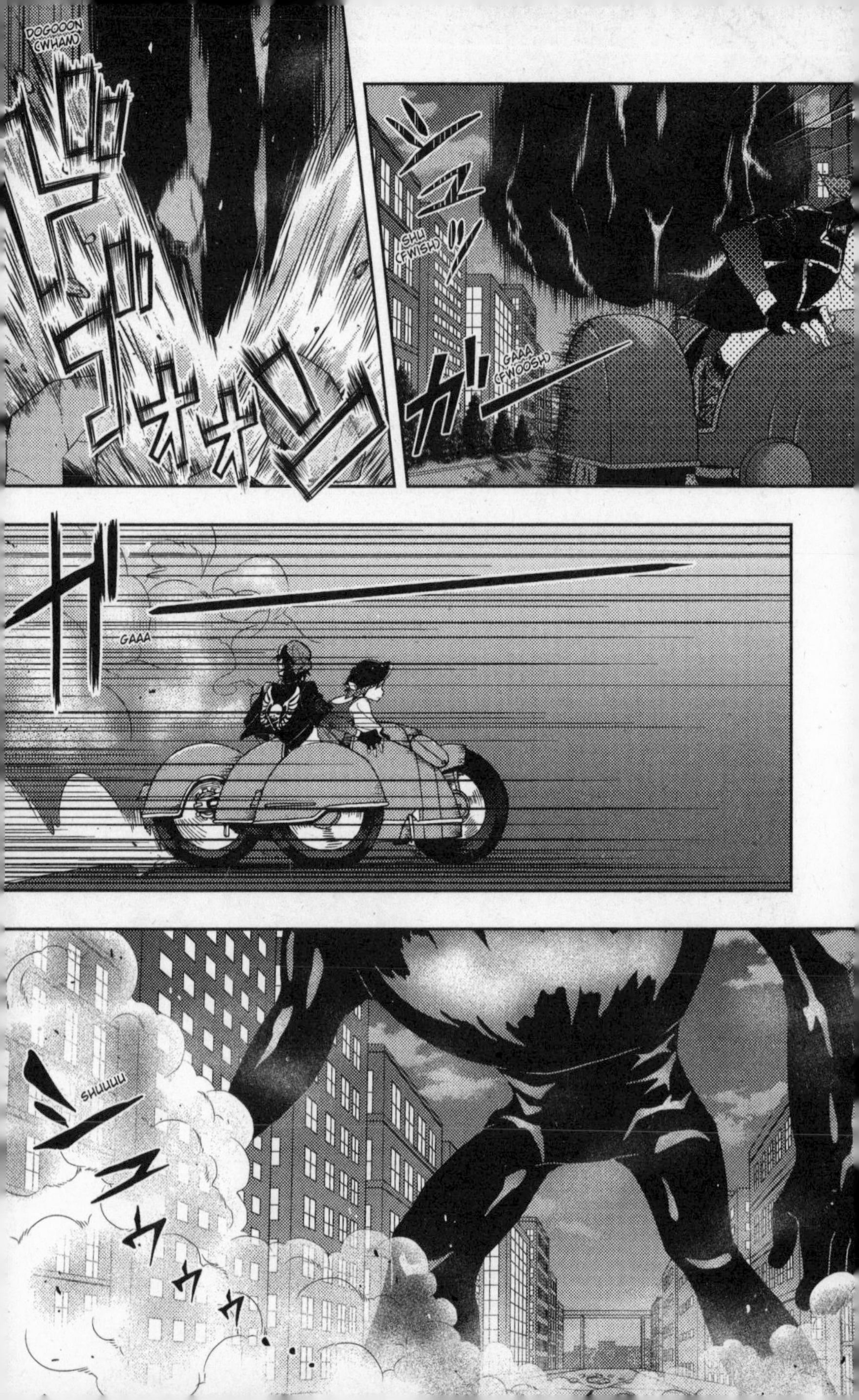
SHU (FWISH)
GAAA (FWOOSH)
DOGOOON (WHAM)
GAAA
SHUUUU

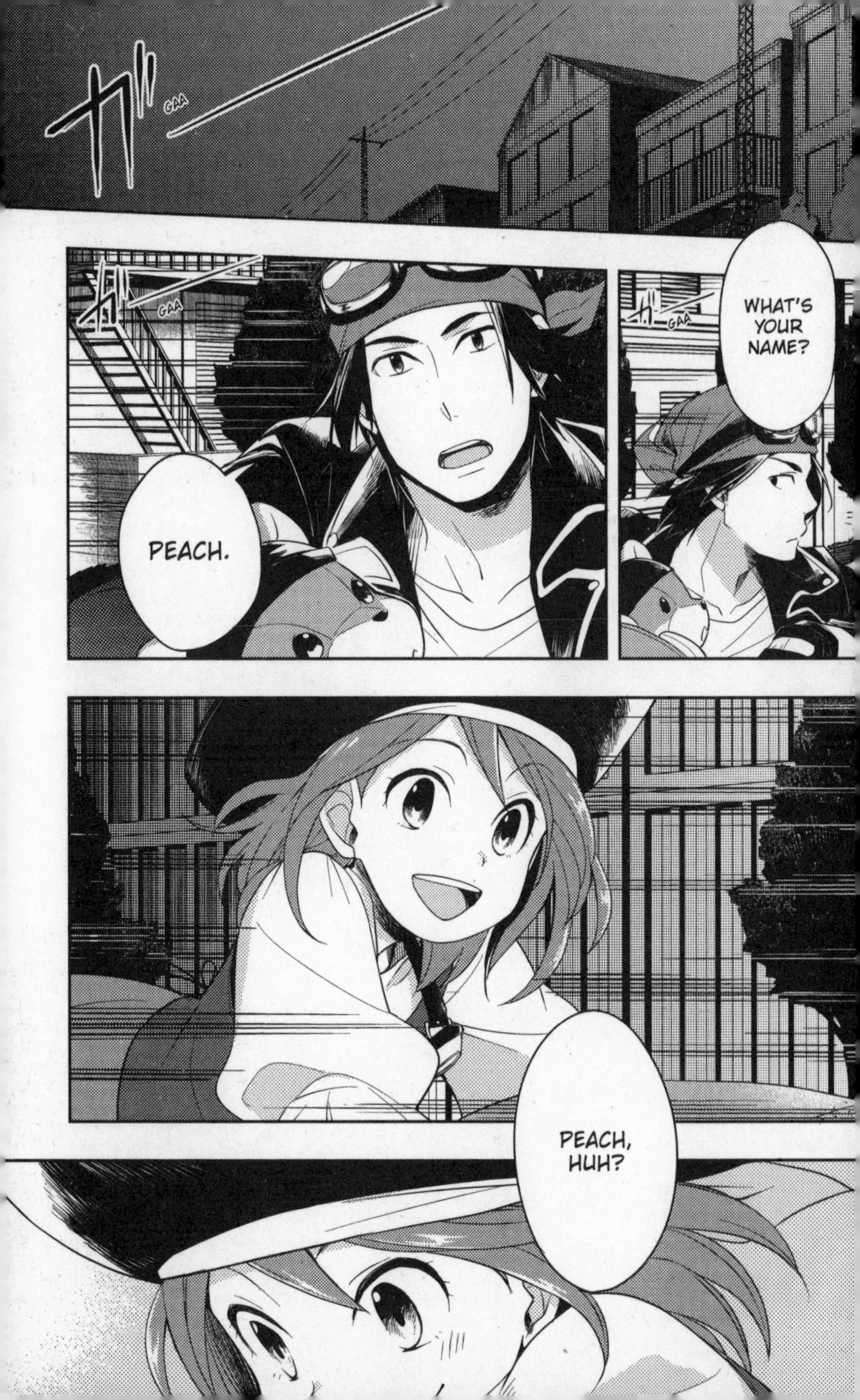
ガ GAA
ガ GAA
WHAT'S YOUR NAME?
ガ GAA
PEACH.
PEACH, HUH?

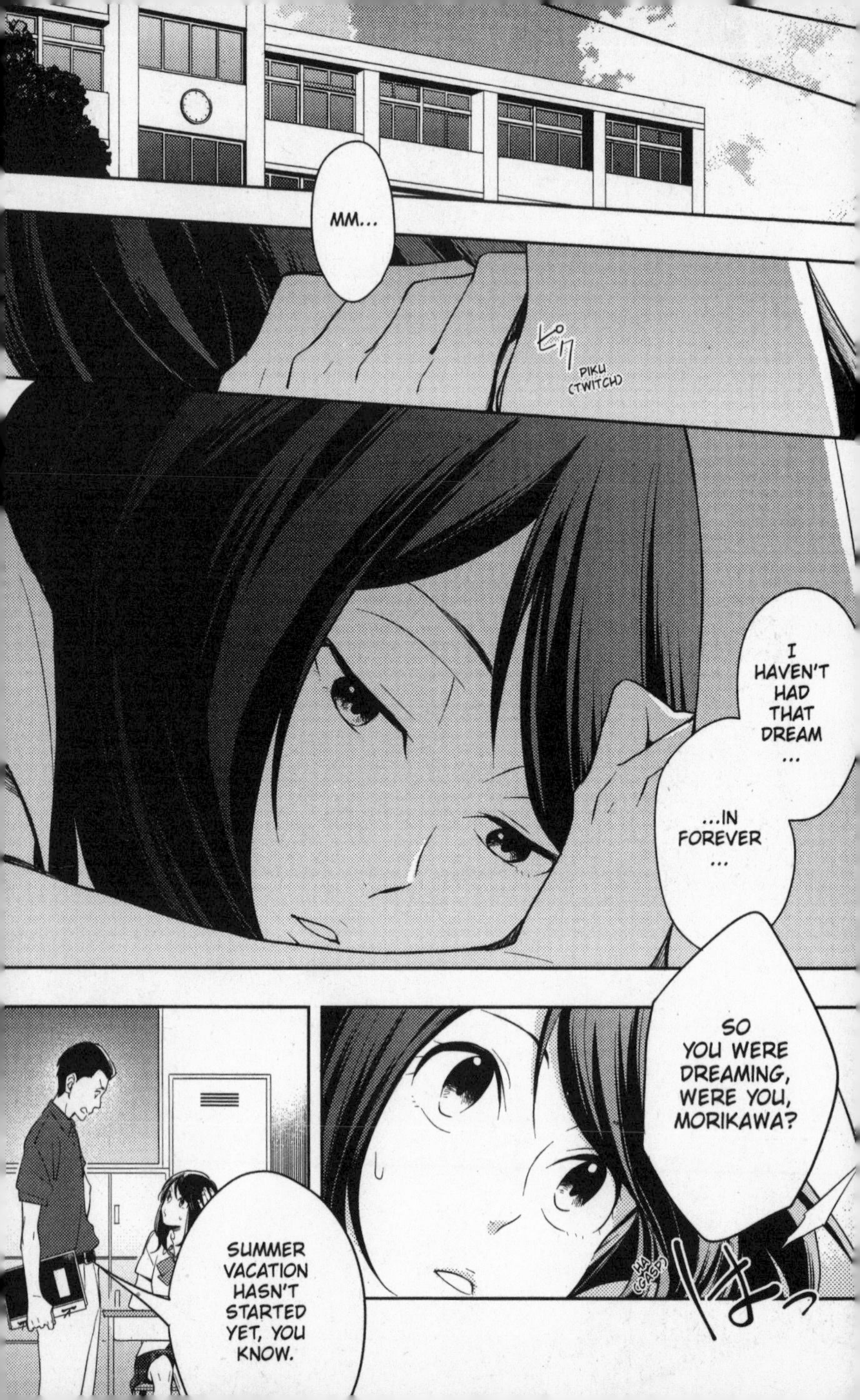
MM...
ピク
PIKU (TWITCH)
I HAVEN'T HAD THAT DREAM ...
...IN FOREVER ...
SO YOU WERE DREAMING, WERE YOU, MORIKAWA?
はっ
HA (GASP)
SUMMER VACATION HASN'T STARTED YET, YOU KNOW.

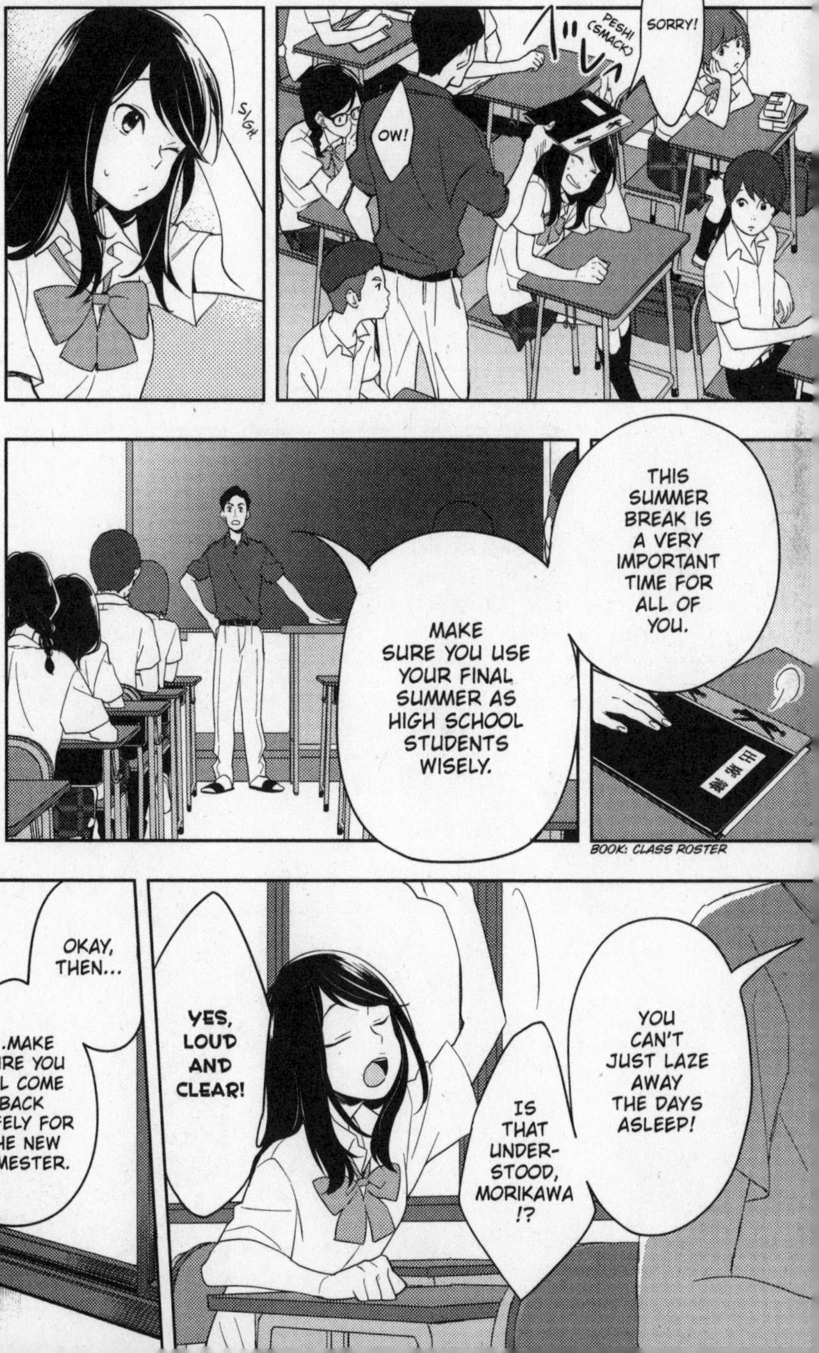
SORRY!
PESHI! (SMACK)
OW!
SIGH
THIS SUMMER BREAK IS A VERY IMPORTANT TIME FOR ALL OF YOU.
MAKE SURE YOU USE YOUR FINAL SUMMER AS HIGH SCHOOL STUDENTS WISELY.
BOOK: CLASS ROSTER
YOU CAN'T JUST LAZE AWAY THE DAYS ASLEEP!
IS THAT UNDER-STOOD, MORIKAWA!?
YES, LOUD AND CLEAR!
OKAY, THEN...
...MAKE SURE YOU ALL COME BACK SAFELY FOR THE NEW SEMESTER.

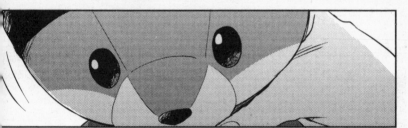

YOU'RE THE ONLY ONE...

...WHO KNOWS EVERYTHING THAT HAPPENED.

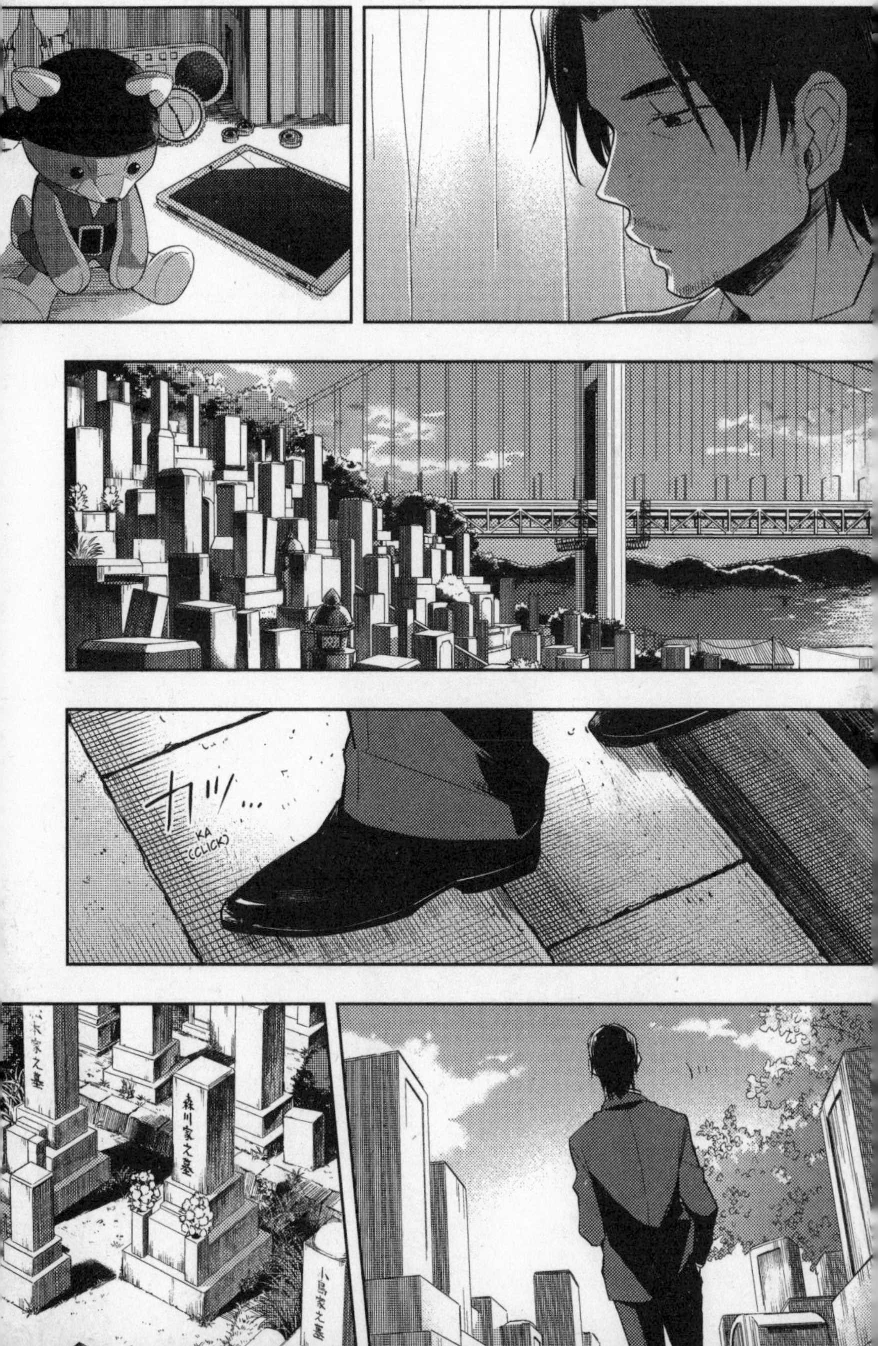
カツ…
KA
(CLICK)
森川家之墓
小島家之墓

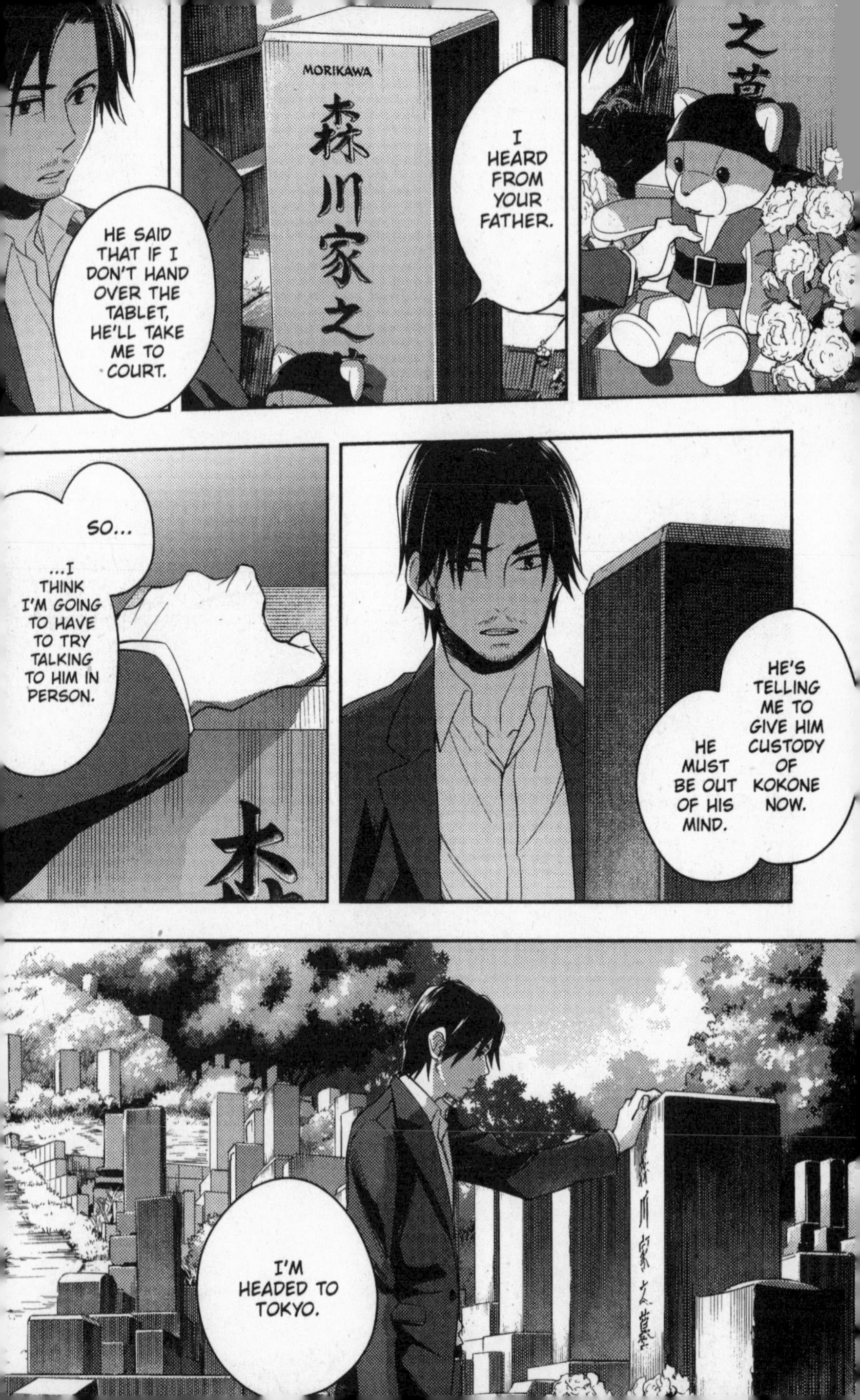
之
I HEARD FROM YOUR FATHER.
MORIKAWA
森川家之
HE SAID THAT IF I DON'T HAND OVER THE TABLET, HE'LL TAKE ME TO COURT.
HE'S TELLING ME TO GIVE HIM CUSTODY OF KOKONE NOW.
HE MUST BE OUT OF HIS MIND.
SO...
...I THINK I'M GOING TO HAVE TO TRY TALKING TO HIM IN PERSON.
I'M HEADED TO TOKYO.

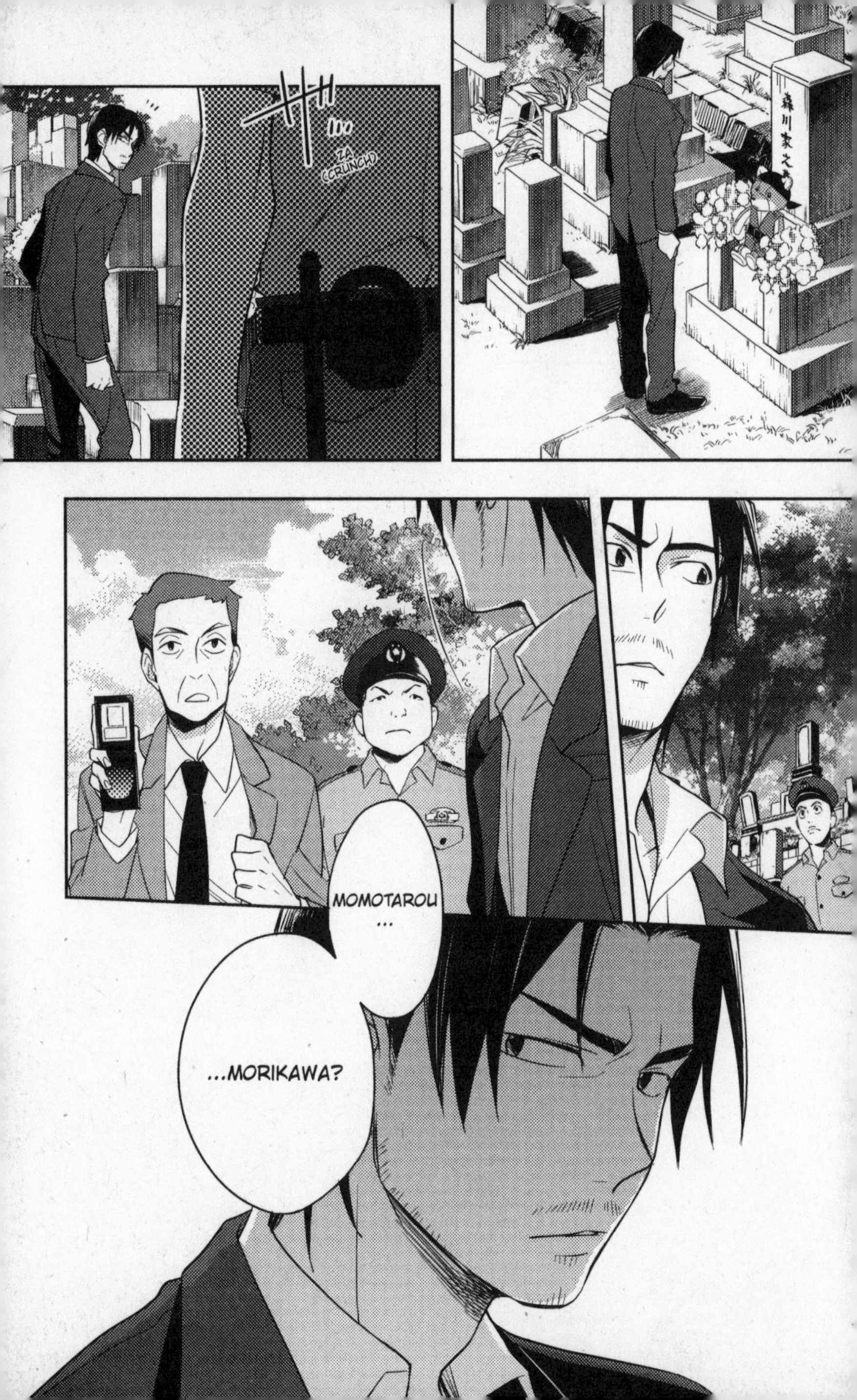
ZA (CRUNCH)
MOMOTAROU ...
...MORIKAWA?

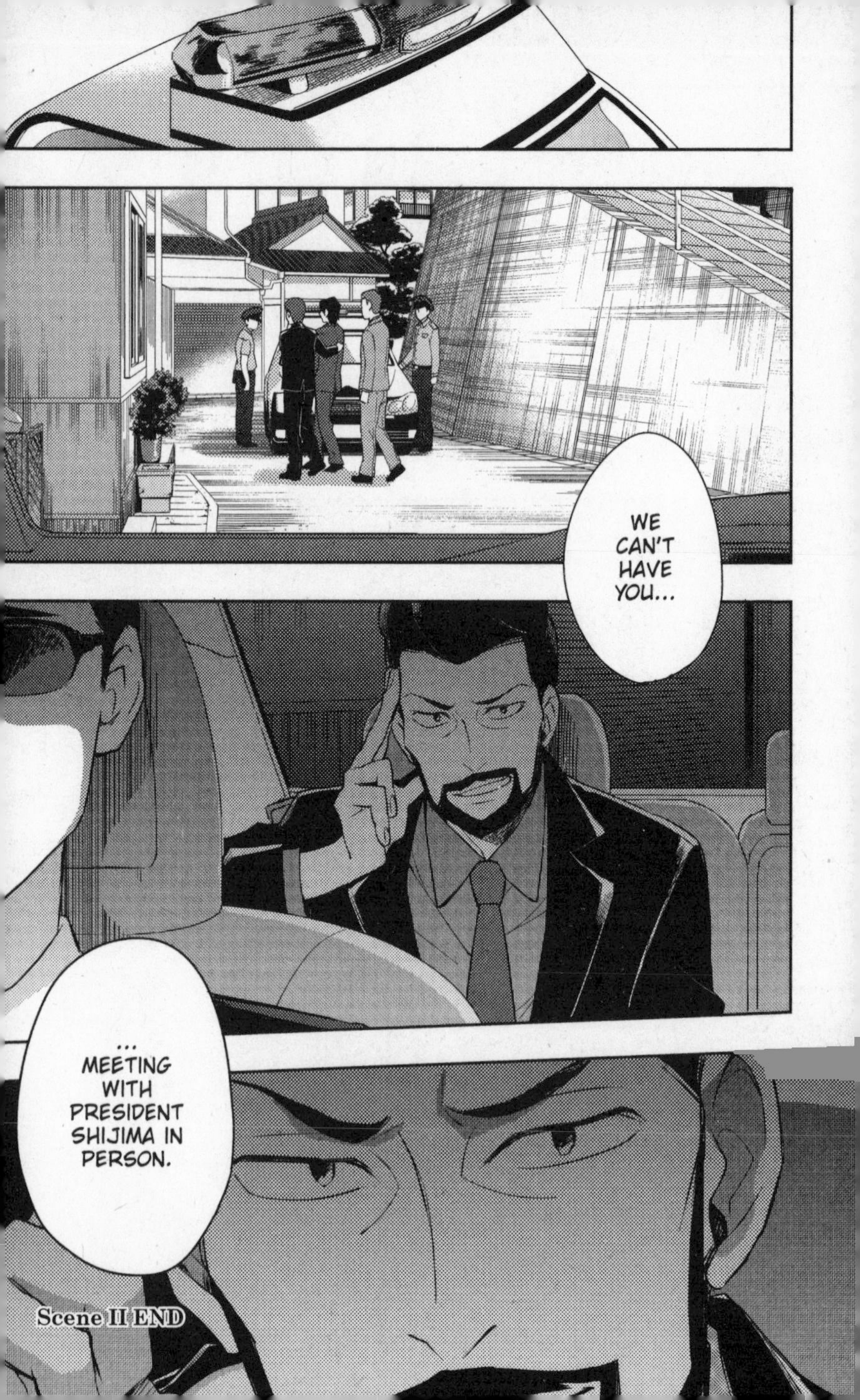
WE CAN'T HAVE YOU...
... MEETING WITH PRESIDENT SHIJIMA IN PERSON.
Scene II END

# Napping Princess

### The Story of the Unknown Me

# Scene III

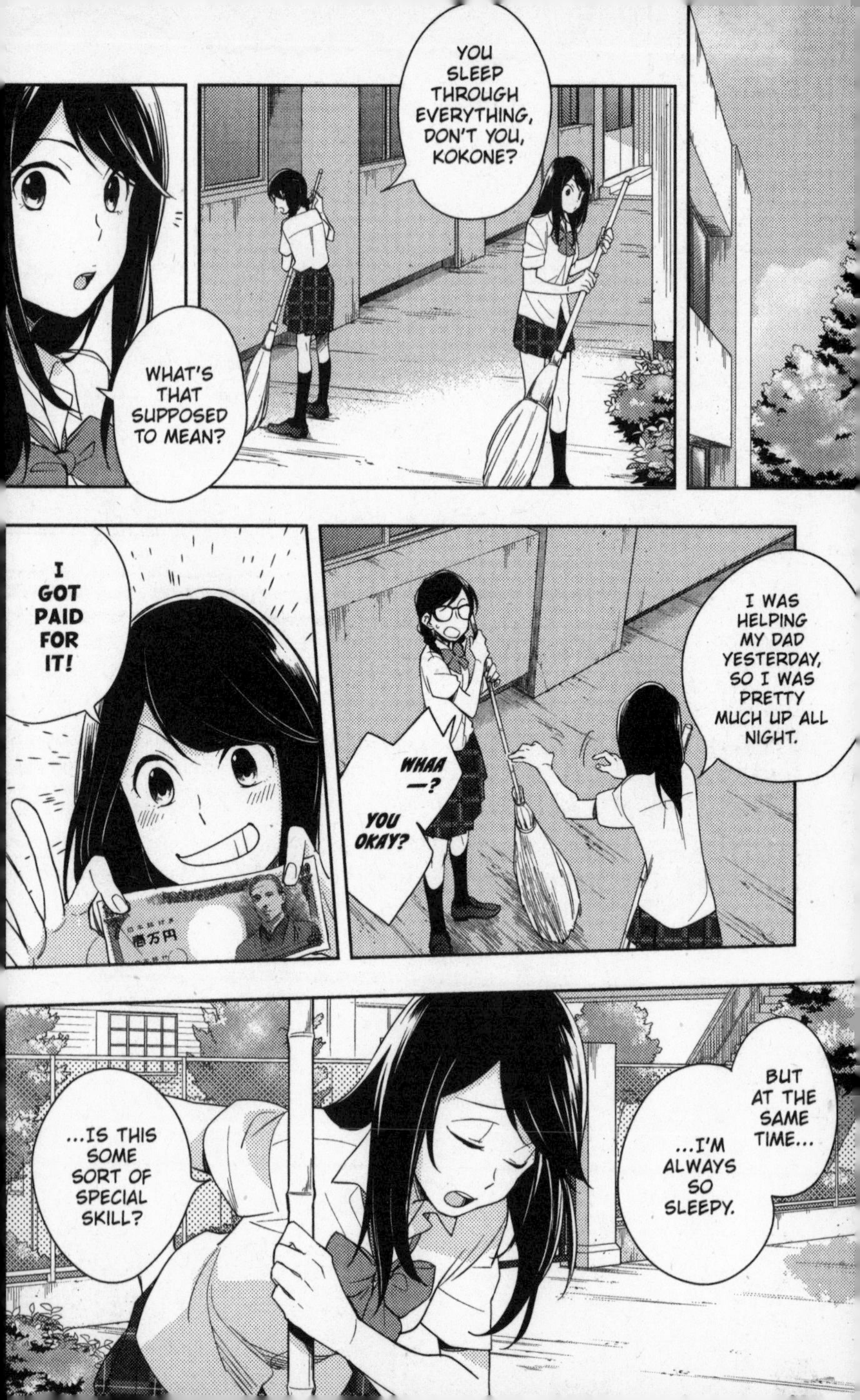
YOU SLEEP THROUGH EVERYTHING, DON'T YOU, KOKONE?
WHAT'S THAT SUPPOSED TO MEAN?
I WAS HELPING MY DAD YESTERDAY, SO I WAS PRETTY MUCH UP ALL NIGHT.
WHAA—?
YOU OKAY?
I GOT PAID FOR IT!
BUT AT THE SAME TIME...
...I'M ALWAYS SO SLEEPY.
...IS THIS SOME SORT OF SPECIAL SKILL?

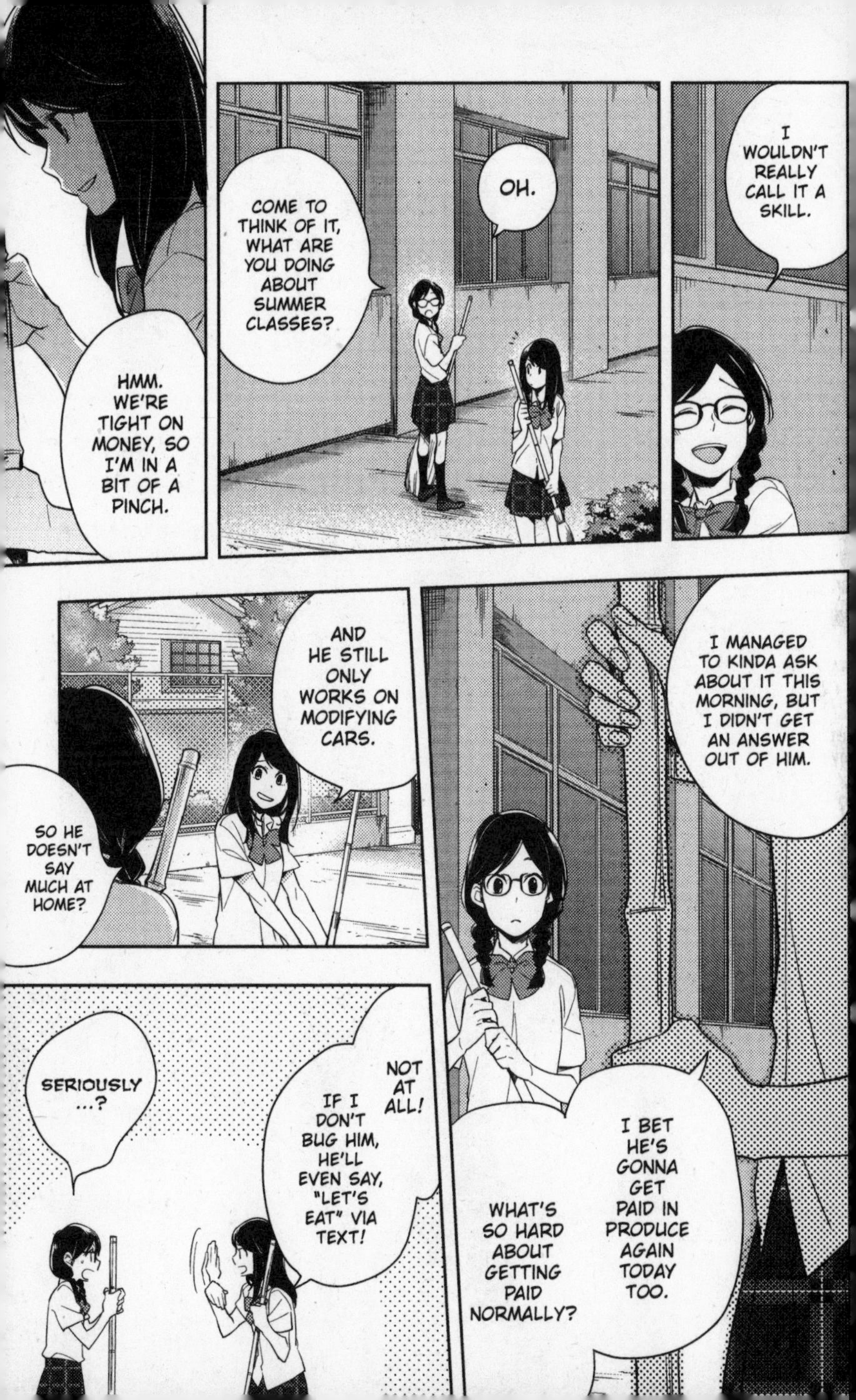
I WOULDN'T REALLY CALL IT A SKILL.
OH.
COME TO THINK OF IT, WHAT ARE YOU DOING ABOUT SUMMER CLASSES?
HMM. WE'RE TIGHT ON MONEY, SO I'M IN A BIT OF A PINCH.
I MANAGED TO KINDA ASK ABOUT IT THIS MORNING, BUT I DIDN'T GET AN ANSWER OUT OF HIM.
I BET HE'S GONNA GET PAID IN PRODUCE AGAIN TODAY TOO.
WHAT'S SO HARD ABOUT GETTING PAID NORMALLY?
AND HE STILL ONLY WORKS ON MODIFYING CARS.
SO HE DOESN'T SAY MUCH AT HOME?
NOT AT ALL!
IF I DON'T BUG HIM, HE'LL EVEN SAY, "LET'S EAT" VIA TEXT!
SERIOUSLY ...?

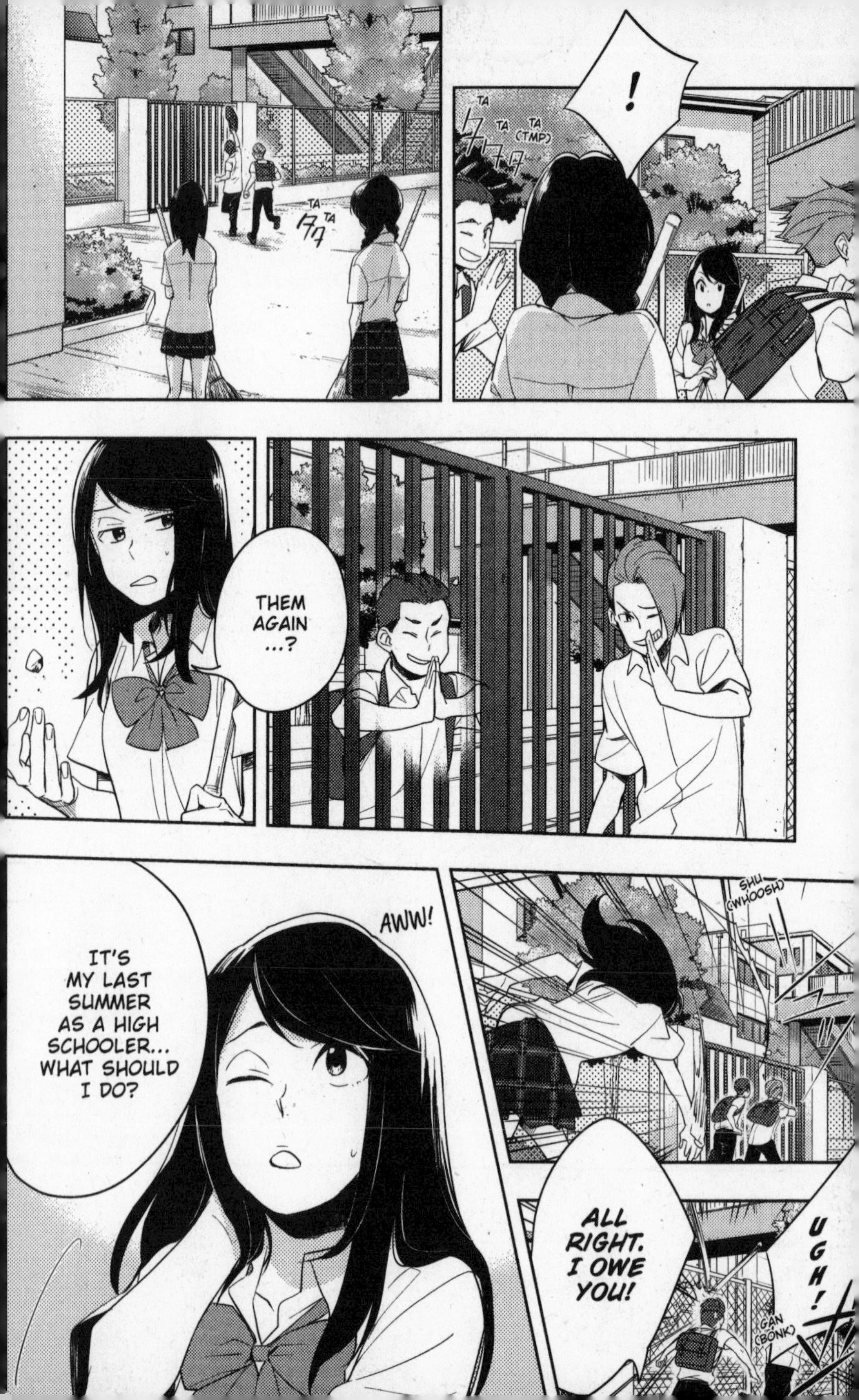
!
TA TA TA (TMP)
TA TA
THEM AGAIN ...?
SHU (WHOOSH)
ALL RIGHT. I OWE YOU!
UGH!
GAN (BONK)
AWW!
IT'S MY LAST SUMMER AS A HIGH SCHOOLER... WHAT SHOULD I DO?

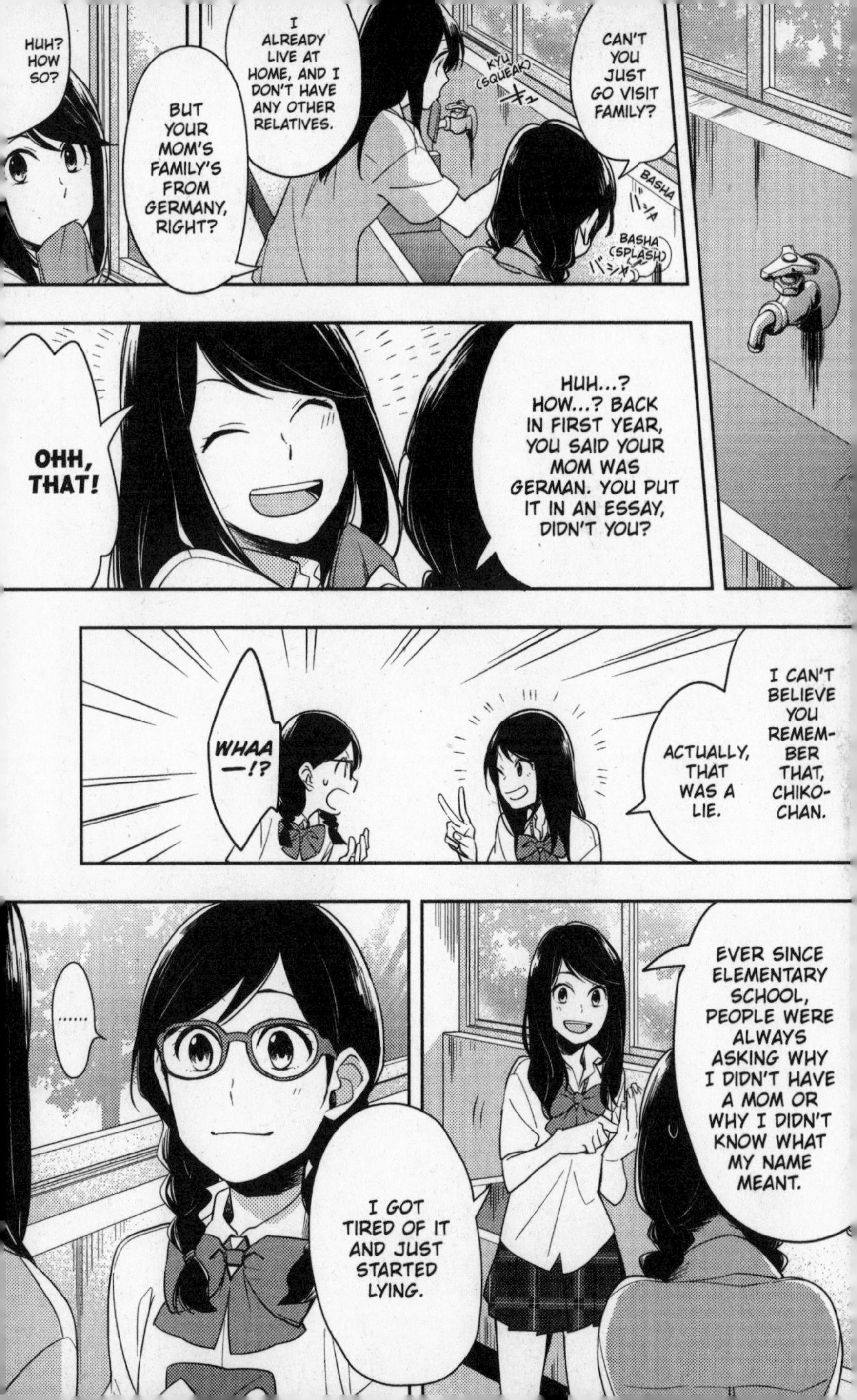
CAN'T YOU JUST GO VISIT FAMILY?
KYU (SQUEAK)
BASHA
BASHA (SPLASH)
I ALREADY LIVE AT HOME, AND I DON'T HAVE ANY OTHER RELATIVES.
BUT YOUR MOM'S FAMILY'S FROM GERMANY, RIGHT?
HUH? HOW SO?
HUH...? HOW...? BACK IN FIRST YEAR, YOU SAID YOUR MOM WAS GERMAN. YOU PUT IT IN AN ESSAY, DIDN'T YOU?
OHH, THAT!
I CAN'T BELIEVE YOU REMEMBER THAT, CHIKO-CHAN.
ACTUALLY, THAT WAS A LIE.
WHAA—!?
EVER SINCE ELEMENTARY SCHOOL, PEOPLE WERE ALWAYS ASKING WHY I DIDN'T HAVE A MOM OR WHY I DIDN'T KNOW WHAT MY NAME MEANT.
I GOT TIRED OF IT AND JUST STARTED LYING.
......

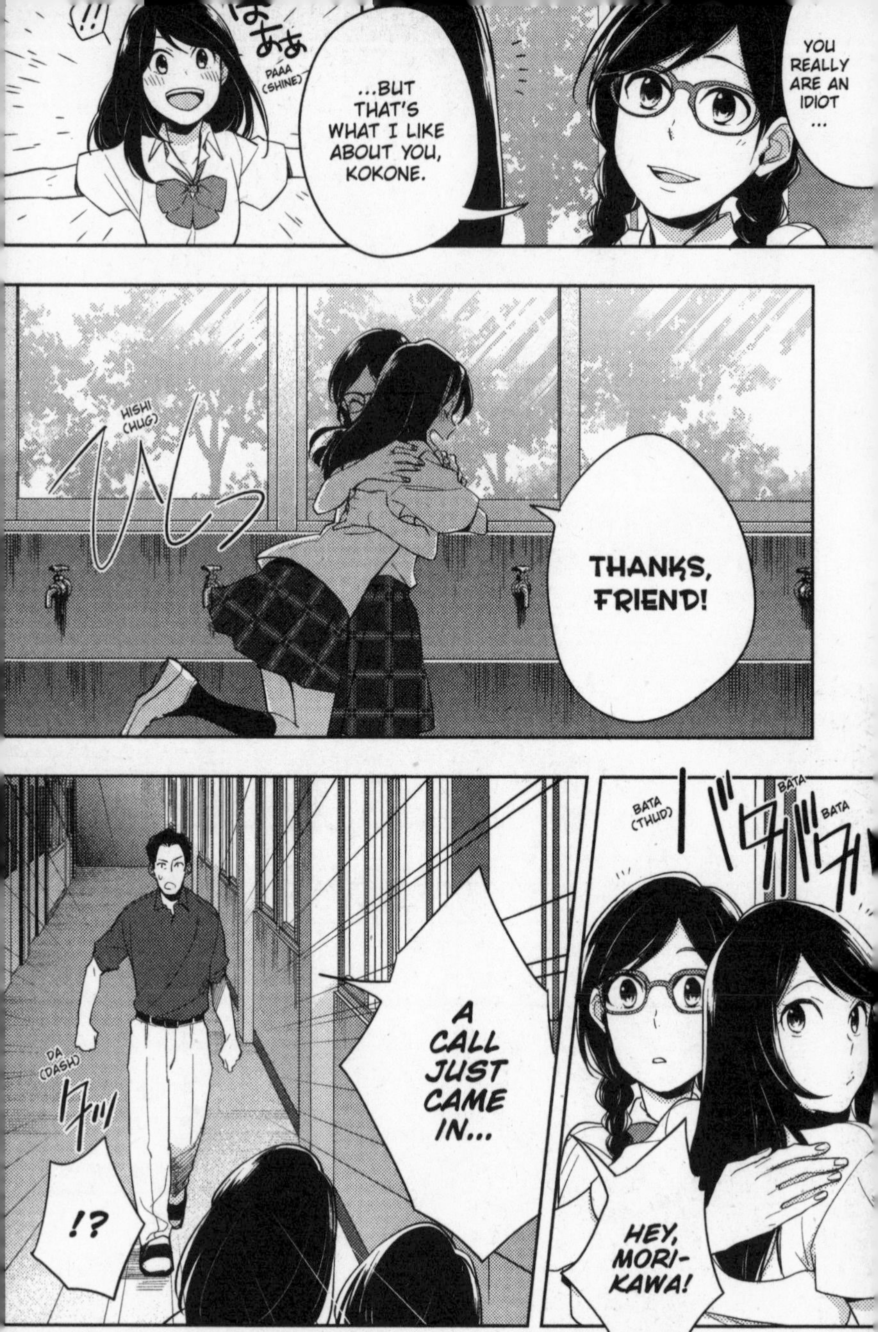
YOU REALLY ARE AN IDIOT ...
...BUT THAT'S WHAT I LIKE ABOUT YOU, KOKONE.
!!
PAAA (SHINE)
HISHI (HUG)
THANKS, FRIEND!
BATA (THUD) BATA BATA
HEY, MORI-KAWA!
A CALL JUST CAME IN...
!?
DA (DASH)

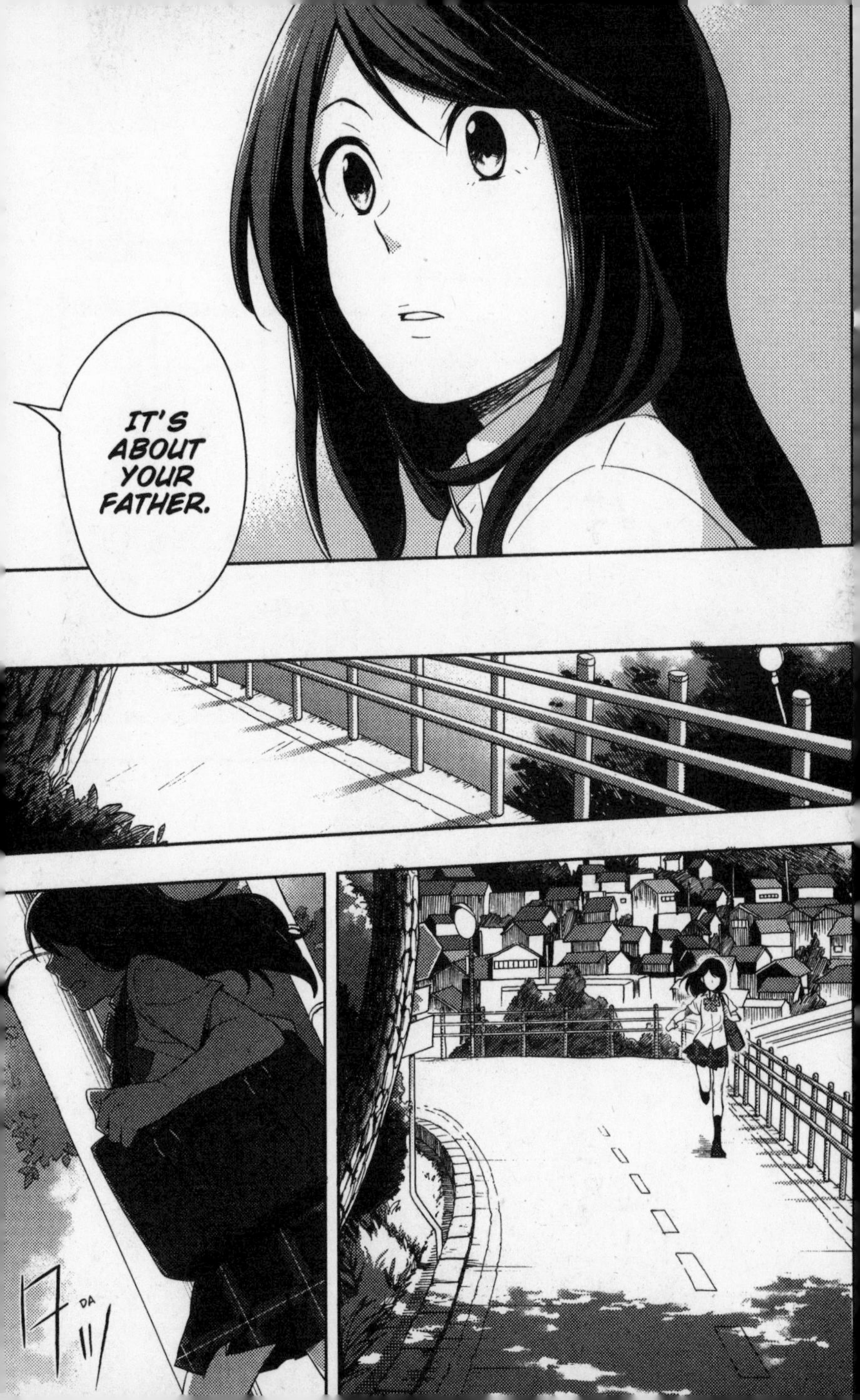
IT'S ABOUT YOUR FATHER.
DA

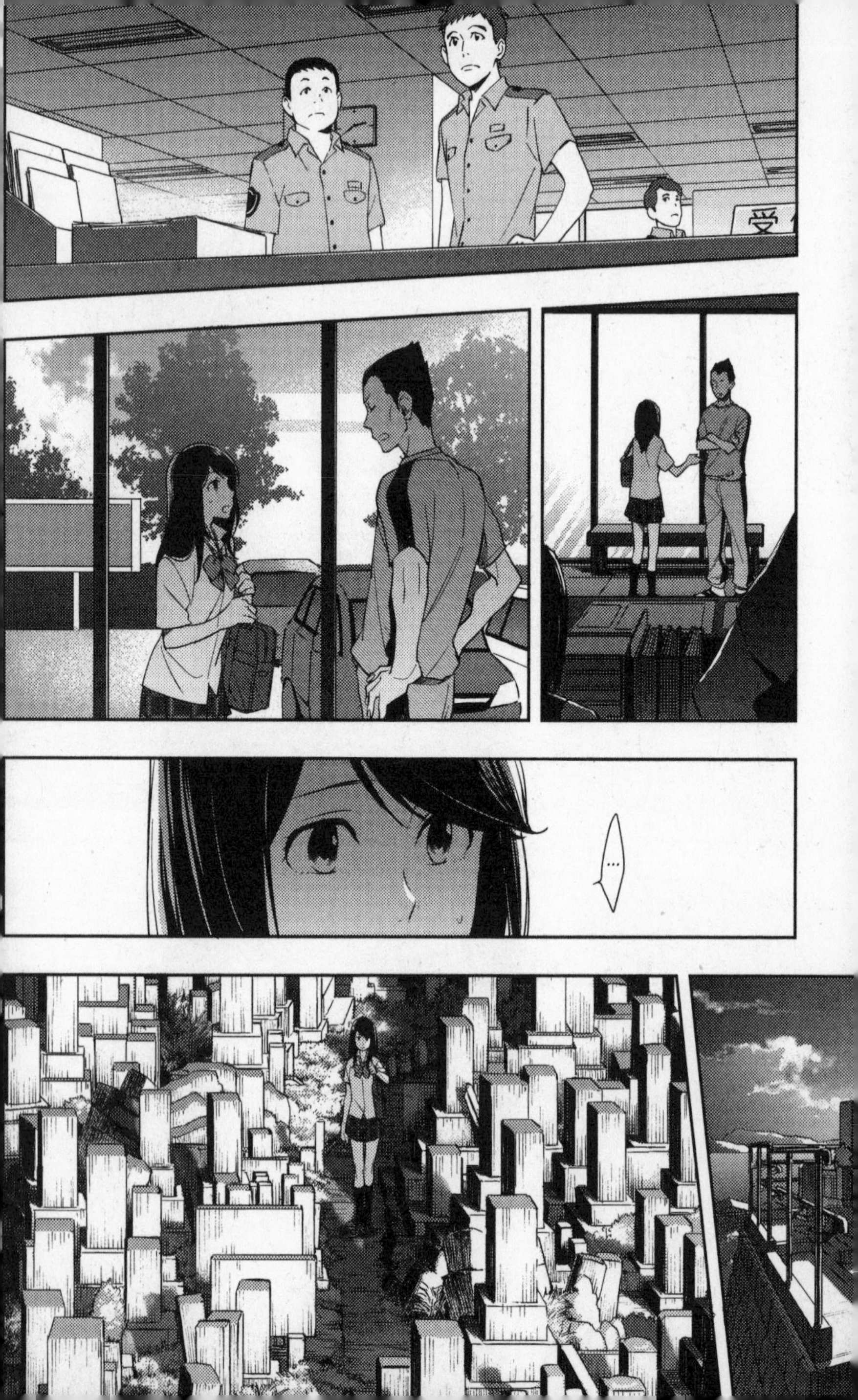
...

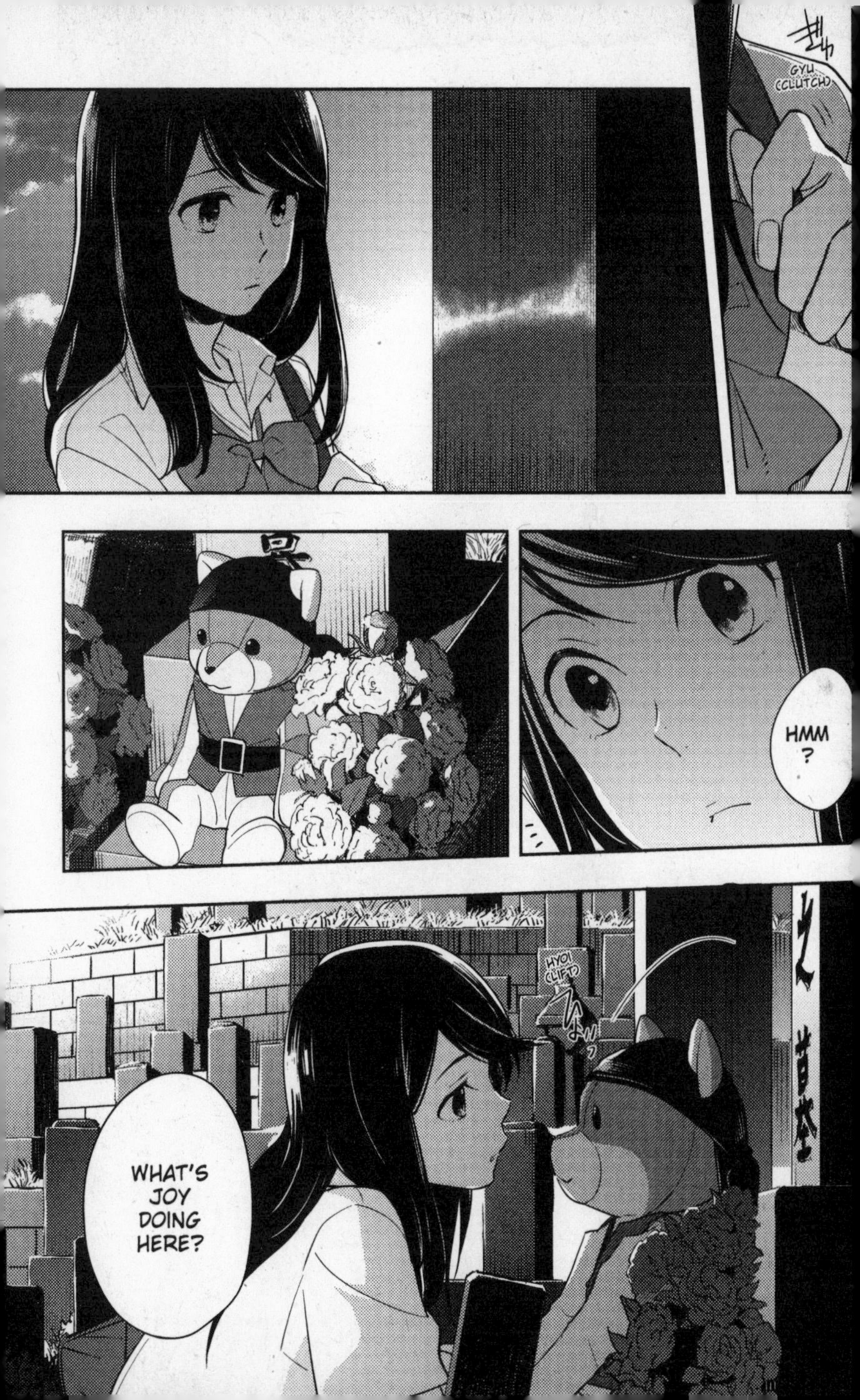
GYU (CLUTCH)
HMM ?
HYOI (LIFT)
WHAT'S JOY DOING HERE?

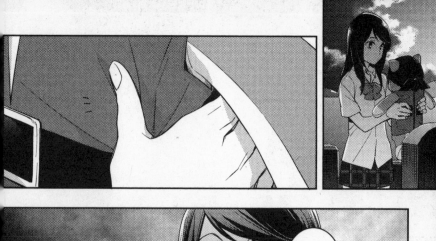

HUH?

A TABLET?

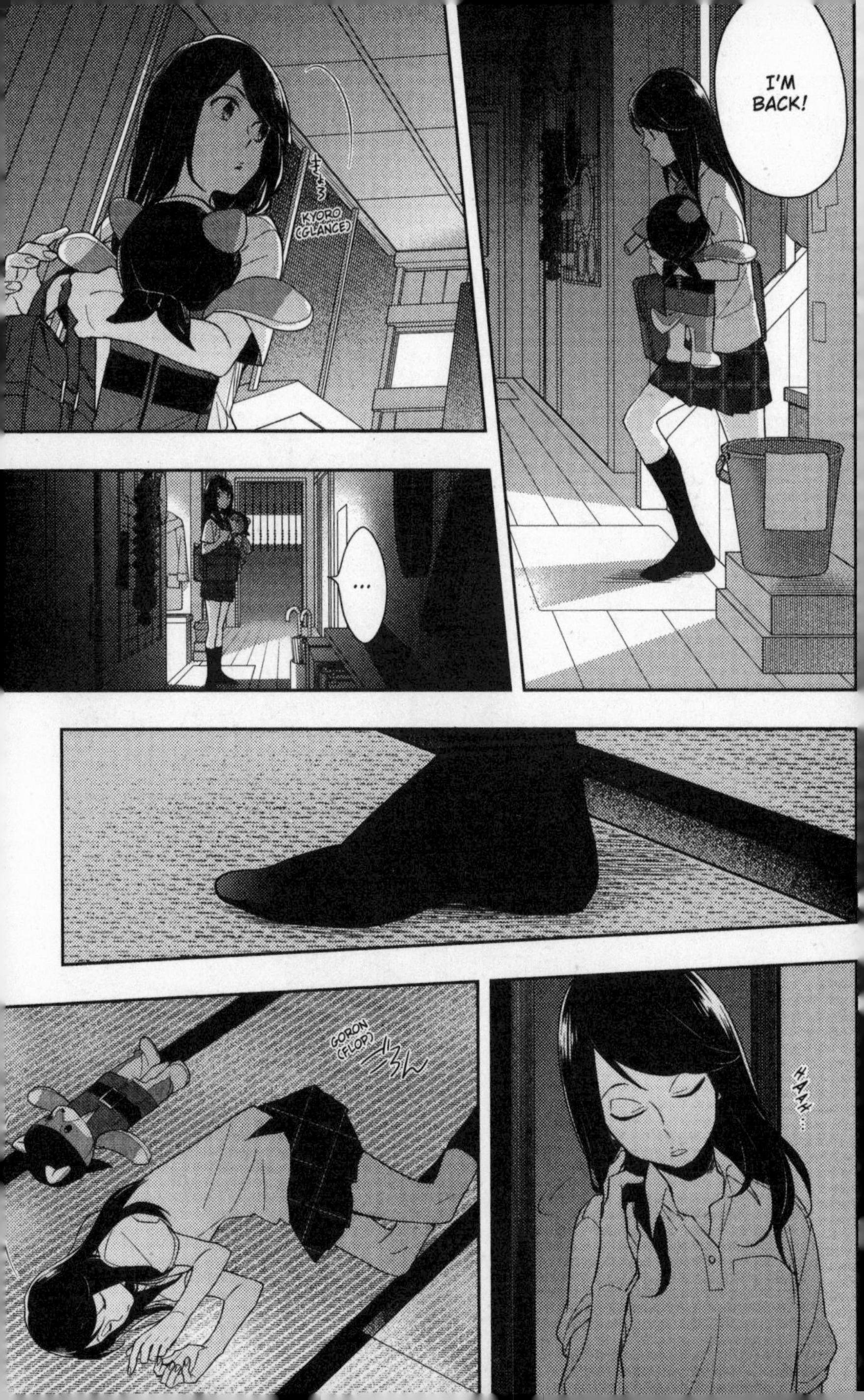
I'M BACK!
きょろ
KYORO (GLANCE)
...
HAAH...
ごろん
GORON (FLOP)

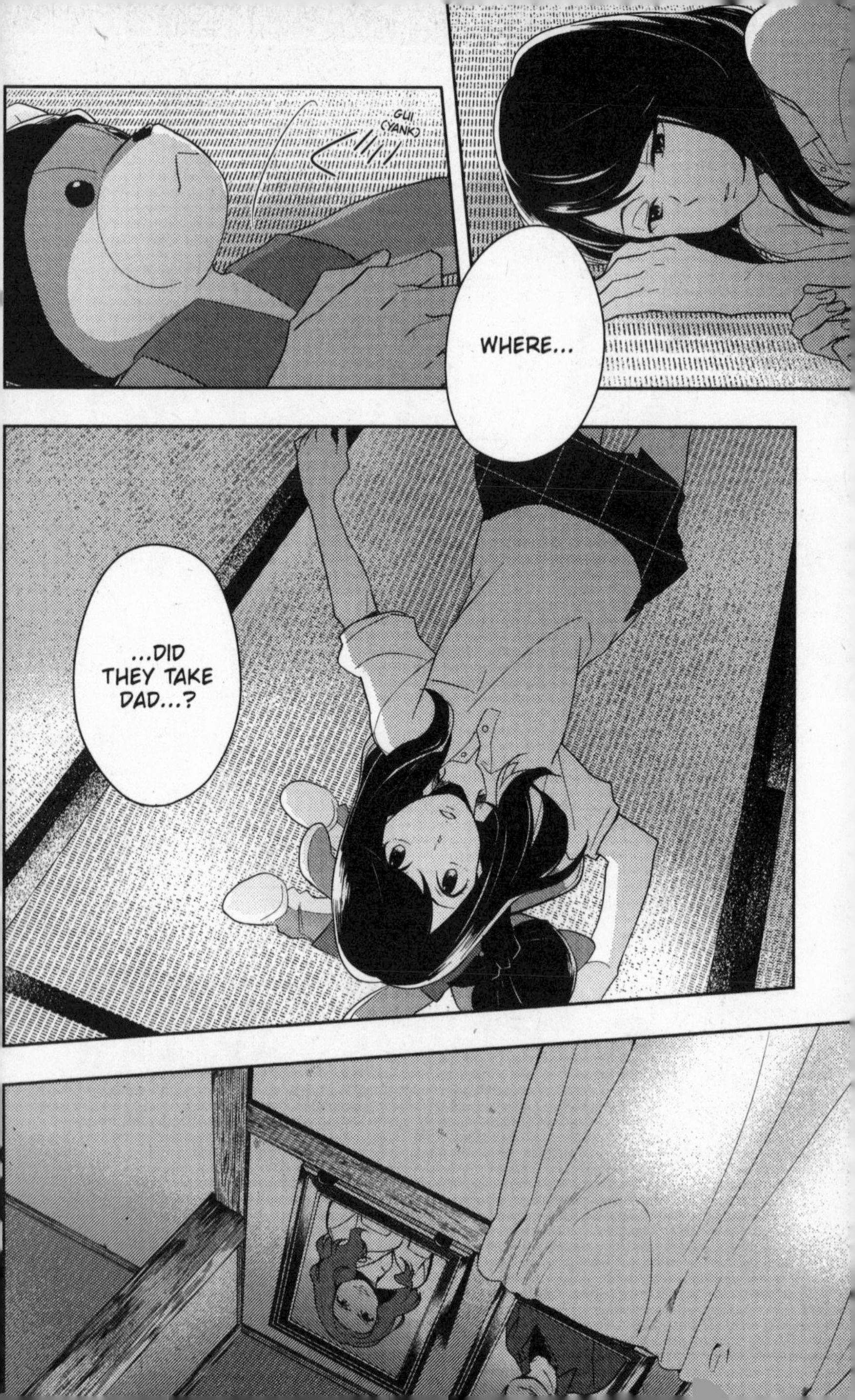
GUI (YANK)
WHERE...
...DID THEY TAKE DAD...?

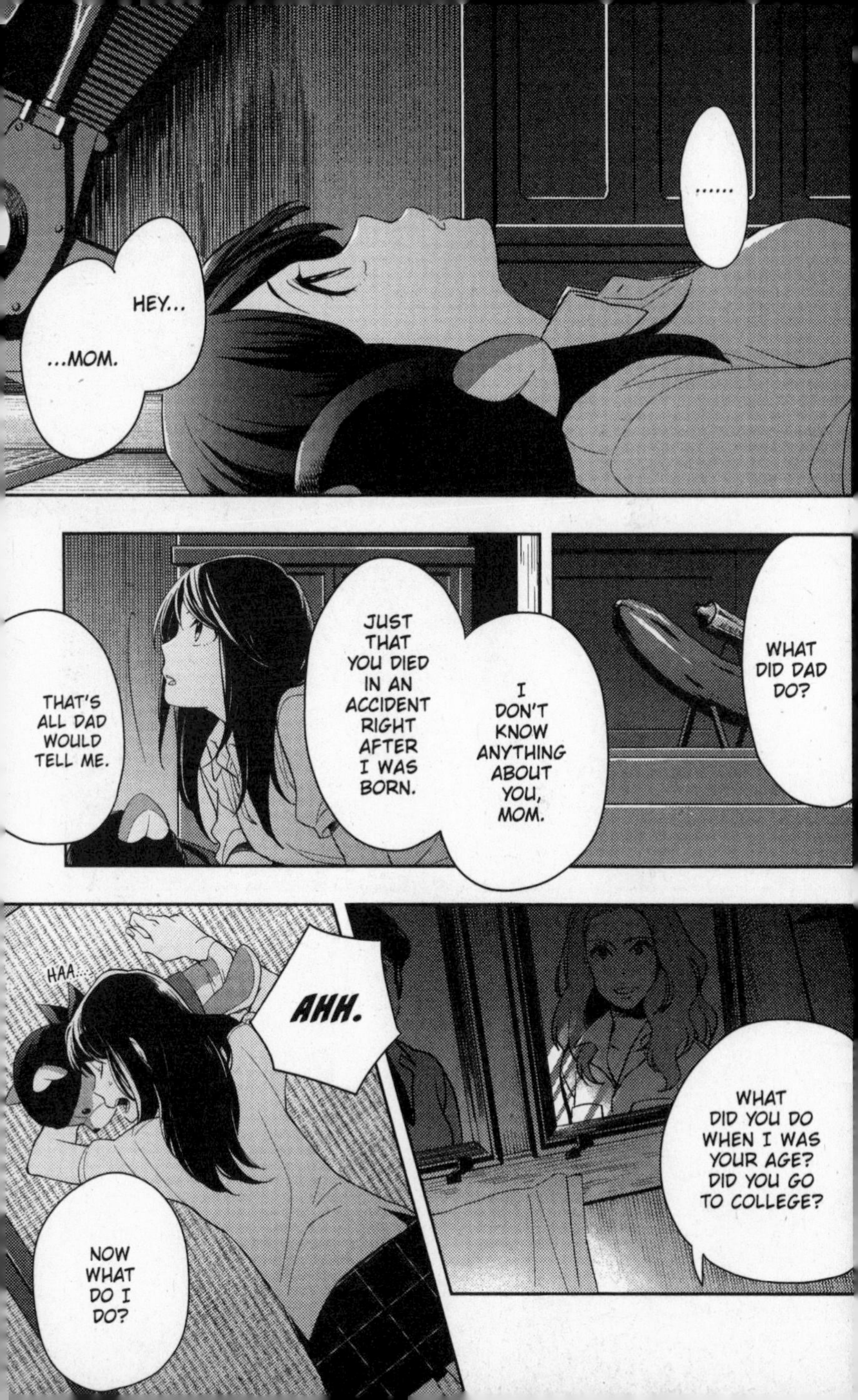
......
HEY... ...MOM.
WHAT DID DAD DO?
I DON'T KNOW ANYTHING ABOUT YOU, MOM.
JUST THAT YOU DIED IN AN ACCIDENT RIGHT AFTER I WAS BORN.
THAT'S ALL DAD WOULD TELL ME.
WHAT DID YOU DO WHEN I WAS YOUR AGE? DID YOU GO TO COLLEGE?
AHH.
HAA...
NOW WHAT DO I DO?

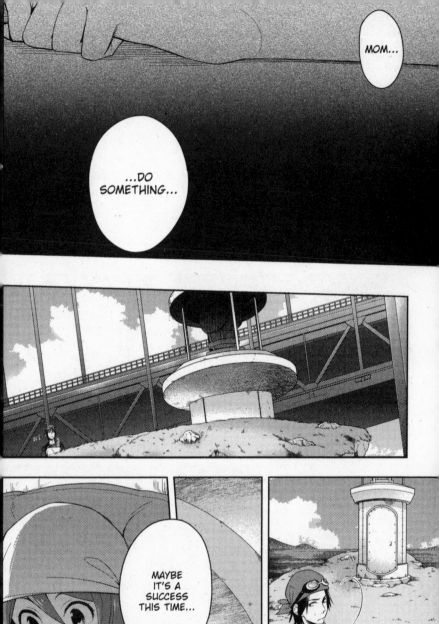

MOM...

...DO
SOMETHING...

MAYBE
IT'S A
SUCCESS
THIS TIME...

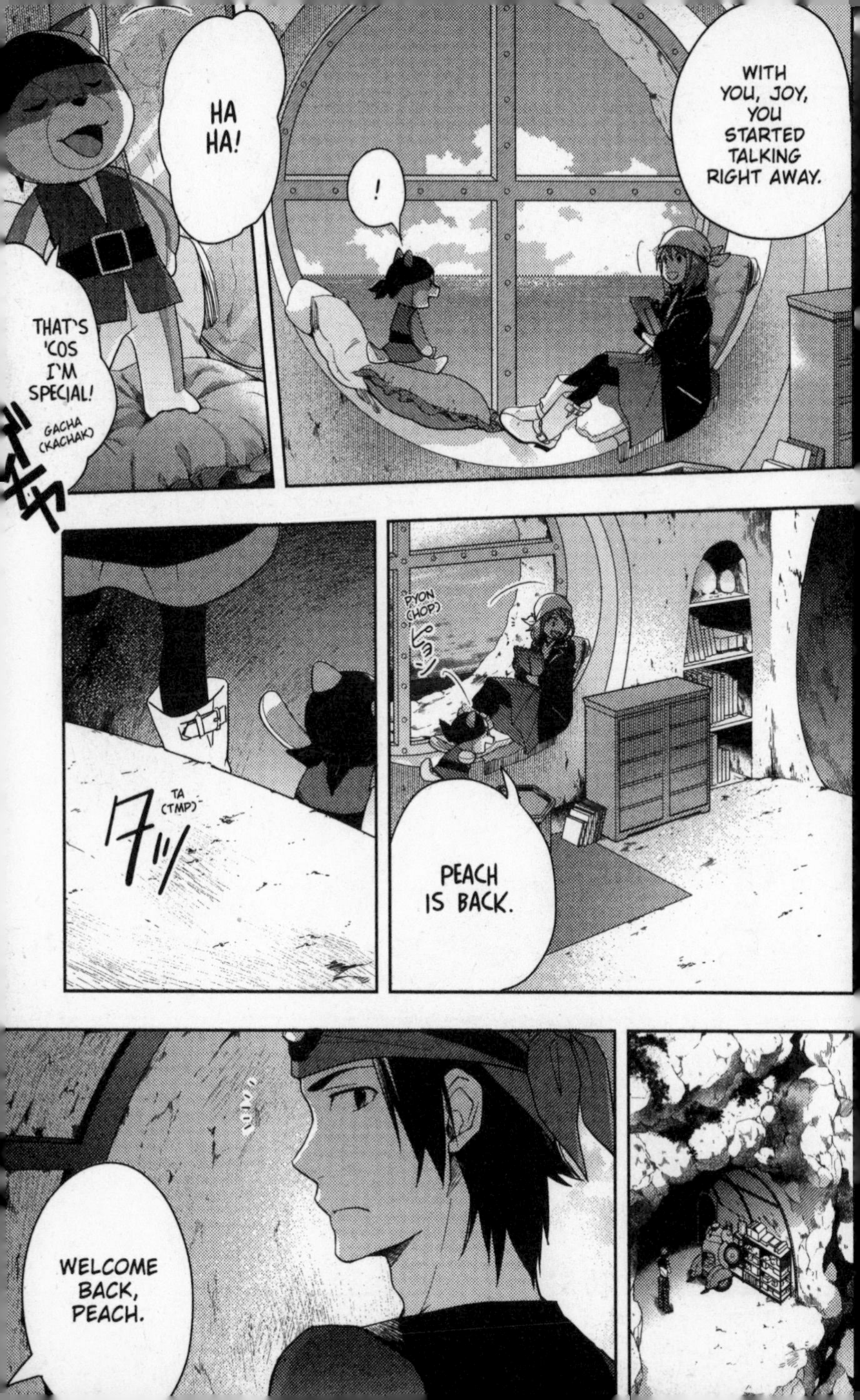
WITH YOU, JOY, YOU STARTED TALKING RIGHT AWAY.
!
HA HA!
THAT'S 'COS I'M SPECIAL!
GACHA (KACHAK)
PYON (HOP)
PEACH IS BACK.
TA (TMP)
WELCOME BACK, PEACH.

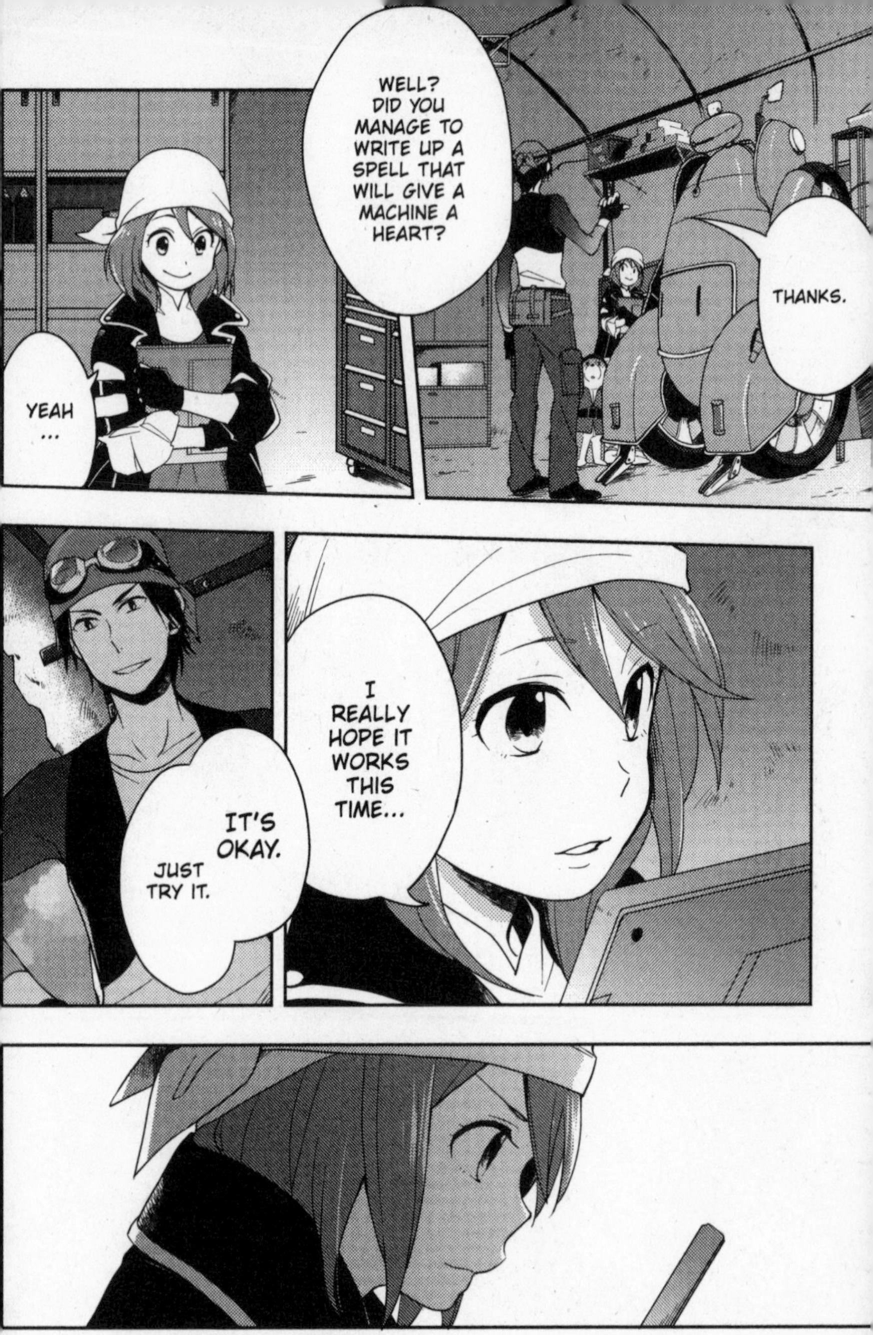
WELL? DID YOU MANAGE TO WRITE UP A SPELL THAT WILL GIVE A MACHINE A HEART?
THANKS.
YEAH ...
I REALLY HOPE IT WORKS THIS TIME...
IT'S OKAY.
JUST TRY IT.

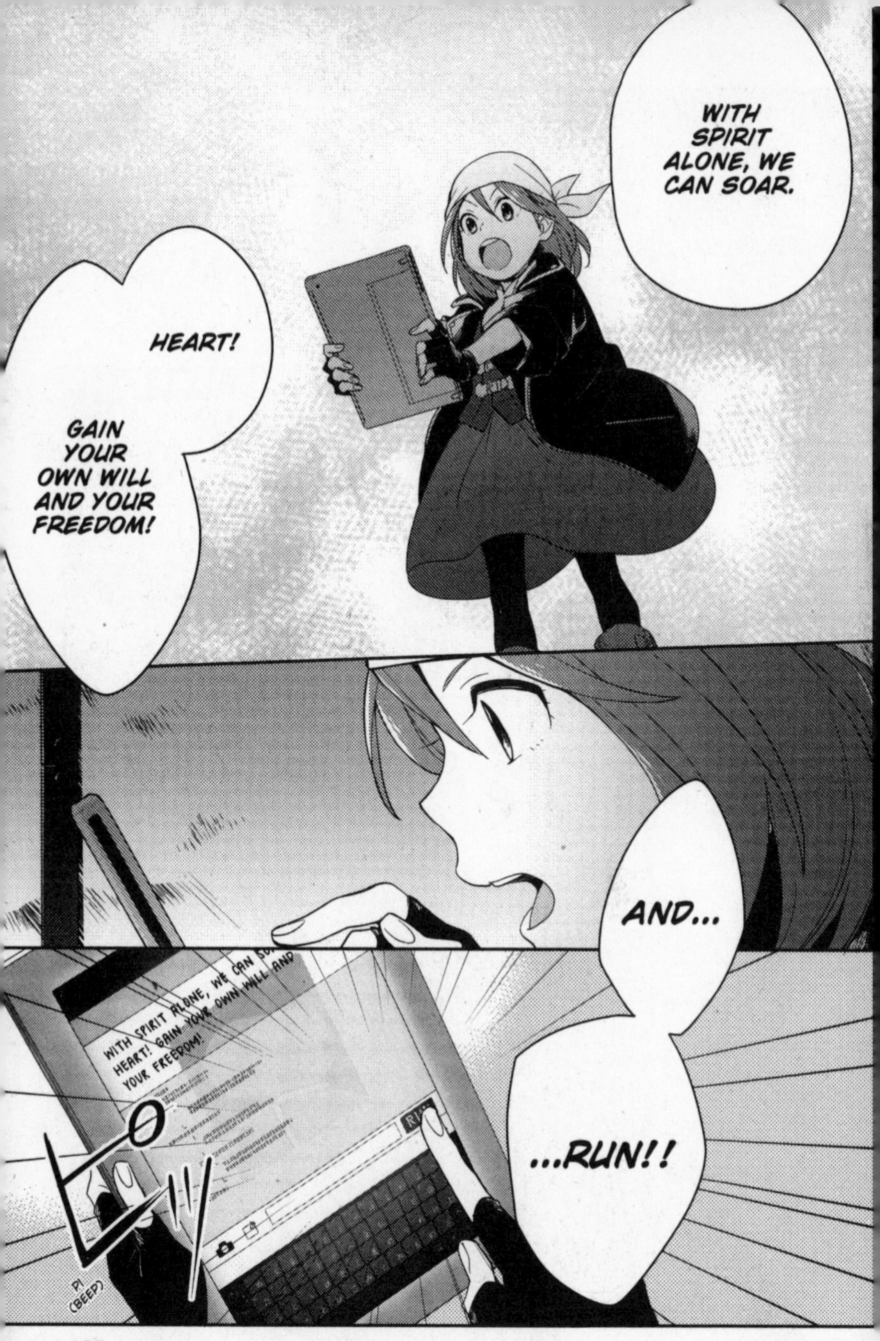
WITH SPIRIT ALONE, WE CAN SOAR.
HEART!
GAIN YOUR OWN WILL AND YOUR FREEDOM!
AND...
...RUN!!
WITH SPIRIT ALONE, WE CAN SO
HEART! GAIN YOUR OWN WILL AND
YOUR FREEDOM!
PI (BEEP)

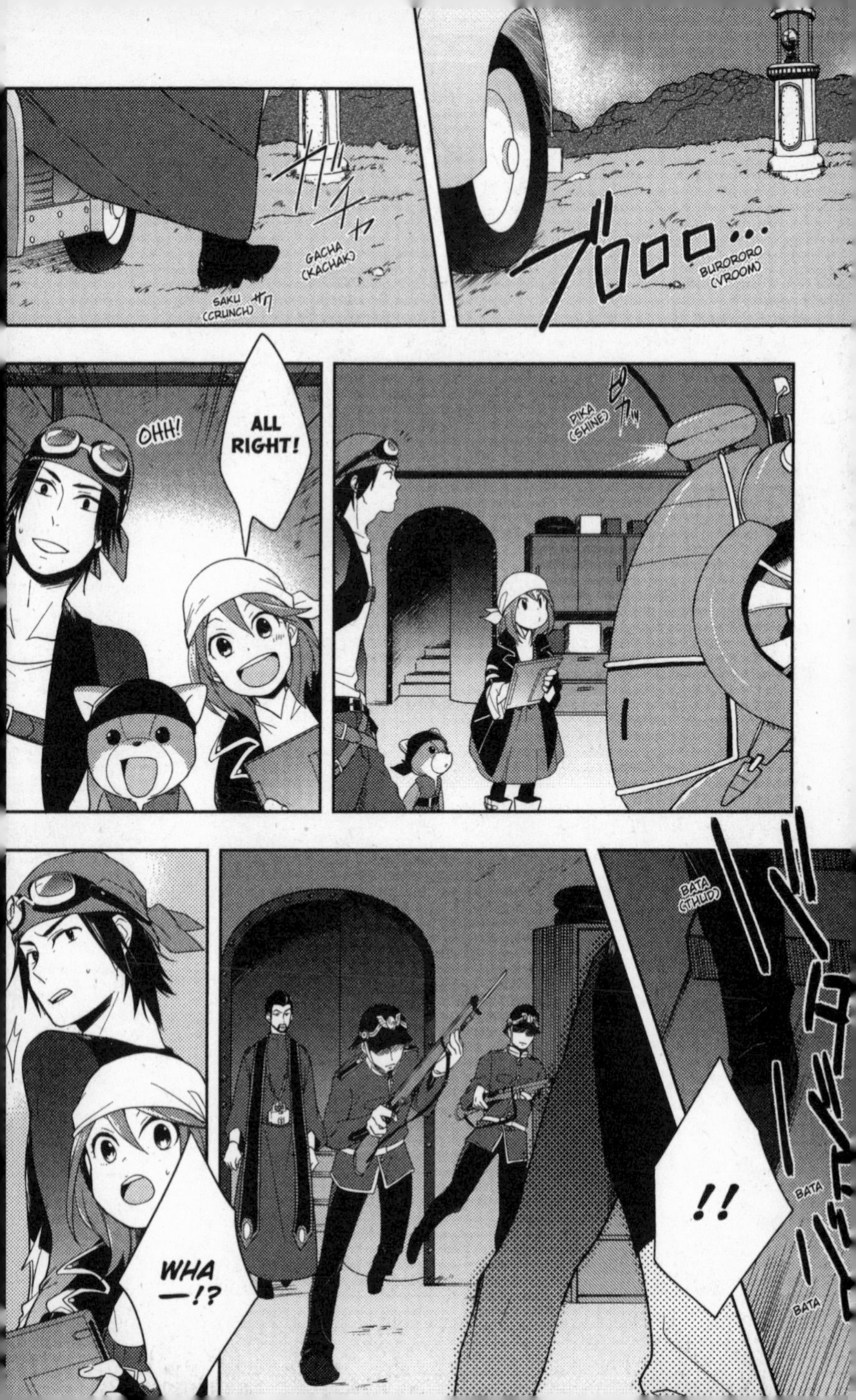
BURORORO (VROOM)
GACHA (KACHAK)
SAKU (CRUNCH)
PIKA (SHINE)
ALL RIGHT!
OHH!
BATA (THUD)
!!
BATA
BATA
WHA—!?

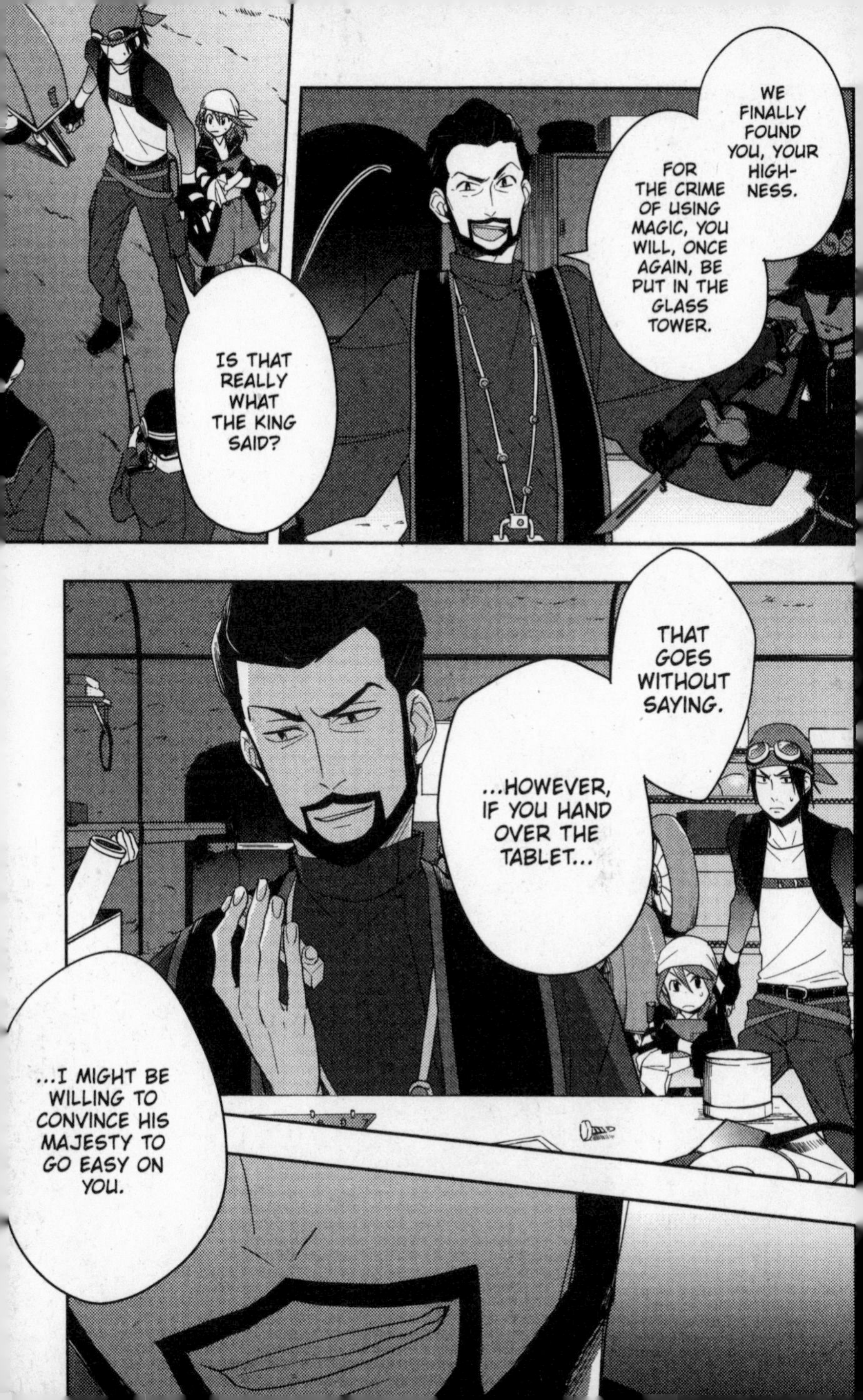
WE FINALLY FOUND YOU, YOUR HIGH-NESS.
FOR THE CRIME OF USING MAGIC, YOU WILL, ONCE AGAIN, BE PUT IN THE GLASS TOWER.
IS THAT REALLY WHAT THE KING SAID?
THAT GOES WITHOUT SAYING.
...HOWEVER, IF YOU HAND OVER THE TABLET...
...I MIGHT BE WILLING TO CONVINCE HIS MAJESTY TO GO EASY ON YOU.

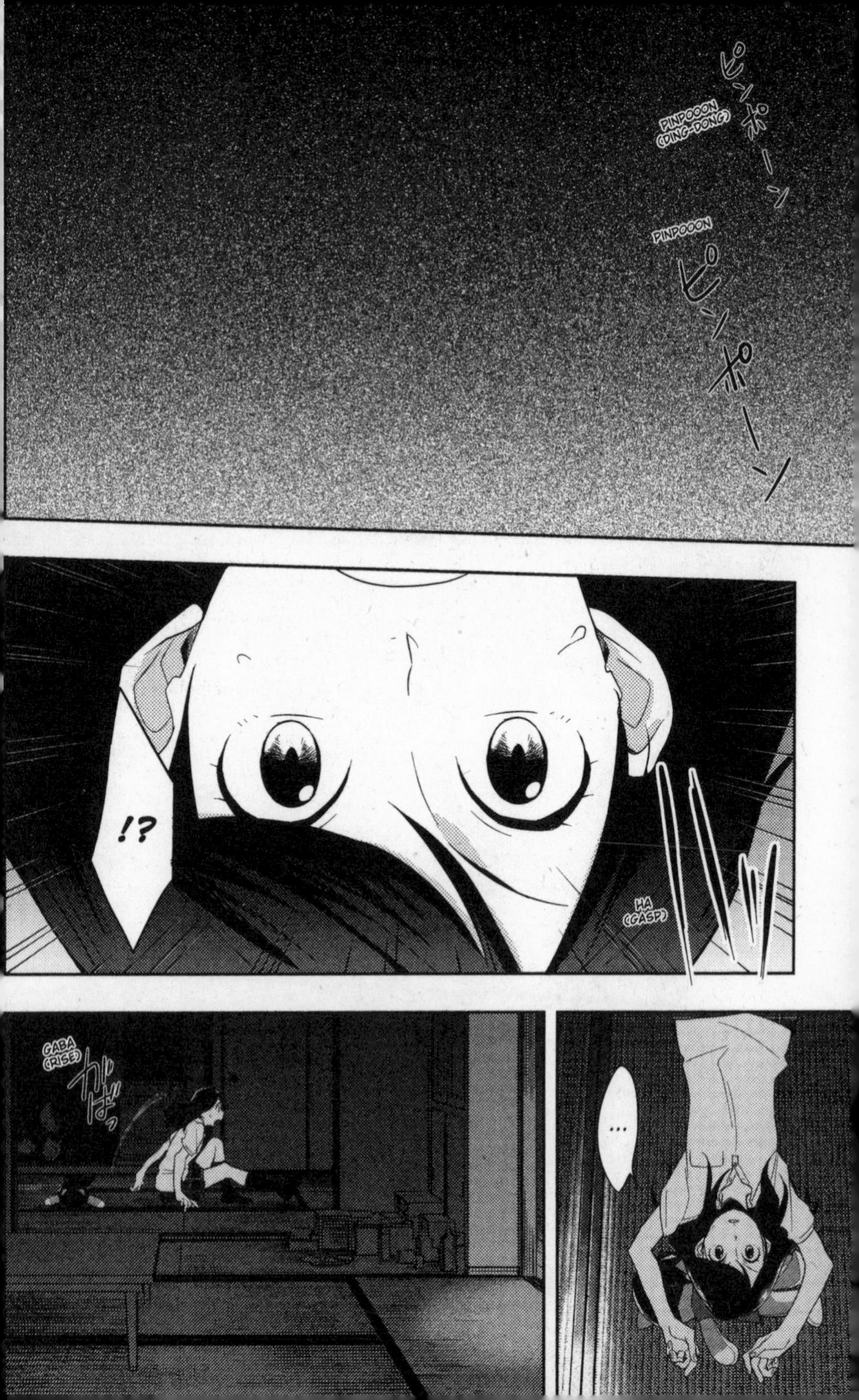
PINPOOON (DING-DONG)
PINPOOON
HA (GASP)
!?
...
GABA (RISE)

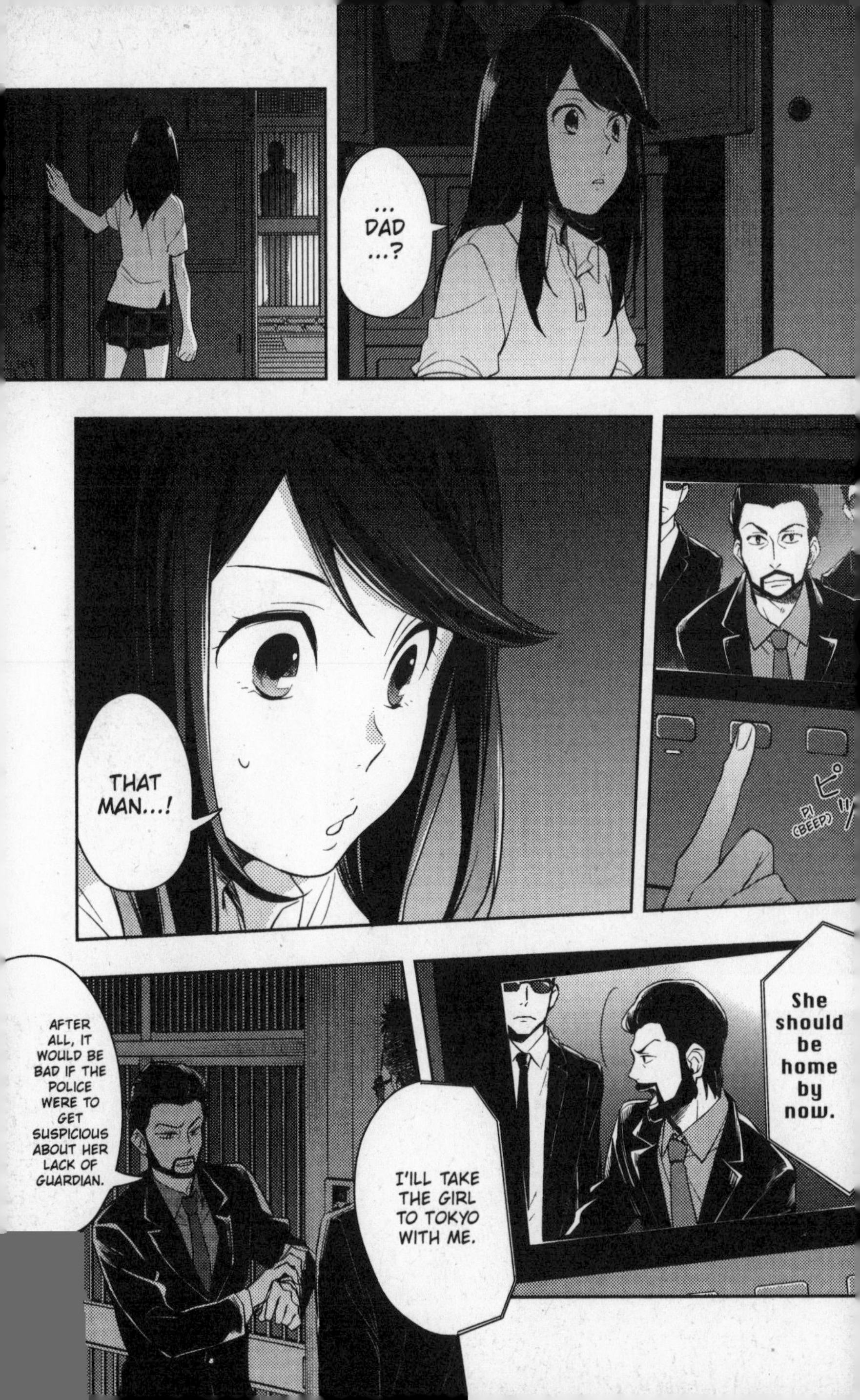
...DAD ...?
ピッ
PI (BEEP)
THAT MAN...!
She should be home by now.
I'LL TAKE THE GIRL TO TOKYO WITH ME.
AFTER ALL, IT WOULD BE BAD IF THE POLICE WERE TO GET SUSPICIOUS ABOUT HER LACK OF GUARDIAN.

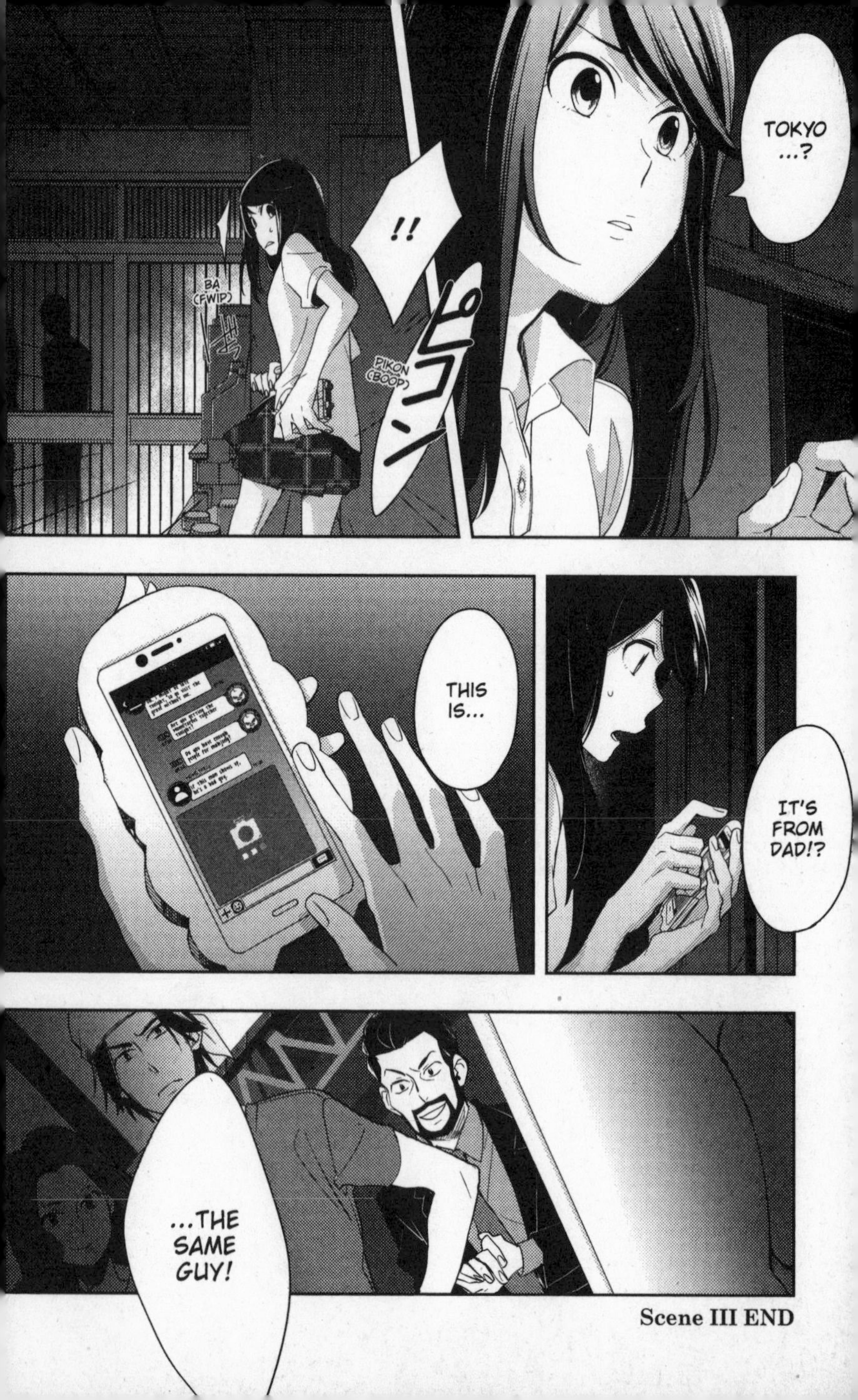
TOKYO ...?
PIKON (BOOP)
!!
BA (FWIP)
IT'S FROM DAD!?
THIS IS...
...THE SAME GUY!

Scene III END

# Napping Princess

## The Story of the Unknown Me

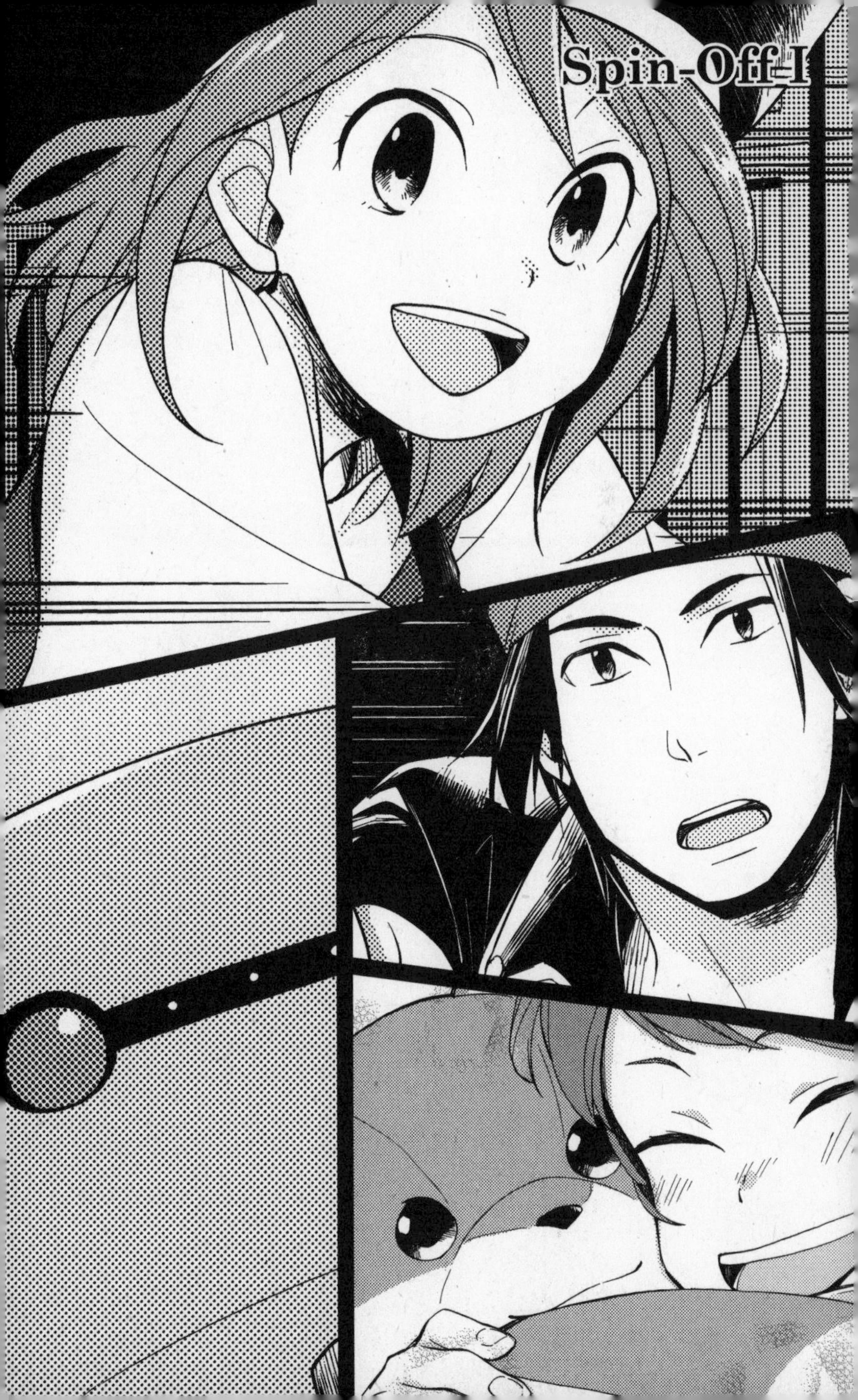
Spin-Off I

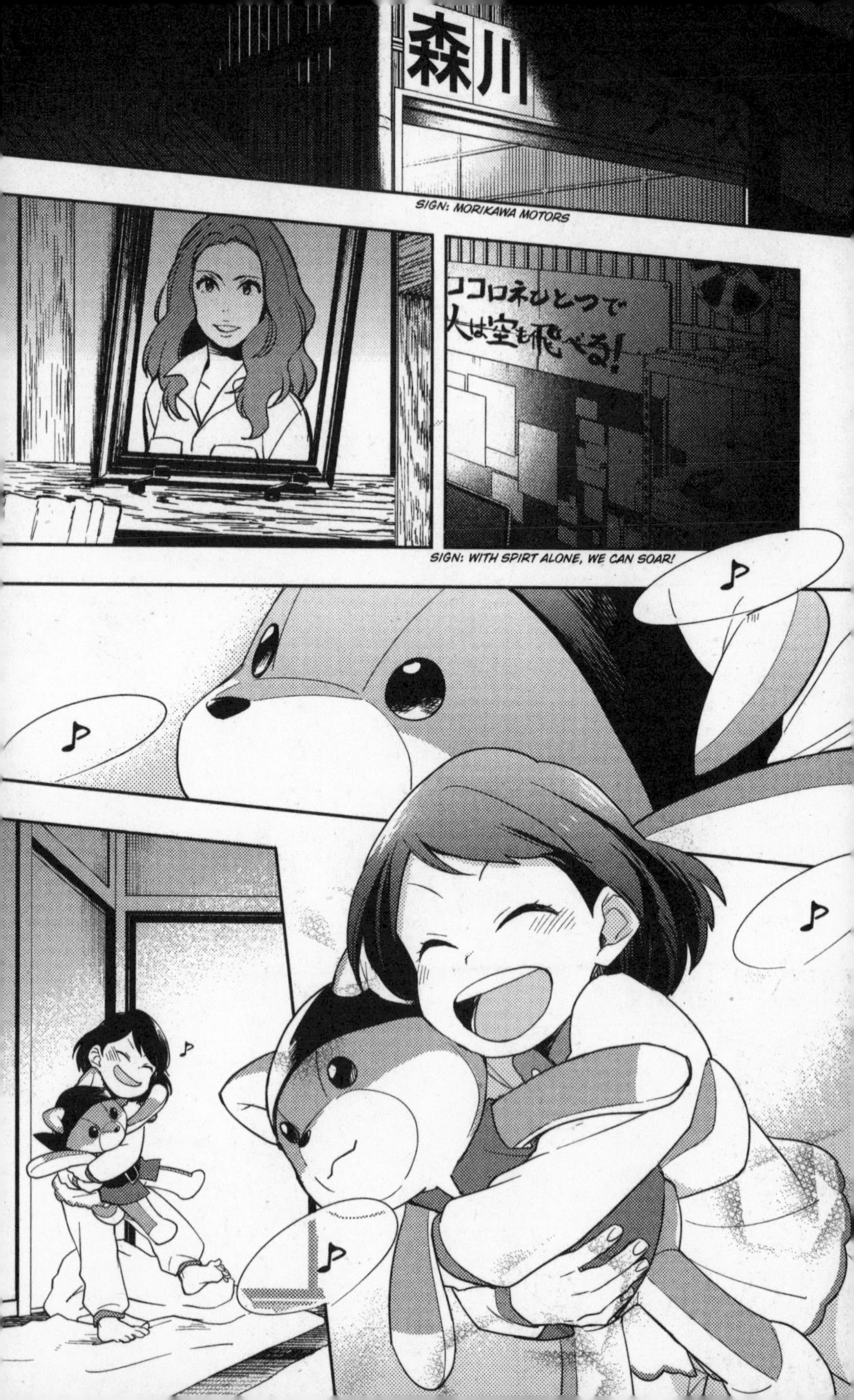
森川
SIGN: MORIKAWA MOTORS
ココロネひとつで
人は空も飛べる!
SIGN: WITH SPIRT ALONE, WE CAN SOAR!
♪
♪
♪
♪
♪

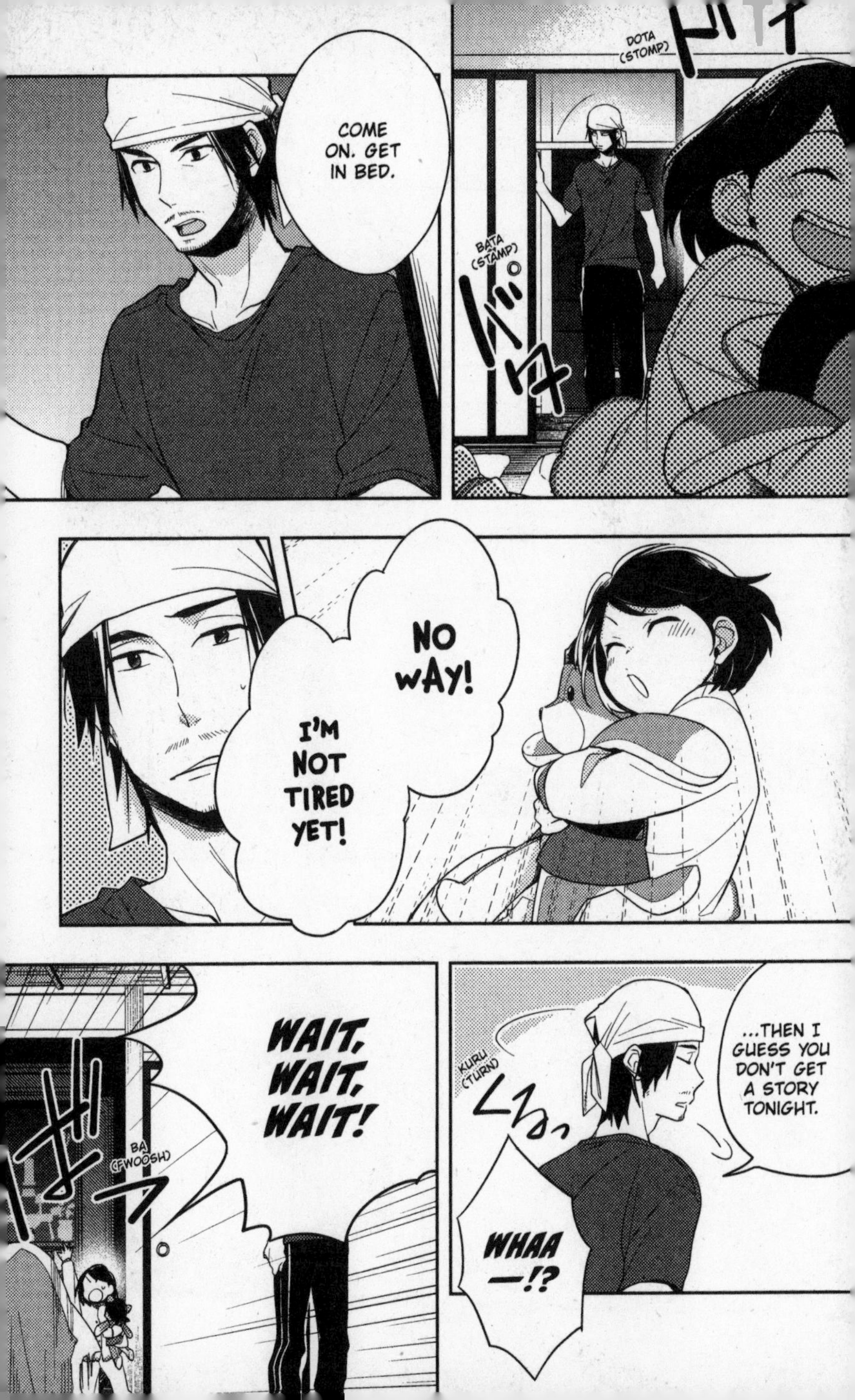
DOTA (STOMP)
BATA (STAMP)
COME ON. GET IN BED.
NO wAY!
I'M NOT TIRED YET!
KURU (TURN)
...THEN I GUESS YOU DON'T GET A STORY TONIGHT.
WHAA—!?
WAIT, WAIT, WAIT!
BA (FWOOSH)

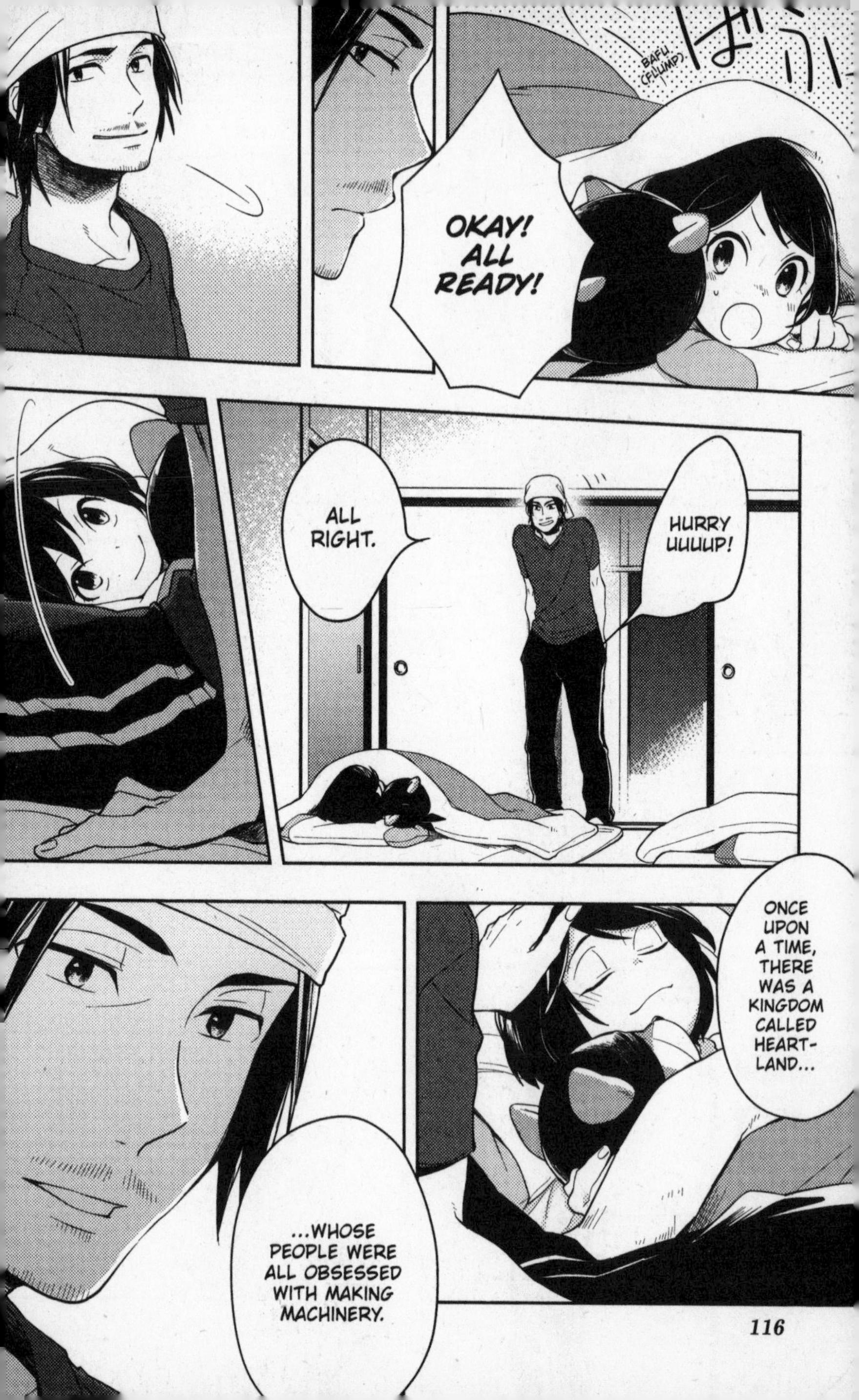
ばふ
BAFU (FLUMP)
OKAY! ALL READY!
HURRY UUUUP!
ALL RIGHT.
ONCE UPON A TIME, THERE WAS A KINGDOM CALLED HEART-LAND...
...WHOSE PEOPLE WERE ALL OBSESSED WITH MAKING MACHINERY.

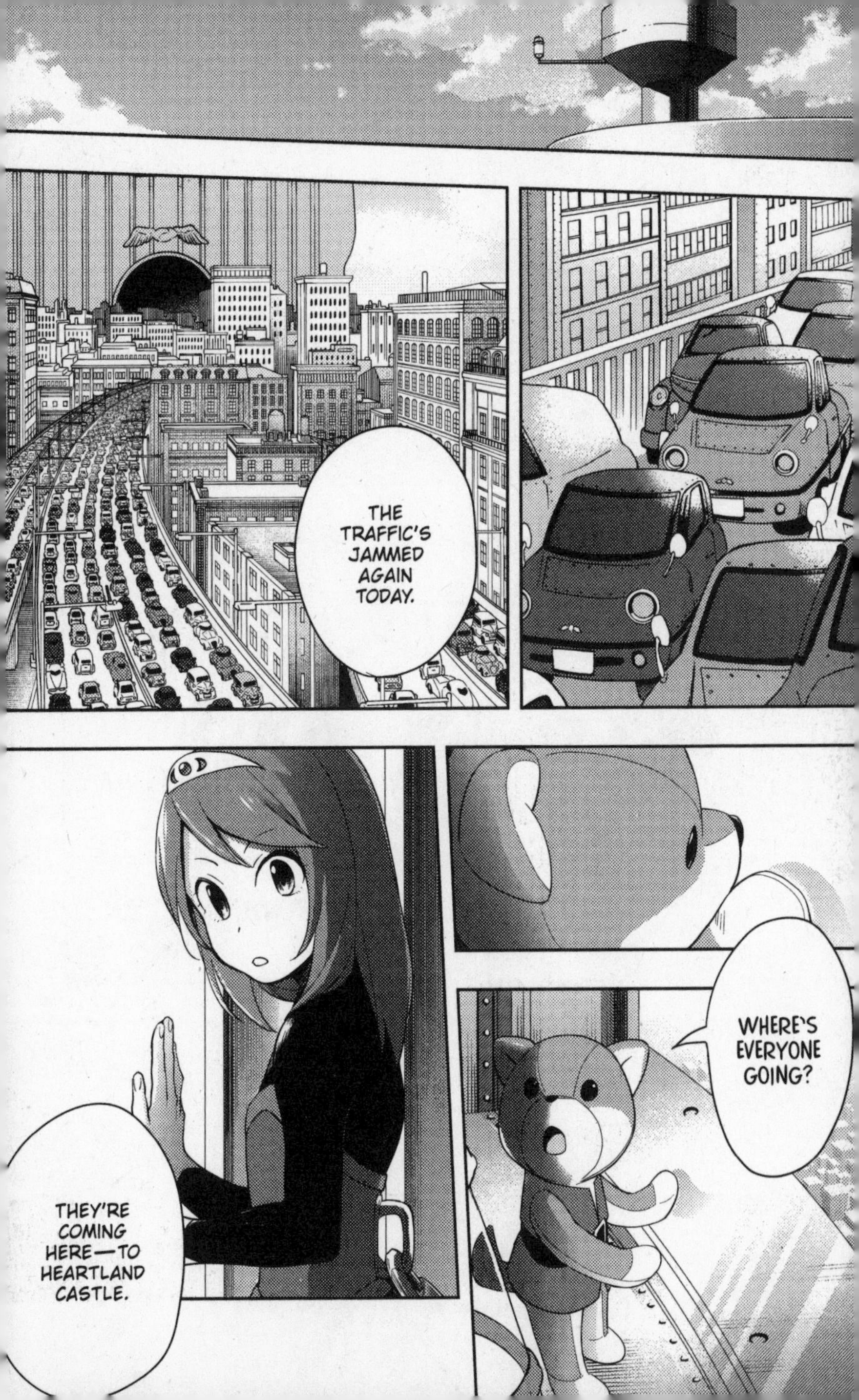
THE TRAFFIC'S JAMMED AGAIN TODAY.
WHERE'S EVERYONE GOING?
THEY'RE COMING HERE—TO HEARTLAND CASTLE.

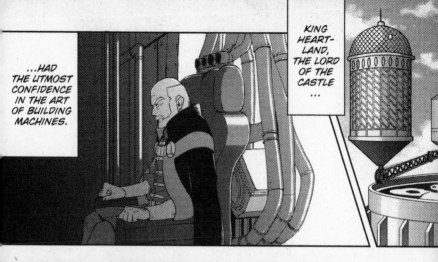

KING HEART-LAND, THE LORD OF THE CASTLE...
...HAD THE UTMOST CONFIDENCE IN THE ART OF BUILDING MACHINES.
HE BELIEVED MACHINES...
...COULD BRING HAPPI-NESS TO ALL.
EXIT
YOU JUST STARTED HERE...
...BUT YOU CAN'T EVEN BOTHER TO COME IN ON TIME?
IT'S COMING OUT OF YOUR PAY.

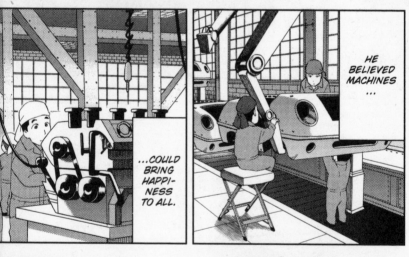

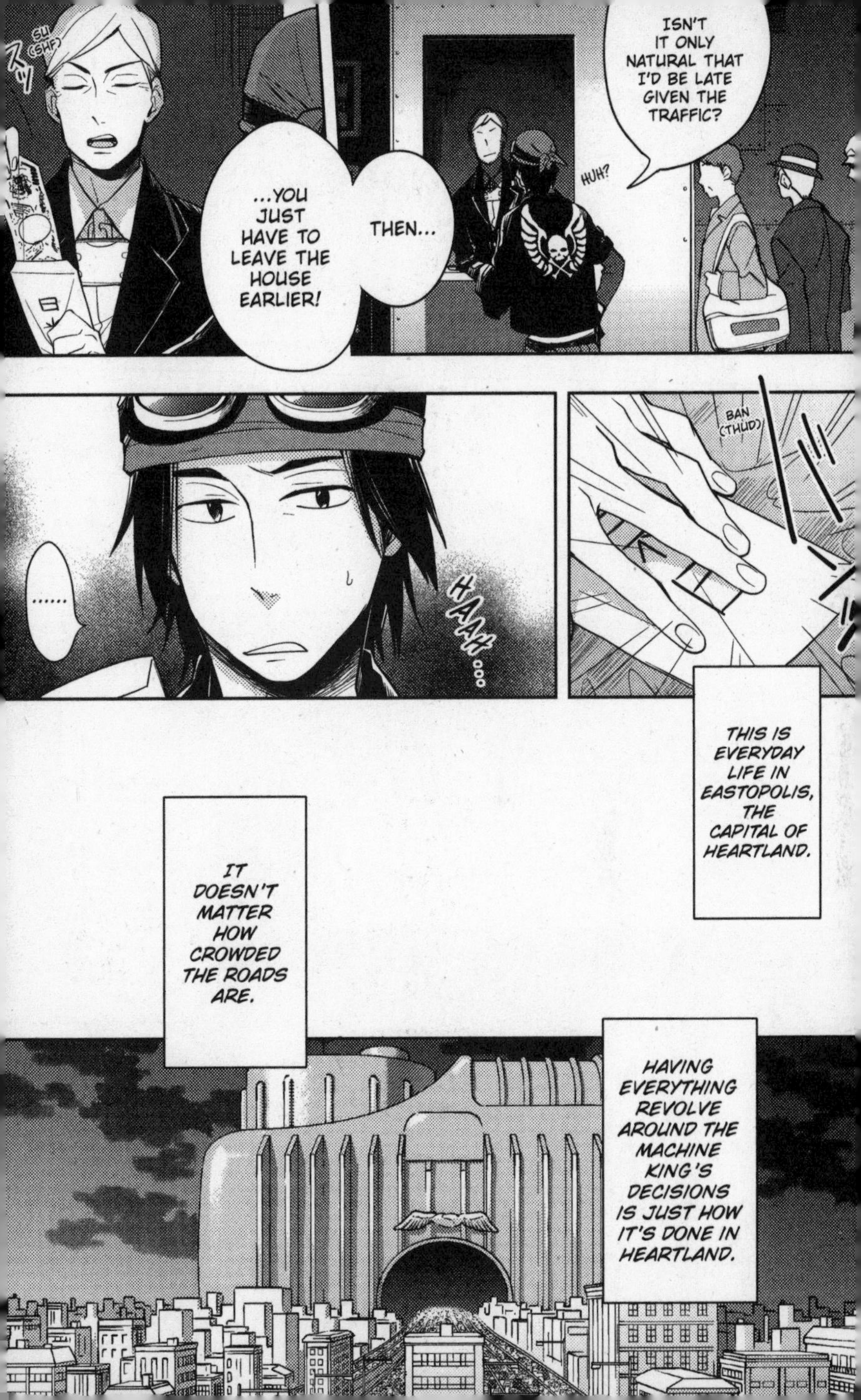
ISN'T IT ONLY NATURAL THAT I'D BE LATE GIVEN THE TRAFFIC?
HUH?
THEN...
...YOU JUST HAVE TO LEAVE THE HOUSE EARLIER!
SU (SHF)
BAN (THUD)
HAAH...
......
THIS IS EVERYDAY LIFE IN EASTOPOLIS, THE CAPITAL OF HEARTLAND.
IT DOESN'T MATTER HOW CROWDED THE ROADS ARE.
HAVING EVERYTHING REVOLVE AROUND THE MACHINE KING'S DECISIONS IS JUST HOW IT'S DONE IN HEARTLAND.

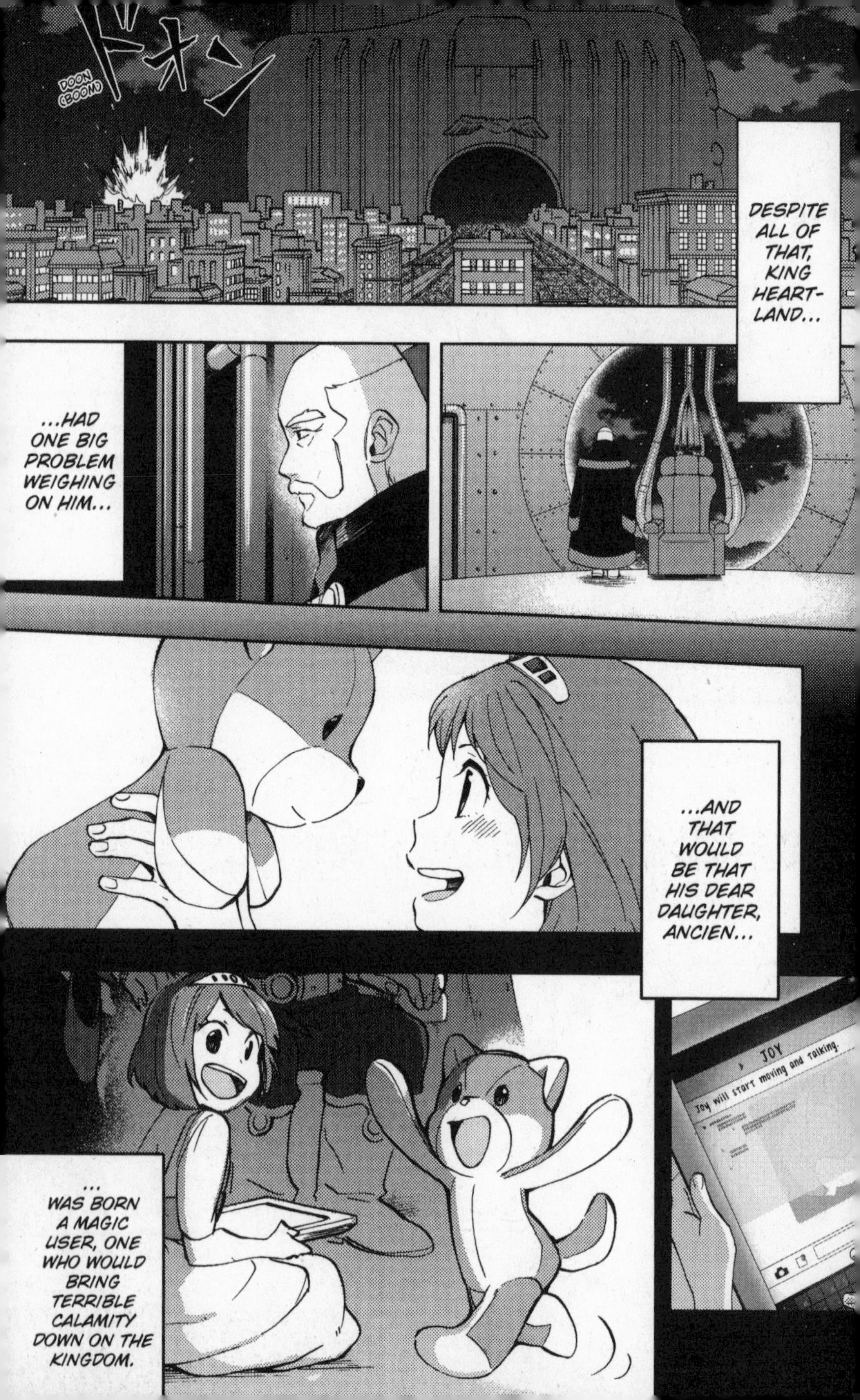
ドォン
DOON (BOOM)
DESPITE ALL OF THAT, KING HEARTLAND...
...HAD ONE BIG PROBLEM WEIGHING ON HIM...
...AND THAT WOULD BE THAT HIS DEAR DAUGHTER, ANCIEN...
JOY
Joy will start moving and talking.
... WAS BORN A MAGIC USER, ONE WHO WOULD BRING TERRIBLE CALAMITY DOWN ON THE KINGDOM.

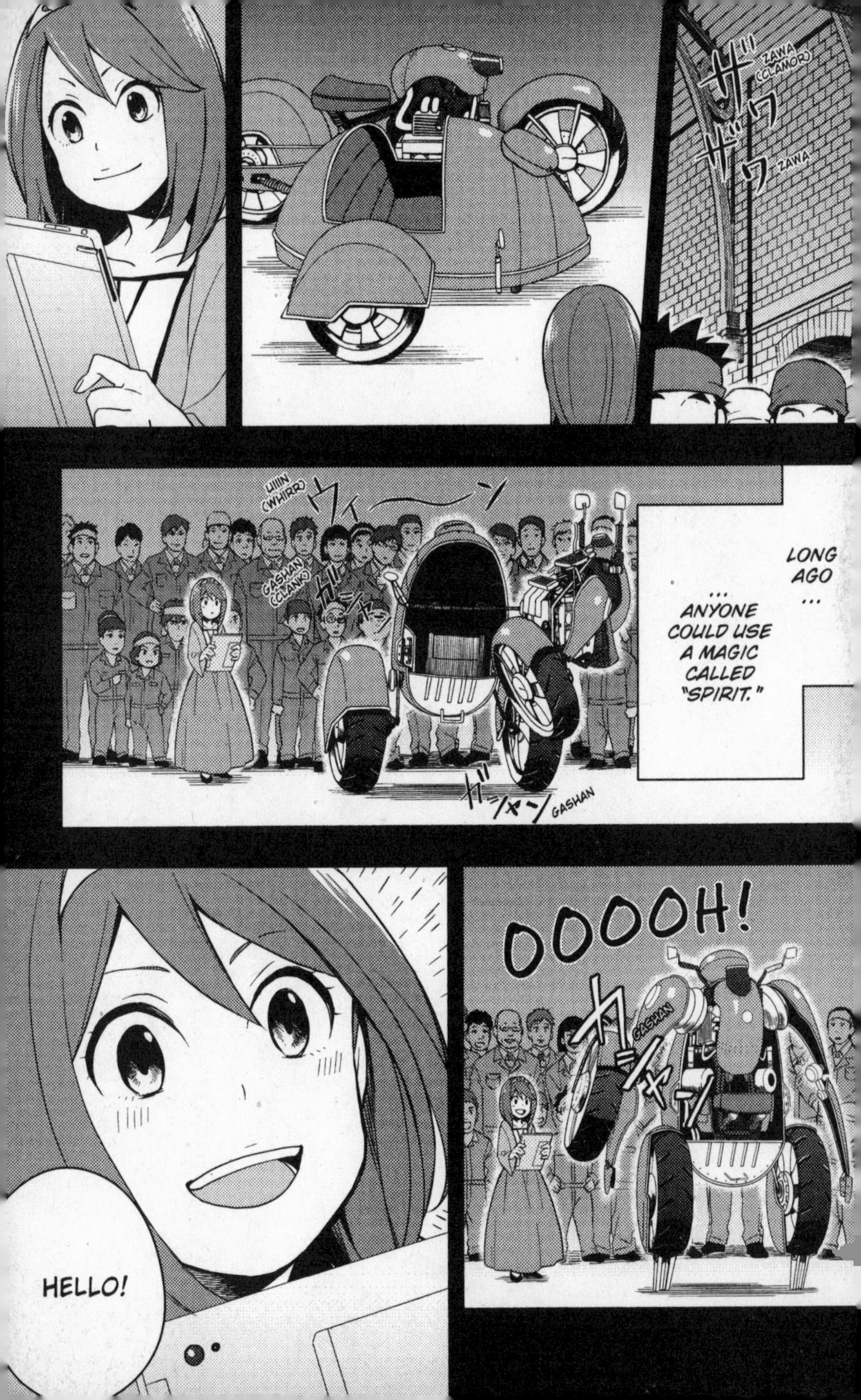
ZAWA (CLAMOR)
ZAWA
LONG AGO ...
... ANYONE COULD USE A MAGIC CALLED "SPIRIT."
UIIIN (WHIRR)
GASHAN (CLANK)
GASHAN
OOOOH!
GASHAN
HELLO!

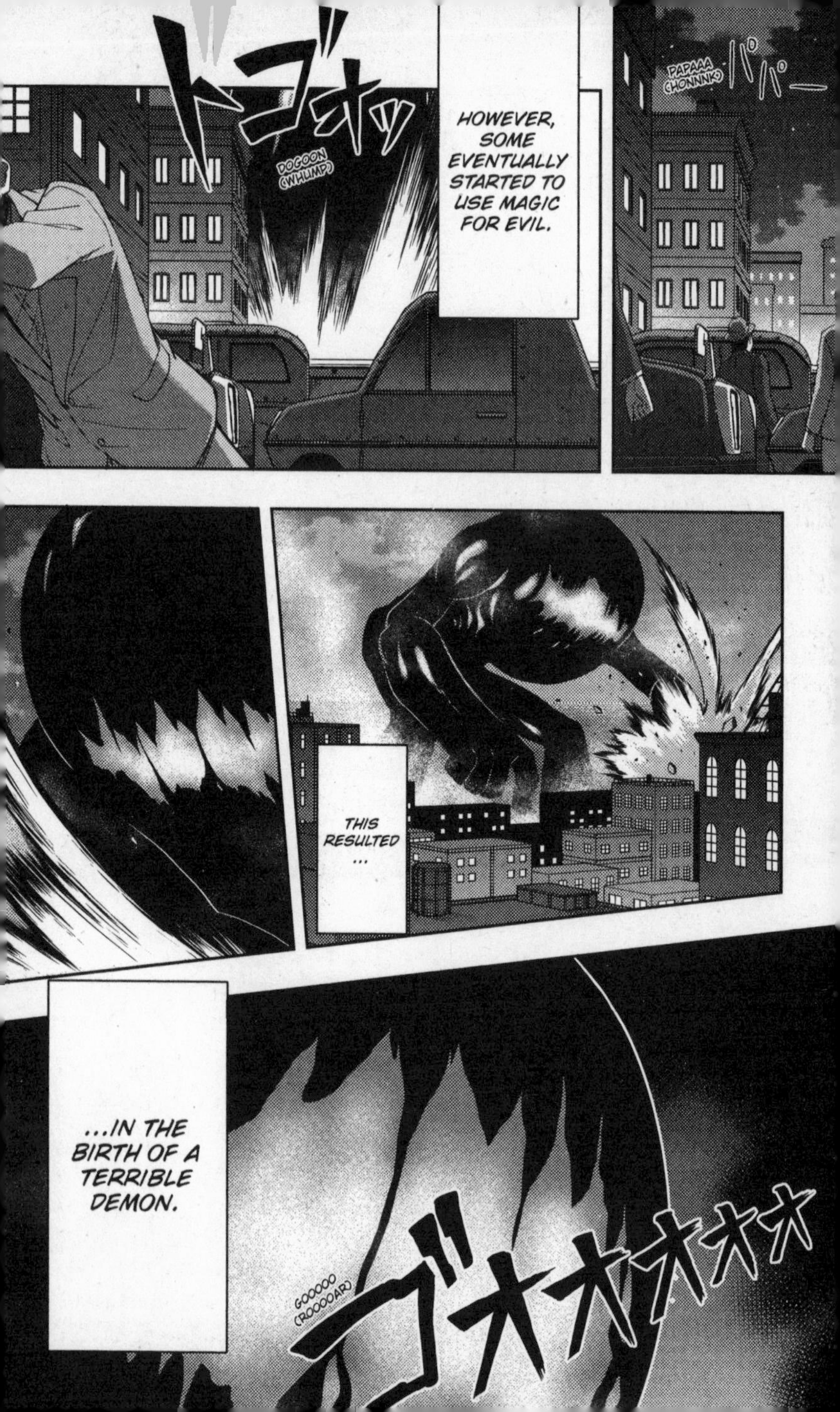
パパー
PAPAAA (HONNNK)
HOWEVER, SOME EVENTUALLY STARTED TO USE MAGIC FOR EVIL.
ドゴオッ
DOGOON (WHUMP)
THIS RESULTED ...
...IN THE BIRTH OF A TERRIBLE DEMON.
ゴオオオオオ
GOOOOO (ROOOOAR)

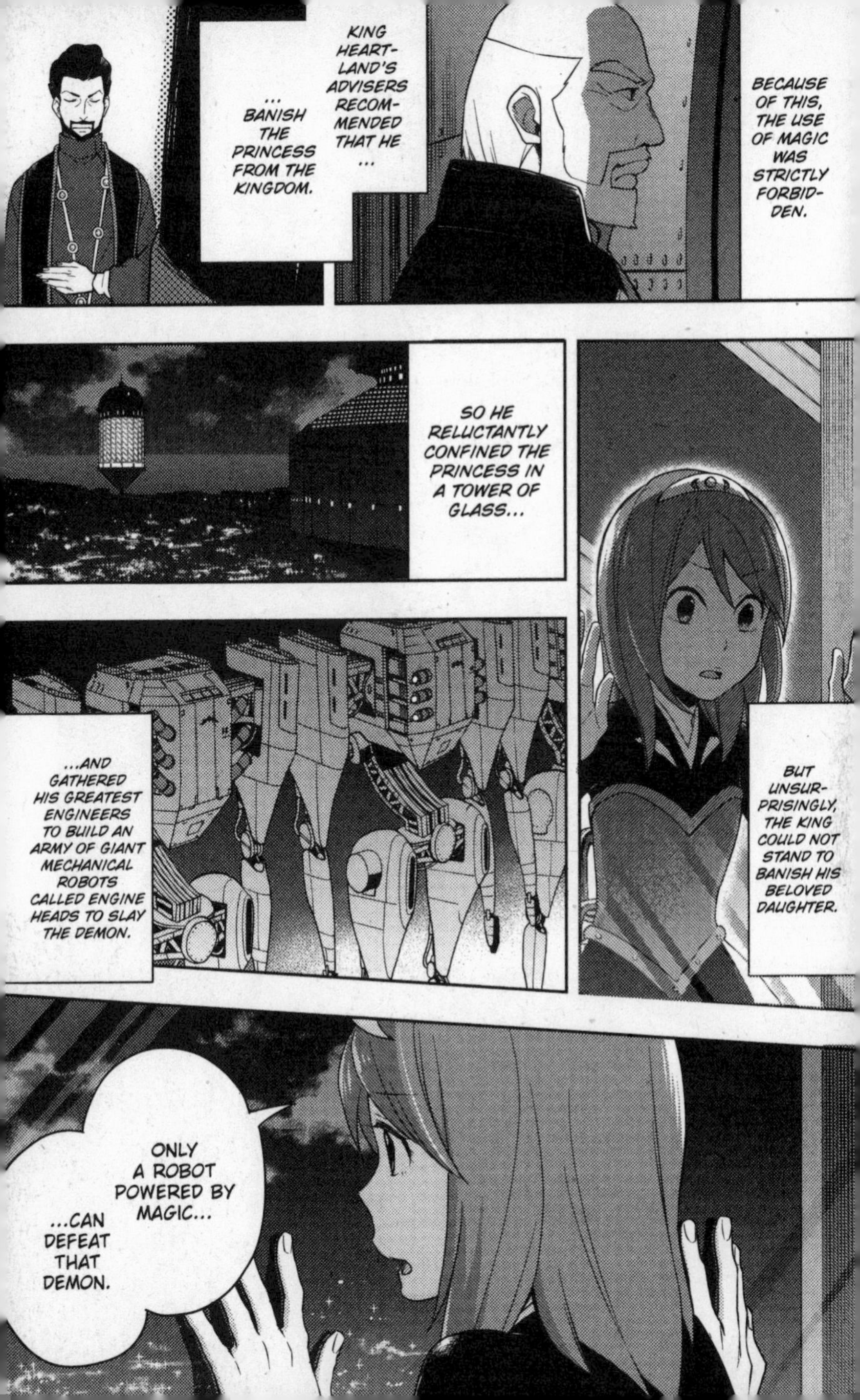
BECAUSE OF THIS, THE USE OF MAGIC WAS STRICTLY FORBIDDEN.
KING HEARTLAND'S ADVISERS RECOMMENDED THAT HE ...
... BANISH THE PRINCESS FROM THE KINGDOM.
BUT UNSURPRISINGLY, THE KING COULD NOT STAND TO BANISH HIS BELOVED DAUGHTER.
SO HE RELUCTANTLY CONFINED THE PRINCESS IN A TOWER OF GLASS...
...AND GATHERED HIS GREATEST ENGINEERS TO BUILD AN ARMY OF GIANT MECHANICAL ROBOTS CALLED ENGINE HEADS TO SLAY THE DEMON.
ONLY A ROBOT POWERED BY MAGIC...
...CAN DEFEAT THAT DEMON.

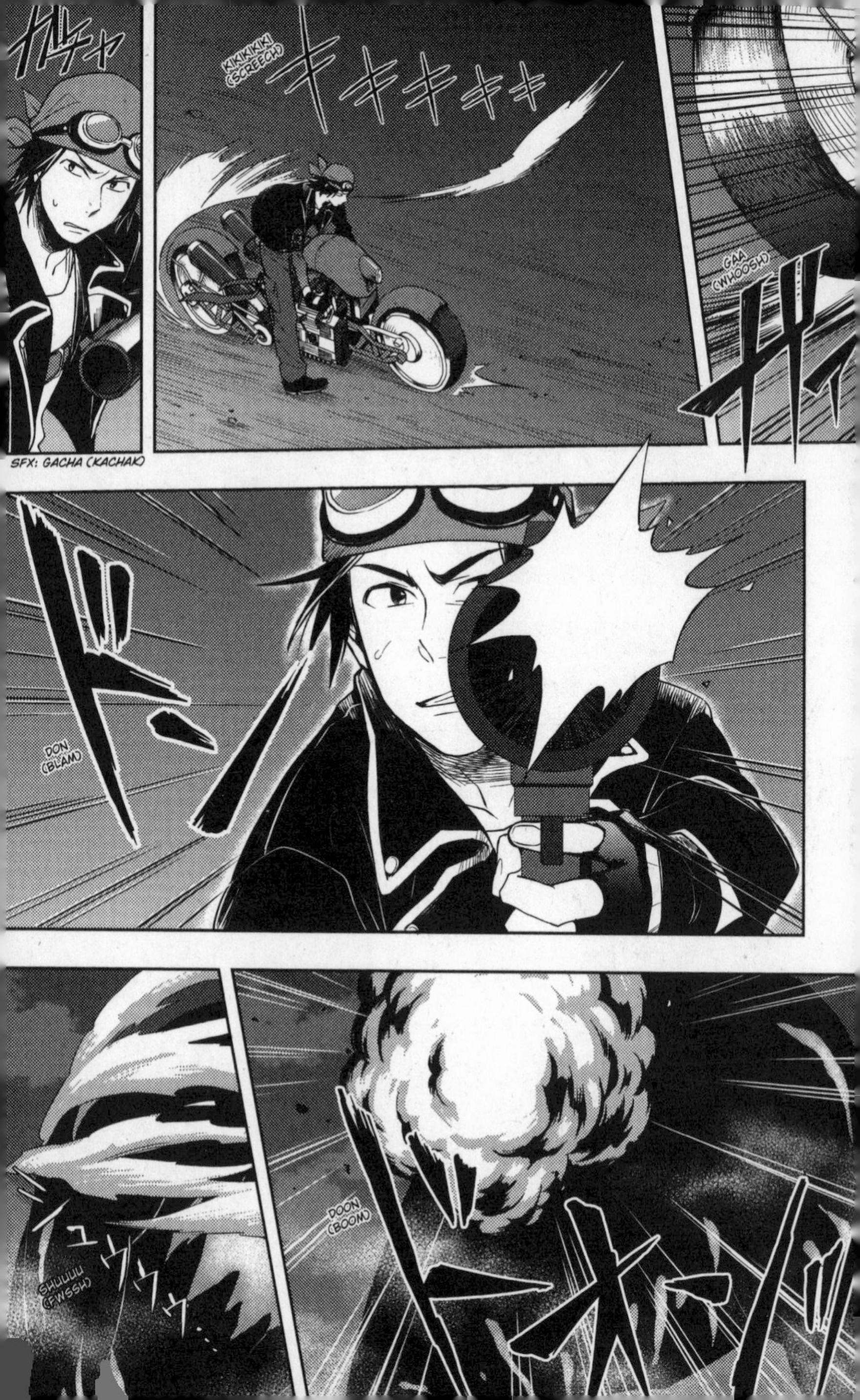
GAA
(WHOOSH)
KIKIKIKI
(SCREECH)
SFX: GACHA (KACHAK)
DON
(BLAM)
DOON
(BOOM)
SHUUUU
(FWSSH)

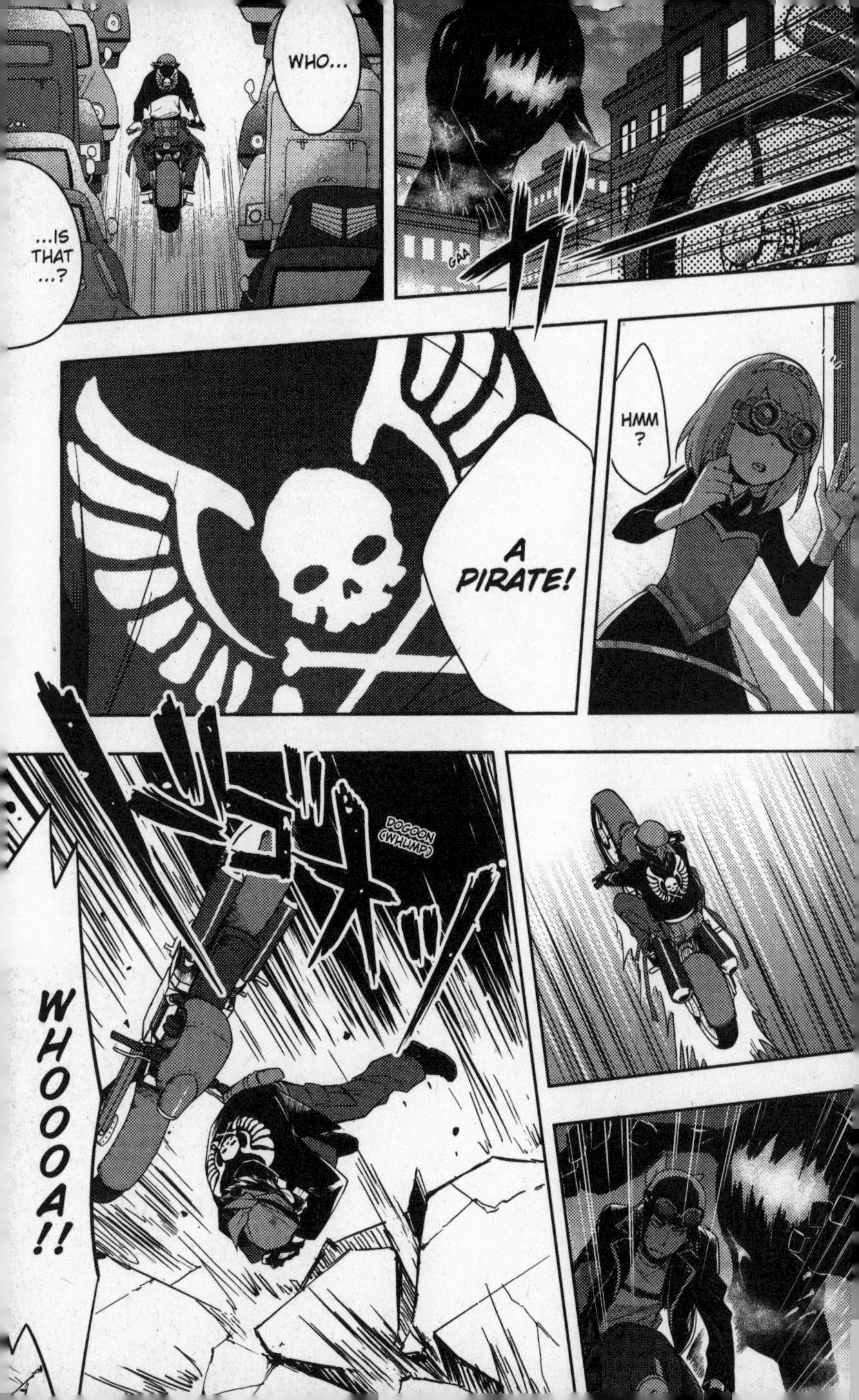
GAA
WHO...
...IS THAT ...?
HMM ?
A PIRATE!
DOGOON (WHUMP)
WHOOOOA!!

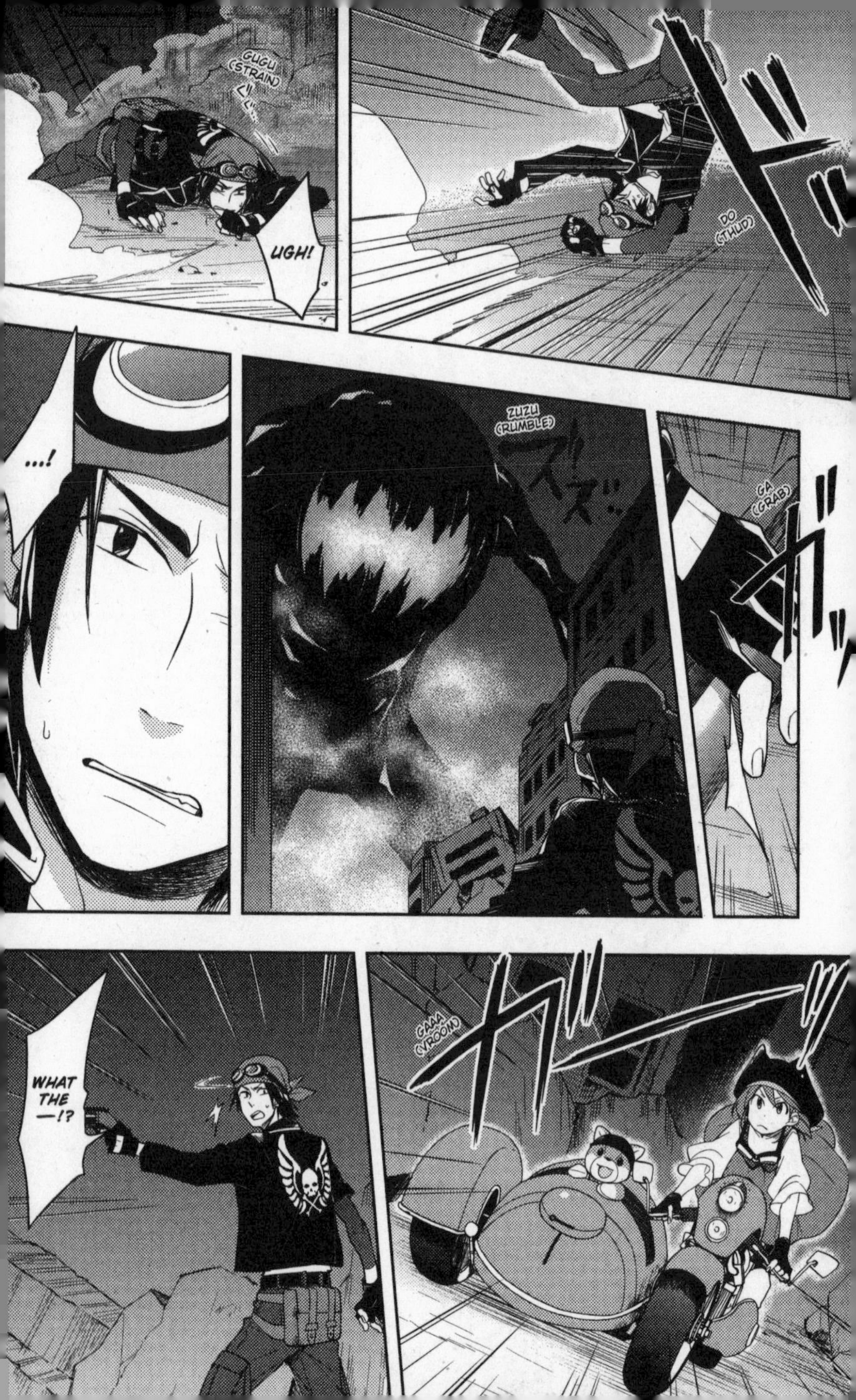
DO (THUD)
GUGU (STRAIN)
UGH!
GA (GRAB)
ZUZU (RUMBLE)
...!
GAAA (VROOM)
WHAT THE—!?

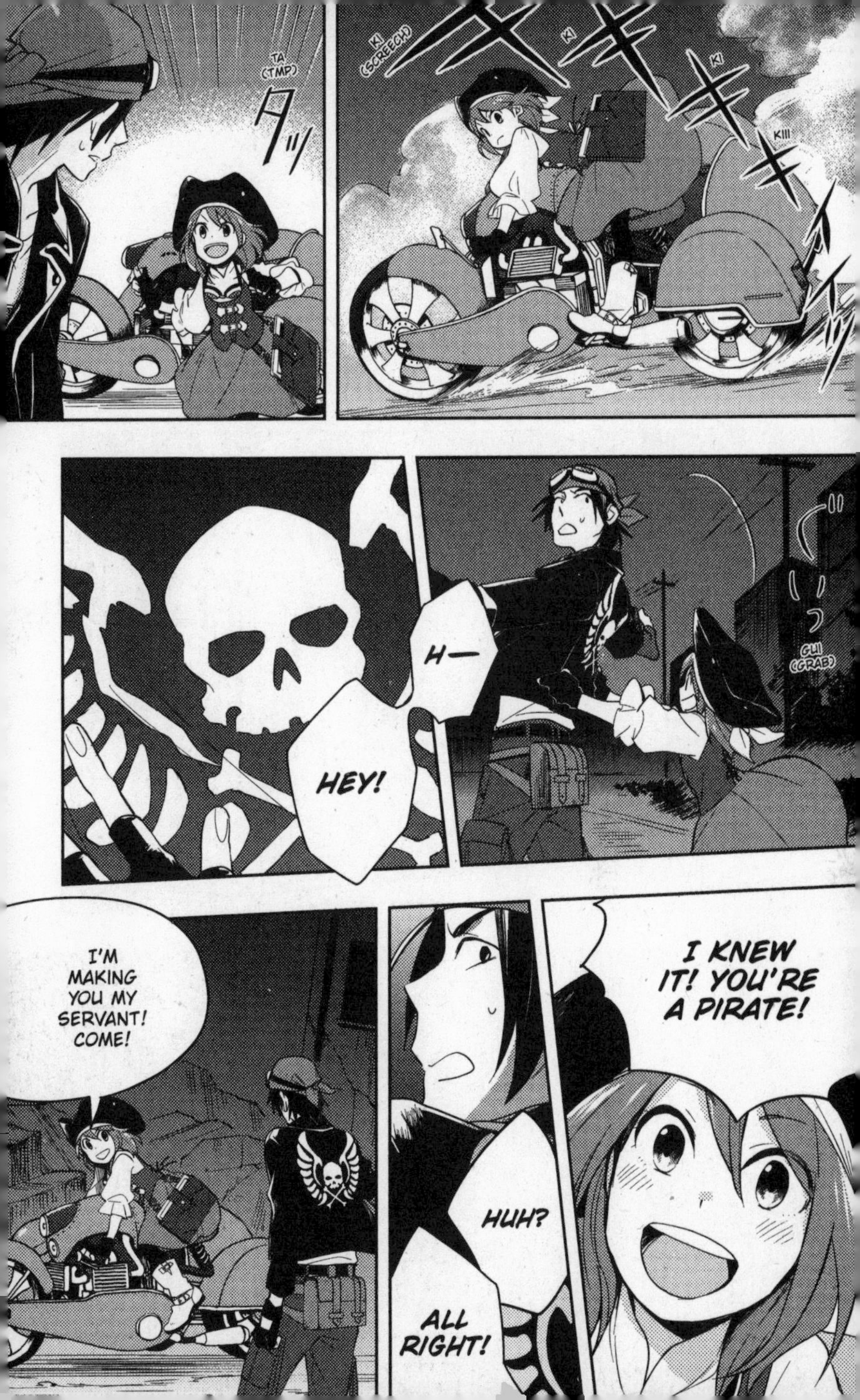
KI (SCREECH)
KI
KI
KIII
TA (TMP)
GUI (GRAB)
H—
HEY!
I KNEW IT! YOU'RE A PIRATE!
HUH?
ALL RIGHT!
I'M MAKING YOU MY SERVANT! COME!

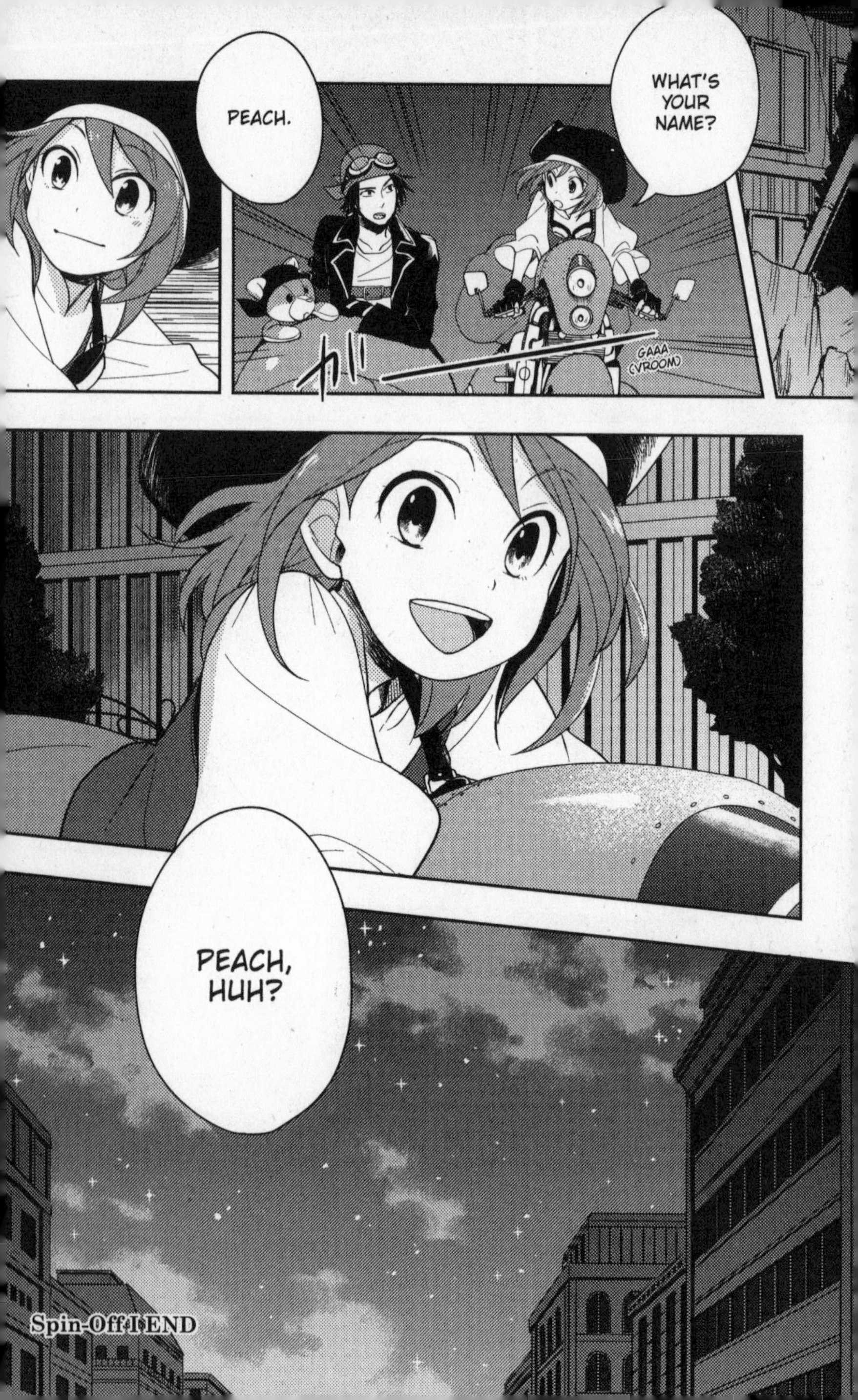
WHAT'S YOUR NAME?
PEACH.
GAAA (VROOM)
PEACH, HUH?
Spin-Off I END

# Napping
# Princess
The Story of the Unknown Me

# Napping Princess
## The Story of the Unknown Me

## Character File

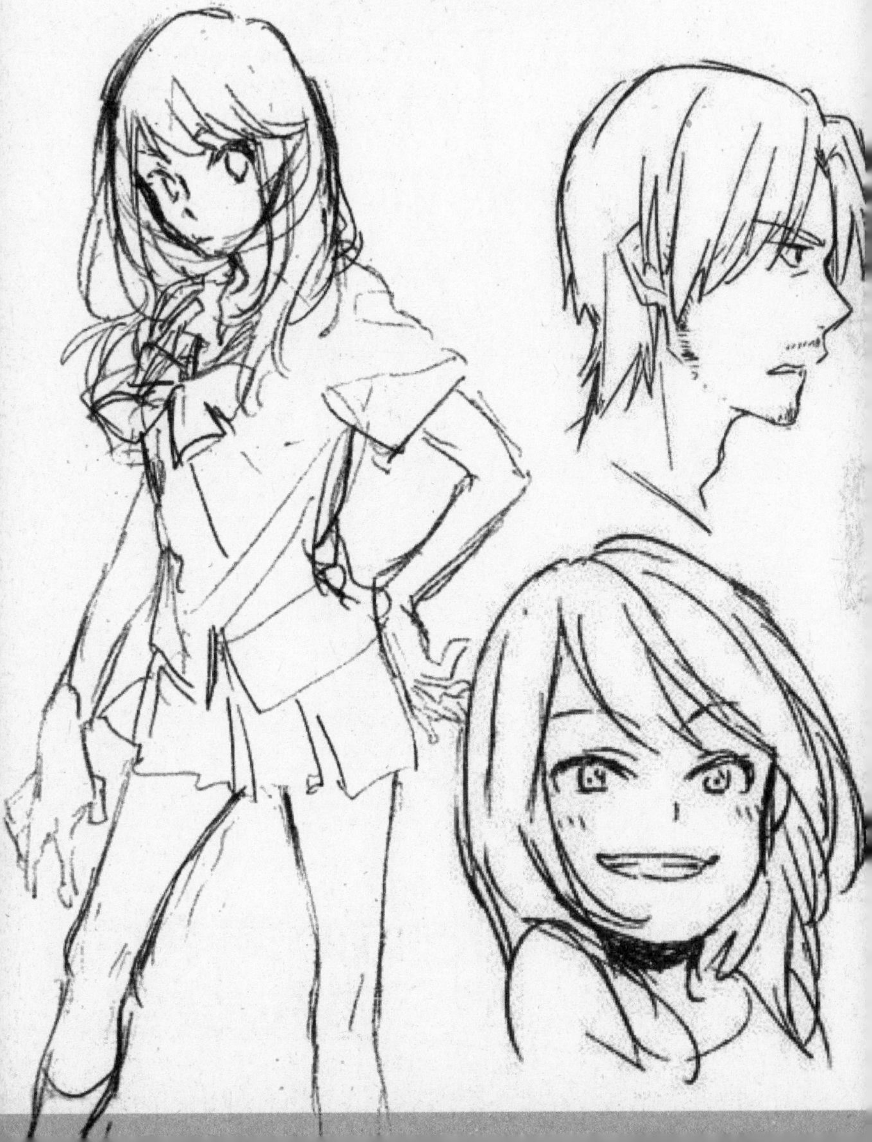

# KOKONE MORIKAWA

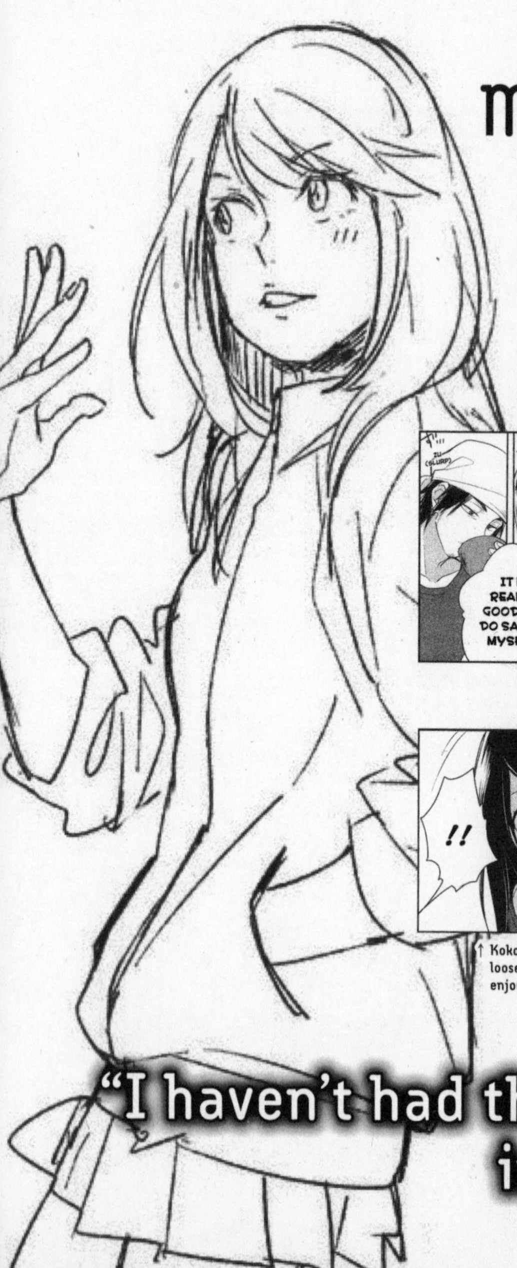

A high school girl living in Okayama with her father. She often dreams of Ancien, the magic-using princess of Heartland. She's not a big fan of studying, but she's a lively girl who really cares about her father.

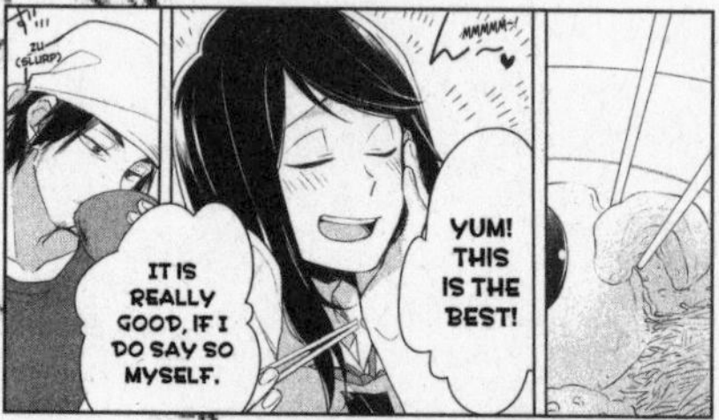
MMMMM~!
YUM! THIS IS THE BEST!
ZU (SLURP)
IT IS REALLY GOOD, IF I DO SAY SO MYSELF.

↑ Kokone singing her own praises after happily making food every day. Momotarou's expressionless face is fun as a contrast to that.

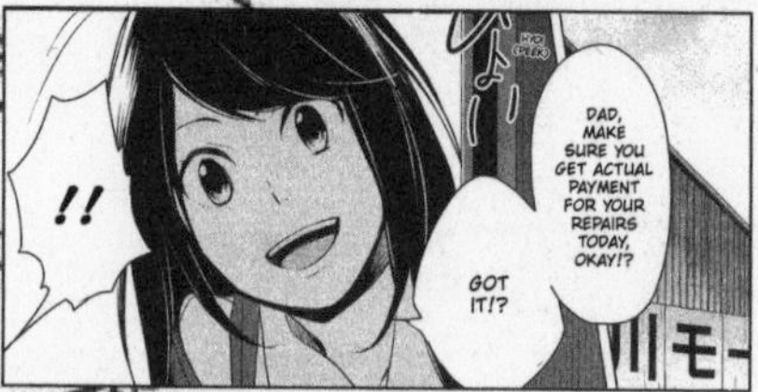
HYO (PEEK)
DAD, MAKE SURE YOU GET ACTUAL PAYMENT FOR YOUR REPAIRS TODAY, OKAY!?
GOT IT!?
!!

↑ Kokone giving a reminder to Momotarou, who is a bit loose when it comes to finances. But she looks like she's enjoying herself, so she doesn't seem to be blaming him.

"I haven't had that dream... in forever..."

# ANCIEN

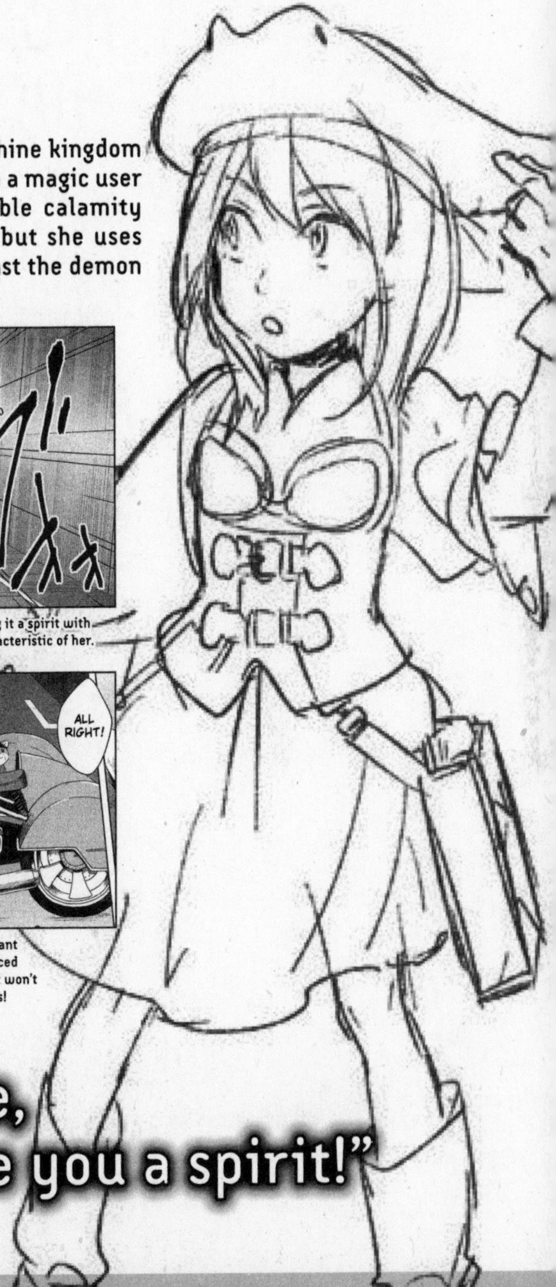

The princess of the machine kingdom Heartland. She was born a magic user who would bring terrible calamity down on the kingdom, but she uses her magic to stand against the demon attacking them.

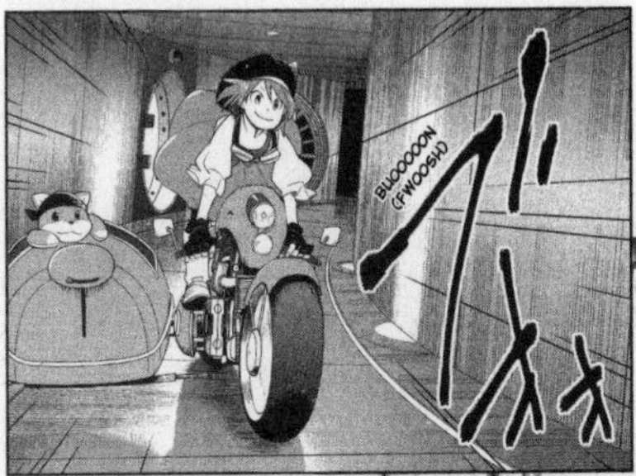
BUOOOOON
(FWOOSH)

↑ Ancien gallantly riding Heart after giving it a spirit with her magic. That proud expression is characteristic of her.

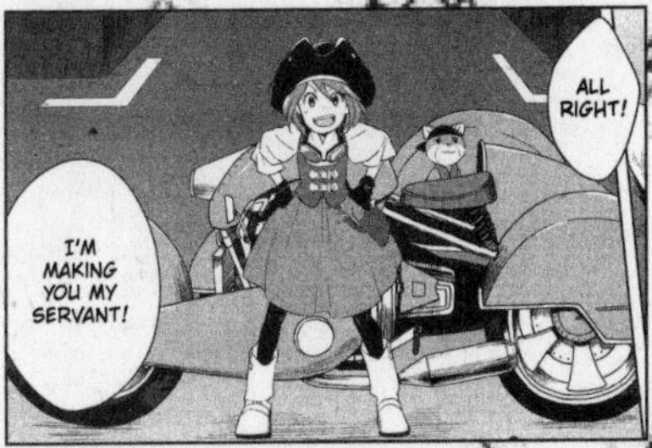
ALL RIGHT!
I'M MAKING YOU MY SERVANT!

↑ Ancien forcing Peach to become her servant after taking a shine to him because he faced off against the demon. She's innocent but won't take no for an answer, just like a princess!

"This time, I will give you a spirit!"

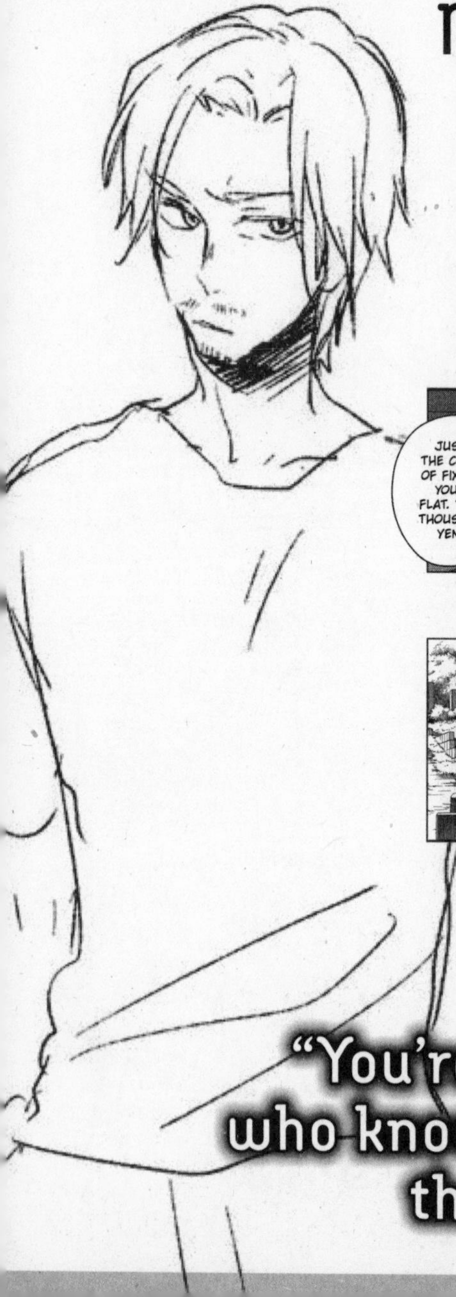

# MOMOTAROU MORIKAWA

Kokone's father. He's an ex-ruffian who the local kids call "Gruff Track." He runs a small mechanic shop. He barely says anything to Kokone most of the time, but he is thinking about the future of her education.

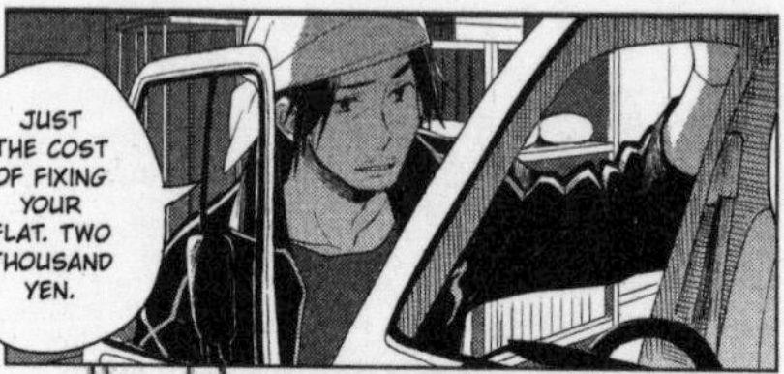
JUST THE COST OF FIXING YOUR FLAT. TWO THOUSAND YEN.

↑ He installed a self-driving system in the car, but he isn't charging for it. He's unsociable but compassionate, and his customers appreciate that.

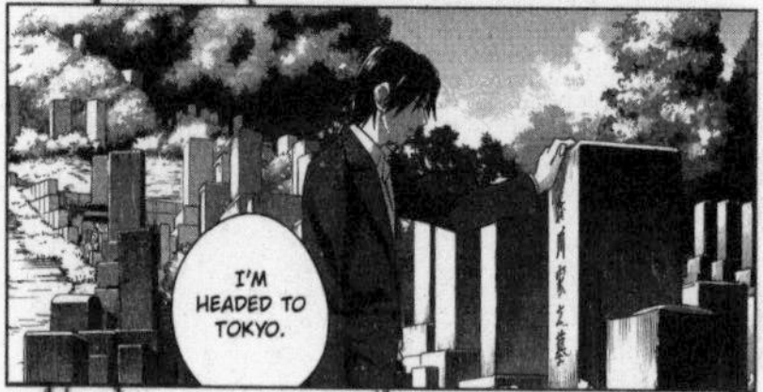
I'M HEADED TO TOKYO.

↑ Momotarou talking in front of his dead wife's grave. He's estranged from his father-in-law, but he's decided to go to Tokyo because of the threat of a lawsuit.

**"You're the only one who knows everything that happened."**

# MORIO SAWATARI

Kokone's childhood friend, two years older than her. A college sophomore attending the Tokyo Institute of Technology. He's always overwhelmed by Kokone's energy.

**"...Would you stop calling me that already?"**

# JOY

A Shiba Inu stuffed animal that Kokone treasures and carries around. In the dream world, he has been given life by Ancien's magic.

**"Aye, aye, sir!"**

# KING HEARTLAND

The king of Heartland, who believes machines can bring happiness to all. He is troubled by the fact that his daughter, Ancien, was born a magic user.

**"Troops! Deploy the Engine Heads!"**

# Napping Princess
### The Story of the Unknown Me

THANK YOU SO MUCH FOR PICKING UP VOLUME 1 OF NAPPING PRINCESS: THE STORY OF THE UNKNOWN ME! I'M HANA ICHIKA. PLEASED TO MEET YOU. I LOVE FAMILIAL LOVE AND BONDS. I FEEL LIKE THE LINK BETWEEN KOKONE'S DREAM WORLD AND THE REAL WORLD IN NAPPING PRINCESS MATCHES UP NICELY WITH THE ACT OF CREATING MANGA. WE TAKE DREAMS, IMAGINATION...AND SOMETIMES DELUSIONS AND GIVE THEM FORM. FOR THE MOST PART, THE DREAM TIME IS FUN, AND REALITY (DEADLINES) IS HARD...

I WORK HARD EVERY DAY CREATING MY MANGA, BUT IN THE END, I ENJOYED DRAWING CHEERFUL KOKONE AND ANCIEN. PEACH, ANCIEN, AND JOY LINE UP IN NICE LITTLE STEPS, SO THAT'S REALLY CUTE.

NAPPING PRINCESS IS MADE UP OF SEVERAL ELEMENTS. I DO HOPE YOU CAN ENJOY BOTH THE MOVIE AND THE MANGA ADAPTATION TOGETHER. I STILL HAVE A LONG WAY TO GO MYSELF, BUT I HOPE YOU'LL CHEER ME ON IN THE END. SWEET DREAMS, EVERYONE!

◊ SPECIAL THANKS ◊
MIKI KAMITANI-SAN • ATSUYA ITOU-SAN •
SATOMI HIKUMA-SAN • MAYUMI IIDA-SAN •
AYUMI OOTSUKA-SAN • ASUKA ENAMI-SAN •
RIHO-CHAN
MY EDITOR, KOUHEI ITOU-SAN

HANA ICHIKA

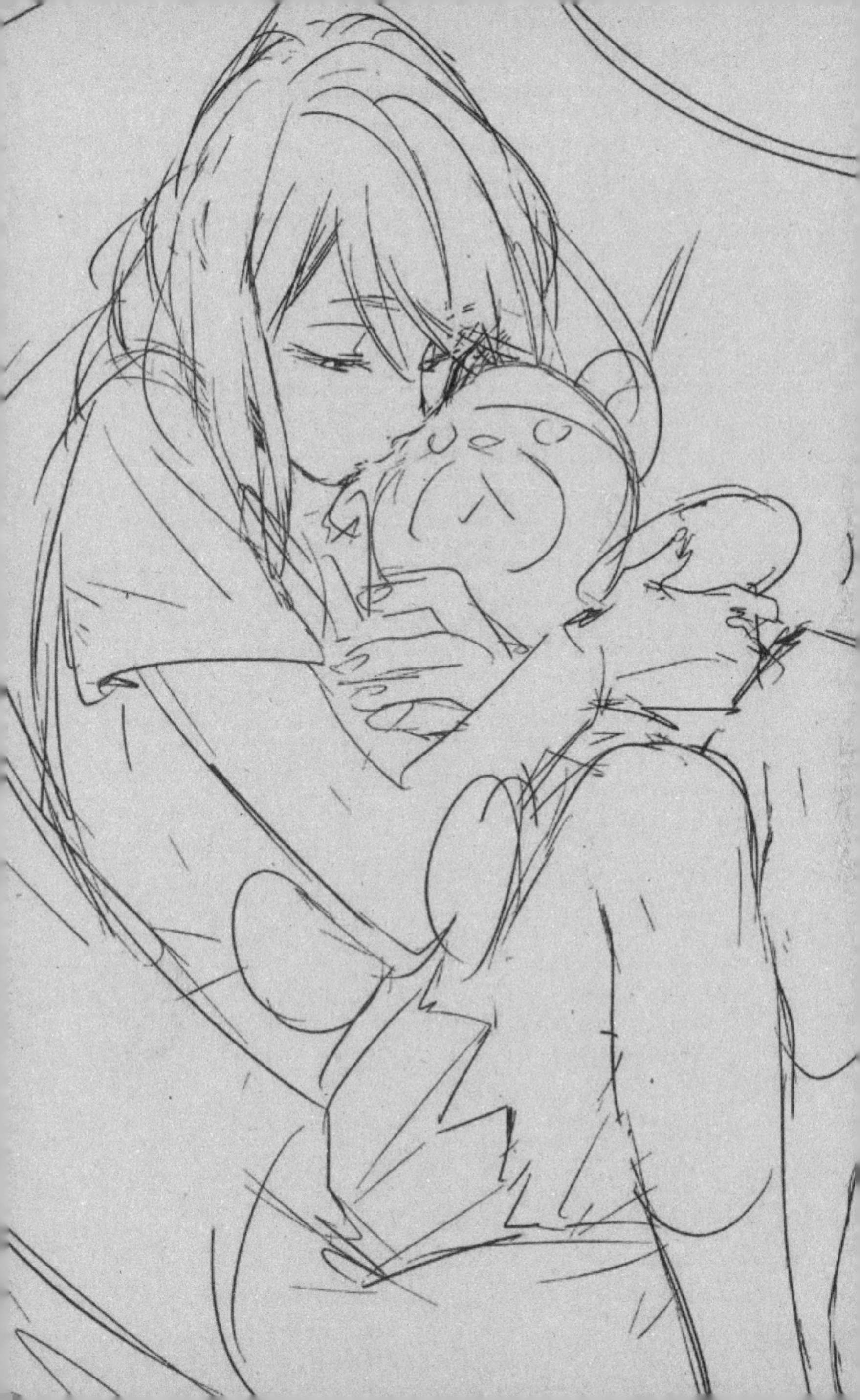

# Translation Notes

## COMMON HONORIFICS

**no honorific:** Indicates familiarity or closeness; if used without permission or reason, addressing someone in this manner would constitute an insult.

**-san:** The Japanese equivalent of Mr./Mrs./Miss. If a situation calls for politeness, this is the fail-safe honorific.

**-sama:** Conveys great respect; may also indicate that the social status of the speaker is lower than that of the addressee.

**-kun:** Used most often when referring to boys, this indicates affection or familiarity. Occasionally used by older men among their peers, but it may also be used by anyone referring to a person of lower standing.

**-chan:** An affectionate honorific indicating familiarity used mostly in reference to girls; also used in reference to cute persons or animals of either gender.

**-sensei:** A respectful term for teachers, artists, or high-level professionals.

### Page 37
**Obon** is a Buddhist custom where one honors their family's ancestral spirits, often by visiting and cleaning graves and household shrines.

### Page 45
The exchange rate for the US dollar to the Japanese yen usually comes out as roughly $1 = ¥100. So **two thousand** yen is about twenty dollars.

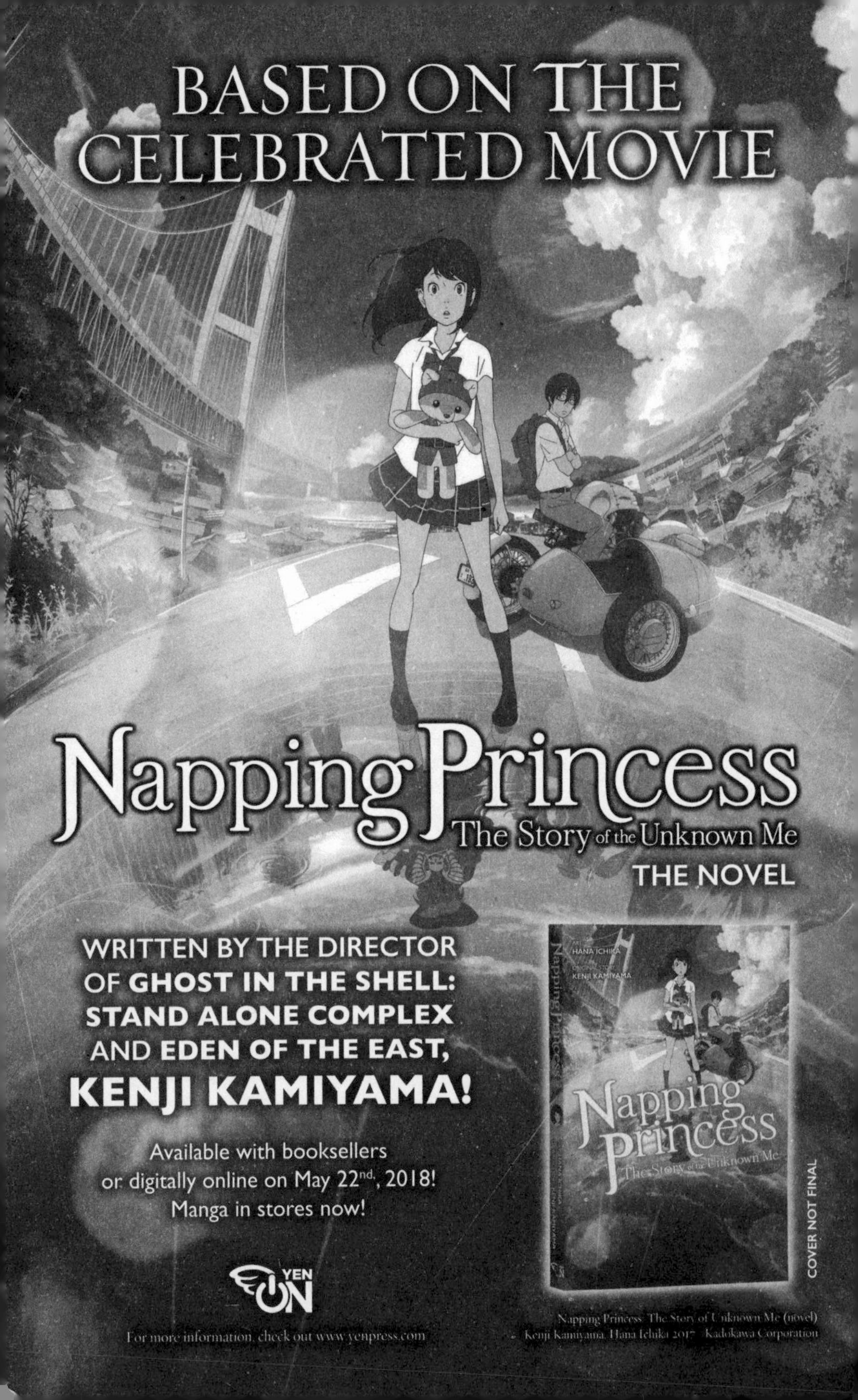

BASED ON THE CELEBRATED MOVIE
Napping Princess
The Story of the Unknown Me
THE NOVEL
WRITTEN BY THE DIRECTOR OF GHOST IN THE SHELL: STAND ALONE COMPLEX AND EDEN OF THE EAST, KENJI KAMIYAMA!
Available with booksellers or digitally online on May 22nd, 2018! Manga in stores now!
COVER NOT FINAL
YEN ON
For more information, check out www.yenpress.com
Napping Princess: The Story of Unknown Me (novel)
© Kenji Kamiyama, Hana Ichika 2017 Kadokawa Corporation

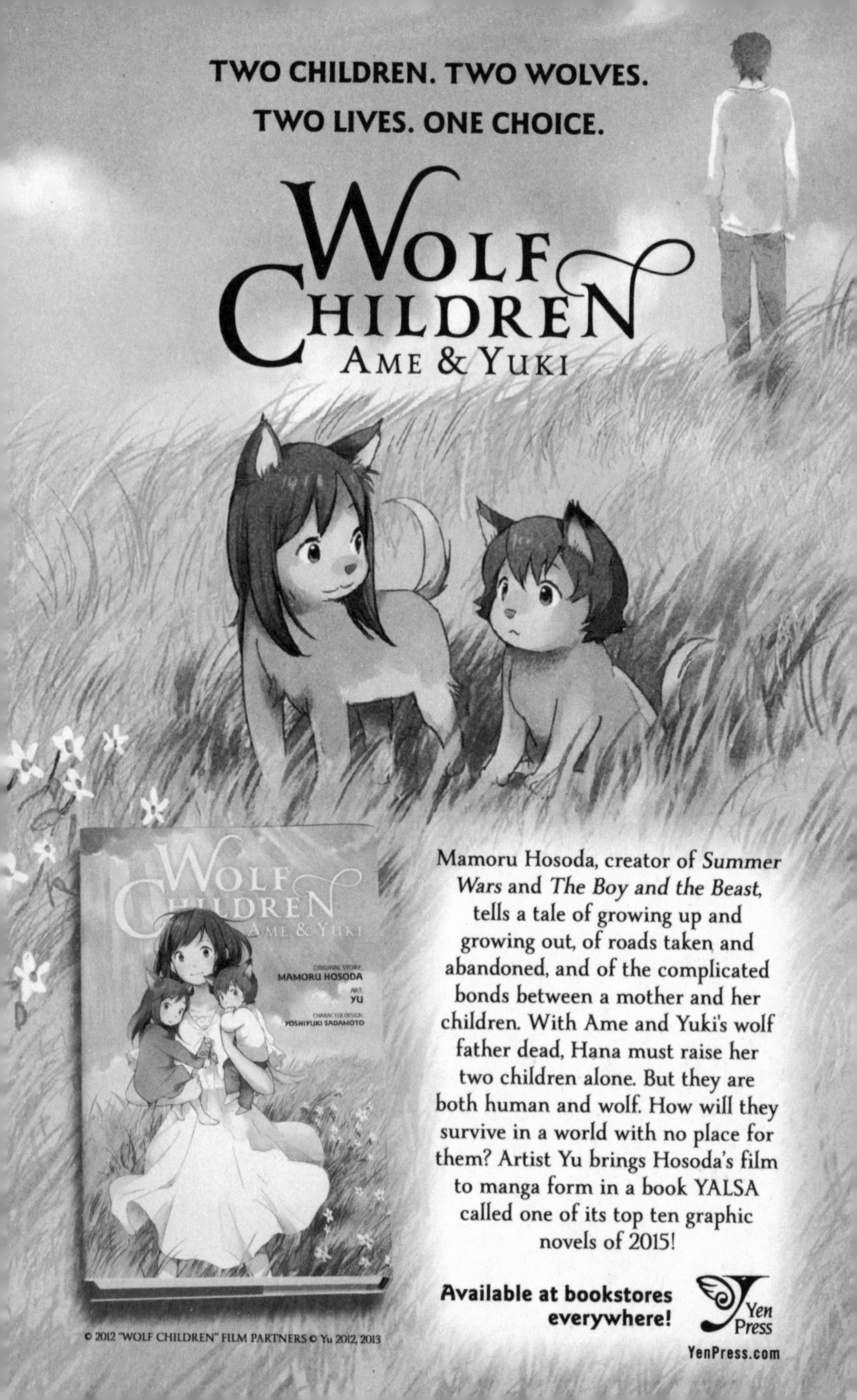

TWO CHILDREN. TWO WOLVES.
TWO LIVES. ONE CHOICE.
WOLF CHILDREN
AME & YUKI
WOLF CHILDREN
AME & YUKI
ORIGINAL STORY:
MAMORU HOSODA
ART:
YU
CHARACTER DESIGN:
YOSHIYUKI SADAMOTO
Mamoru Hosoda, creator of Summer Wars and The Boy and the Beast, tells a tale of growing up and growing out, of roads taken and abandoned, and of the complicated bonds between a mother and her children. With Ame and Yuki's wolf father dead, Hana must raise her two children alone. But they are both human and wolf. How will they survive in a world with no place for them? Artist Yu brings Hosoda's film to manga form in a book YALSA called one of its top ten graphic novels of 2015!
Available at bookstores everywhere!
Yen Press
YenPress.com
© 2012 "WOLF CHILDREN" FILM PARTNERS © Yu 2012, 2013

# Two girls, a new school, and the beginning of a beautiful friendship.

## *Kiss & White Lily for My Dearest Girl*

In middle school, Ayaka Shiramine was the perfect student: hard-working, with excellent grades and a great personality to match. As Ayaka enters high school she expects to still be on top, but one thing she didn't account for is her new classmate, the lazy yet genuine genius Yurine Kurosawa. What's in store for Ayaka and Yurine as they go through high school...together?

# BUNGO STRAY DOGS

Volumes 1–6
available now

## BUNGO STRAY DOGS 01

STORY BY KAFKA ASAGIRI    ART BY SANGO HARUKAWA

**If you've already seen the anime, it's time to read the manga!**

Having been kicked out of the orphanage, Atsushi Nakajima rescues a strange man from a suicide attempt— Osamu Dazai. Turns out that Dazai is part of a detective agency staffed by individuals whose supernatural powers take on a literary bent!

# ENJOY EVERYTHING.

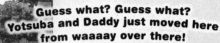

# Hello! This is YOTSUBA!

**Guess what? Guess what?
Yotsuba and Daddy just moved here
from waaaay over there!**

**And Yotsuba met these
nice people next door and made
new friends to play with!**

**The pretty one took
Yotsuba on a bike ride!**
(Whoooa! There was a big hill!)

**And Ena's a good drawer!**
(Almost as good as Yotsuba!)

**And their mom always
gives Yotsuba ice cream!**
(Yummy!)

**And...
        And...   OHHHH!**

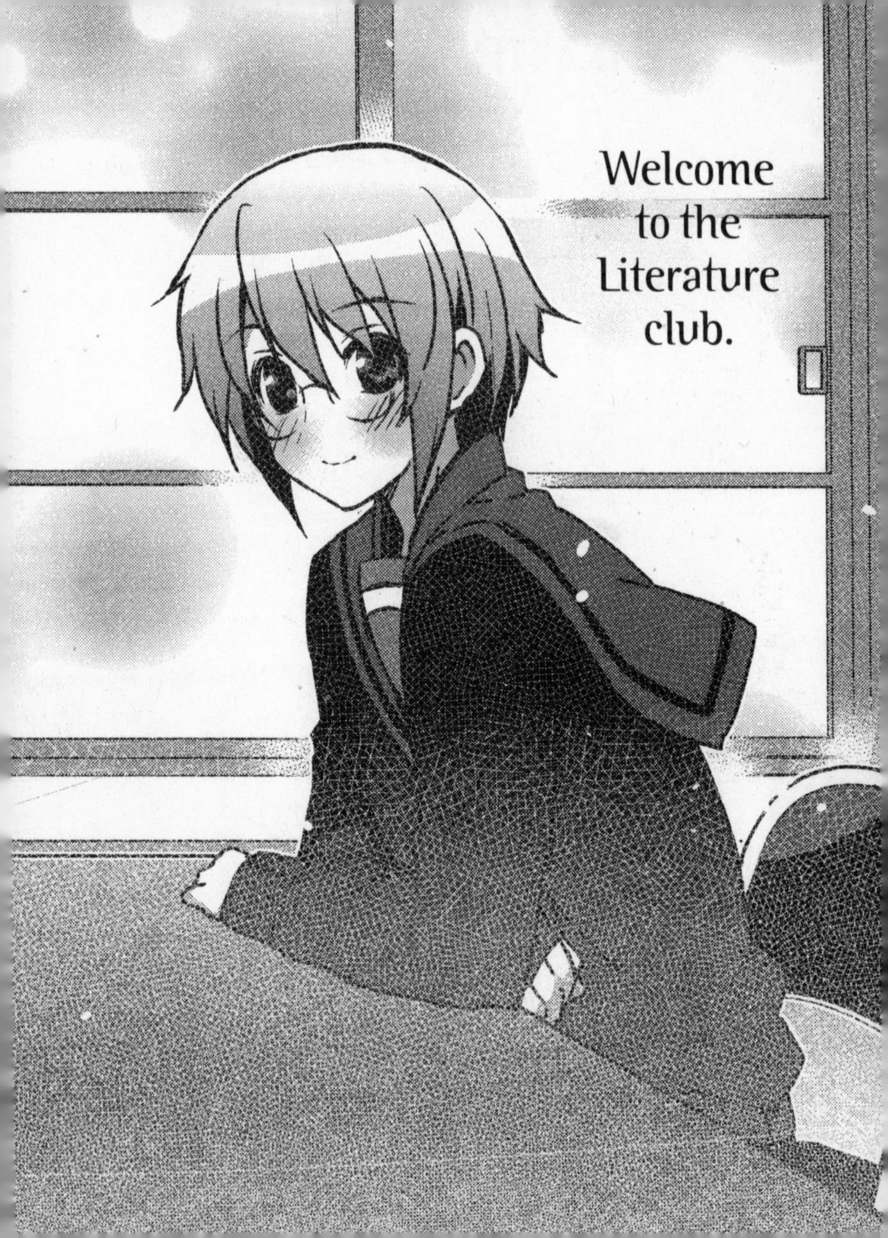
Welcome to the Literature club.

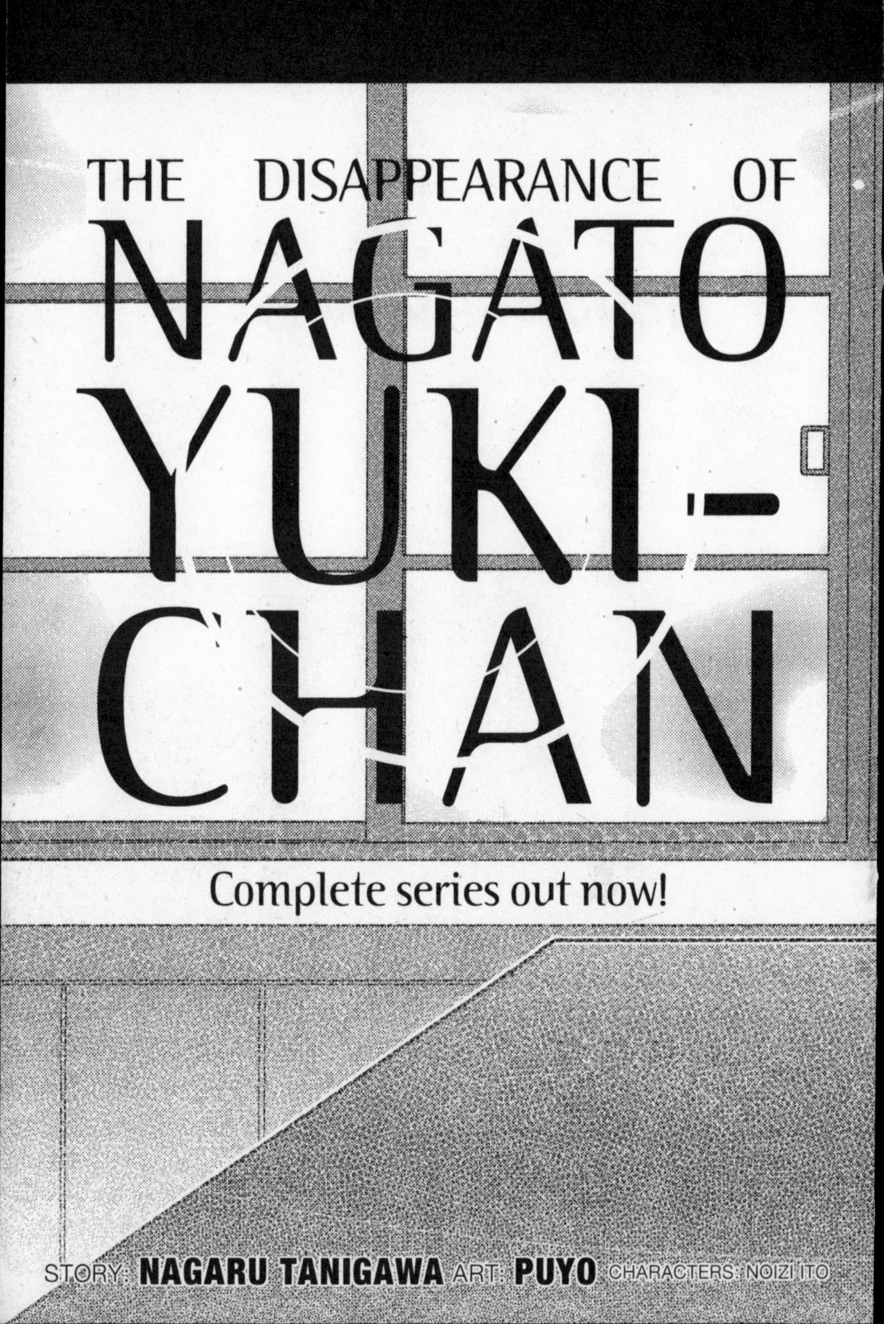
THE DISAPPEARANCE OF NAGATO YUKI-CHAN
Complete series out now!
STORY: NAGARU TANIGAWA ART: PUYO CHARACTERS: NOIZI ITO

# Napping Princess
## The Story of the Unknown Me

1

Original Story KENJI KAMIYAMA

Art HANA ICHIKA

Translation: Leighann Harvey · Lettering: Bianca Pistillo

Napping Princess "The Story of the Unknown Me," Volume 1
©Hana ICHIKA 2017
©Kenji Kamiyama/2017 "ANCIEN AND THE MAGIC TABLET" Film Partners
First published in Japan in 2017 by KADOKAWA CORPORATION, Tokyo. English translation rights arranged with KADOKAWA CORPORATION, Tokyo, through TUTTLE-MORI AGENCY, INC., Tokyo.

English translation © 2017 by Yen Press, LLC

Yen Press
1290 Avenue of the Americas
New York, NY 10104

Visit us at yenpress.com
facebook.com/yenpress
twitter.com/yenpress
yenpress.tumblr.com
instagram.com/yenpress

First Yen Press Print Edition: April 2018
The chapters in this volume were originally published as eBooks by Yen Press.

Yen Press is an imprint of Yen Press, LLC.
The Yen Press name and logo are trademarks of Yen Press, LLC.

Library of Congress Control Number: 2018931542

ISBNs: 978-1-9753-2607-4 (paperback)
978-1-9753-2605-0 (ebook)

10 9 8 7 6 5 4 3 2 1

WOR

Printed in the United States of America